FLYFISHING
SKILL ON STILLWATERS

FLYFISHING SKILL ON STILLWATERS

Third Edition

Peter Mackenzie-Philps

BLANDFORD

Blandford Press
a Cassell imprint
Villiers House
41/47 Strand
London WC2N 5JE

First published 1986

Paperback edition 1989
Reprinted 1990
Revised 1987 and 1994

Distributed in the United States by
Sterling Publishing Co. Inc.
387 Park Avenue South
New York, NY 10016

Distributed in Australia by
Capricorn Link (Australia) Pty Ltd
2/13 Carrington Road, Castle Hill, NSW 2154

British Library Cataloguing-in-Publication Data
A catalogue entry for this title is available from the British Library

ISBN 0-7137-2459-5

Printed and bound in Great Britain by
Mackays of Chatham PLC, Chatham, Kent

This book is dedicated to my wife Sue,
whom I have neglected for many years,
and who has treated me with
amused tolerance and much love
which I have sometimes been
too busy or preoccupied
to show in return.

Contents

Acknowledgements

My sincerest thanks go to my old fishing pal, Ewart Clay, ex-editor of the Yorkshire Evening Post, who encouraged me to believe that I was capable of writing a fishing book.

To our good friends Leslie and Sheila whose kind hospitality gave me a haven of peace and quiet in which to concentrate.

To my sons Tony and Gordon, who have often taken a fresh enquiring look at something which I have taken for granted, and discovered a better way of doing it.

To every angler I have ever talked to – from nearly every one I have learned.

To John Harris, Don Hyde, and Kathy, who tied all the flies pictured in this book.

All photographs by the author.

Introduction: What Kind of Angler Do You Want To be?

Let me start by saying that there are good anglers, and there are lucky anglers. Some anglers are both good and lucky on the same day, and they have a ball. Next time out, if they rely on luck alone, they have a blank day while the good angler manages to catch at least some trout. This book is designed to help you become a good angler – and then your own natural luck can help afterwards!

Let us consider two anglers, turning up at a stillwater for a day's fishing. They both arrive at an early hour, eager for the fray, having left home at the time the sparrows are clearing their throats, and driven just over the legal speed limit in their keenness to be fishing again after the rigours of a week at work.

Our *unthinking* angler has listened to loud music while driving. He had a few beers last night, didn't bother to shave this morning and feels a bit jaded as he pulls up in the reservoir car park. Once there, he realises that he has not got the necessary pound coins for the ticket machine, and has to wait for twenty minutes for another angler to arrive who has change to swop.

Tackling up his favourite rod – a powerful nine footer – with a sinking, shooting head line, a level 15 foot leader of 8 lb breaking strain and a large marabou lure, he grabs his tackle bag, slings it hurriedly over one shoulder and tramps, heavily laden, down to the water's edge. Dumping his bag on the shingle, he wades steadily out until he has only an inch of freeboard left at the top of his waders, and then lengthens line in an expert double-haul cast until he reckons he has as much as he can manage. Letting it go in a long cast towards the middle, he lights his sixth cigarette of the morning and has a good cough while waiting for the line to sink for the necessary twenty seconds. The last time he fished here he caught a double bag limit by letting the line sink for twenty seconds, so it should work now. . . He ignores the fact that his previous visit had been on opening day, in temperatures close to freezing!

Two hours later he has not moved from the spot he first occupied. His net is still stuck into the bottom beside him, the mesh still dry, and steady hurling of that shooting head out as far as it will go has made him feel even more jaded than when he started. He decides it is time for a sandwich for breakfast and so turns and starts to wade ashore. He leaves his net where it is, as that marks his spot for the day; and having taken all the trouble to be there early and book that spot, he reckons he is entitled to occupy a fishy place all day if necessary. To his amazement, just as he turns round, he sees a fish rise within two yards of the bank, between him and his bag on the shingle.

Quickly plonking his lure in the rise rings, he sees the fish swirl at his fly. Lifting the rod tip in a sweep and pulling down with his left hand on the loose line he feels a solid resistance, and then everything goes slack. Swearing, he realises that the fish has broken his leader. Must have been a whopper - only whoppers break leaders like that one did. 'Smashed me rotten,' he thought.

Arriving at his fishing bag he looks into his flybox for another lure to match the one just lost, there isn't one. Muttering, he pours a coffee from the flask and chooses another lure, a Whisky Fly. After a quarter of an hour he notices that fish are rising from time to time within a couple of yards of his net, stuck forlornly out in the water in front of him. Scrambling to his feet he wades out, perhaps half-way to the net, lengthening the line in the air as he goes. By the time he is ready to cast, an observer would have seen that twelve false casts had flickered over the area of those rises, and by the time his fly finally lands the rises have stopped. 'Never mind, they'll still be there,' he thinks, and continues to cast and work the lure through the area. After ten minutes he arrives again beside his net, feels secure in its company and fishes hard until his stomach tells him it is lunchtime.

After two cans of beer and a pile of sandwiches, he feels a lot better. No fish have moved that he could see, and the now-glassy surface of the reservoir looks dead so, planning his activities, our unthinking angler decides to have a sleep in the sunshine. After all he may as well save his energies for the evening rise - the fish always rise well in the evening - so he finds a comfortable hollow for his hip and in two minutes is fast asleep. Out in the water, his net marks the spot where, in his dreams, he will catch a bagful tonight once the sun goes down.

He wakes feeling thoroughly chilled. Sitting up he sees another angler fishing ten yards to the left of his net. 'Cheeky perisher,' he thinks, 'that's my spot,' and scrambling stiffly to his feet and grabbing his rod, he wades purposefully out to his net to make the point that he had squatter's rights over that section of bank. No sooner has he arrived beside his net and the waves have spread fifteen yards outwards on the calm surface, than the other angler winds in his line and wades gently ashore. 'G'night,' the other angler says and walks steadily away to the car park. 'Good riddance,' our angler mutters, and for the next hour he fishes steadily with his Whisky Fly. Hadn't this month's fishing magazine said that this was the best fly for this particular month?

Finally, in desperation, our hopeful looks into his flybox. It's getting dusk -

surely a white fly will work? So a white marabou lure is tied on and, impatiently, is not allowed to sink. Wham! A fish explodes into the air, is immediately classed as just a small stockie and horsed along the surface towards the angler. With an expert scoop of the net, the fish is enmeshed and the angler, net in one hand and rod in the other, quickly wades ashore.

Putting his net down beside his bag, he removes the hook from the jaw of the one pound trout, and rummages in his bag for his priest. Not there. . .must be there,. . . no, not there, so the fish is smashed down on the stones to stun it. After the third bash it stops wriggling and is wrapped in a plastic bag. It is now getting dark so, deciding that enough is enough, our unthinking angler packs up his tackle and trudges slowly uphill to the car park. The gear stowed in the boot, he decides that thirst is the better part of valour and turns his car towards a pub in the local village. Two hours and four pints later, he has agreed with at least another six anglers that the stocking policy leaves much to be desired, and that at the next meeting of the local consultative committee, he will make sure that his protests about the cost of the tickets, the lack of trout and the general 'couldn't care less' attitude of the Water Authority are attacked vigorously.

He drives home, fighting sleep. The beer fumes in the car are noticed by his small son, eager to see Dad's fish, who rushes out to greet him. Grunting that the place wasn't much good anyway, he goes indoors and demands his evening meal. His wife, with a sigh, turns towards the kitchen, leaving our *unthinking* angler to fall rapidly asleep in his armchair before the fire.

★ ★ ★

Our *thinking* angler has planned his trip carefully. He has spent a happy evening going through his flyboxes, checking for rusty hooks, loose dressings and missing patterns. He has watched the farming weather forecast the previous Sunday lunchtime, and has formed a picture of the likely conditions at the reservoir for his eagerly anticipated fishing day. He has gone to bed an hour earlier the night before, setting the alarm clock for one hour before his departure time.

His fishing clothes are laid out in the order in which he will get dressed. He sleeps fitfully but forces himself not to get too excited at the thought of the morrow. He stabs the button on the alarm as it gives its first buzz, and slides quietly out of bed. Getting dressed in the dark, he creeps out of the door, only to hear his wife say 'Have a nice day, drive carefully.' Grinning to himself that he can't do a thing without her knowing, he goes back, kisses her cheek, tucks her in and promises to be home about eight.

Going downstairs, he lets the dog out and stands for a moment sniffing the air. Just as the forecast promised – hardly a breath of wind – and a lovely rosy glow in the East speaks silently of a warm day and cloudless sky. 'Should be some good hatches,' he thinks. Back in the kitchen, he has a good breakfast of cereal, fried egg, toast and marmalade, and coffee. The kettle is refilled for two flasks of coffee and that done, he creeps into the bathroom and shaves. Feeling fresh, well-fed and with mounting excitement, he checks again the tackle in the car. . . Yes, he has remembered the bag of spare clothes, his 'falling-in kit' he calls it. Pointing the car down the motorway, he tunes the radio to the weather forecast. This confirms what he thought, and he starts to plan his day. Any wind – and it would be light – will be from the East. The wind will probably be warmer than the water, last week the water was still very cold. So the warmest water would be on the West side of the reservoir, which is where he will go first. He checks again that he has the right coins on the dashboard for the ticket machine. Singing softly to himself, he draws up in the Western car park, gets his permit from the machine and walks quietly down to the water's edge. Bending down he sees the midge pupae skins floating in the margins, and after a bit of a search he finds a midge which had failed to hatch, floating drowned amid the scum of empty skins. Looking at it carefully, he decides that it is a standard kind of black midge, of which he has several imitations in his flybox. Going back to the car, he gets his binoculars out of the glove locker and has a good look around the reservoir. A few anglers are scattered here and there, but nobody seems to be playing a fish. Watching their casting styles, he decides that they are lure fishing, so he will stay well away from them.

A mile off, he thinks he can see a disturbance on the surface in a small bay, sheltered by trees. Watching closely, he is positive that the ripples in the bay must be caused by fish, there is no breeze to speak of nor any diving birds surfacing. He will start there, he decides. Getting back into the car, he drives around the perimeter road until he is as near as he can get to that little bay. Taking his rod out of its case and shouldering his bag and landing net, he sets off to walk down the faint footpath which leads to the bay.

Ambling along quietly, he spots a fox mousing at the edge of the trees. He pauses to admire the cartoon-like way the fox leaps into tufts of grass, scrabbles for a moment, then pounces. Walking quietly down through the trees, he comes out onto a little beach of gravel, perhaps ten yards long. On either side the trees hang down to the water, and on a branch is a patch of the brightest blue. It moves, and then there is an iridescent blue streak as a kingfisher flashes away, round the wooded point to his right.

Our angler wonders why he has never seen a kingfisher here before, but even as he thinks this, he sees a sparkling ripple on the surface of the water where the kingfisher had been poised on its overhanging branch. Tiny fry are leaping out of the water in the shallows, and obviously some form of mass panic is driving them.

Abandoning all thought of fly life, he tackles up as quickly as he can. Telling himself not to be so like a kid at Christmas, he tries to control the trembling of his fingers as he checks the leader for wind knots. Taking out his flybox, he chooses a small Baby Doll, ties it on and checks the knot.

Carefully he creeps to within fifteen yards of the shoal of fry – still leaping out of the water in a raindrop patter on the surface – he pulls line off the reel, kneels down and with one careful backcast, puts his fly straight out in front of him. Judging the distance to be correct, he then does a careful roll-cast to the edge of the terrified fry shoal, and lets the fly sink. Nothing happens for several minutes, and just as he is starting to think that perhaps he has imagined it all, he sees the end of the floating line slowly draw to one side. Lifting the rod smoothly, he feels the surge of power as a rainbow takes off in panic as it feels the hook. The reel screams as the line tears out, and he sees with amazement the little bow wave where the line enters the water. The line even makes a tearing noise as it is torn through the surface. Keeping his rod upright, the angler tries to apply a braking effect by palming the rim of the reel, but after another ten yards of line has gone and the backing knot has disappeared out through the tip ring, he takes his hand away from the reel. Leaning his rod to the side, parallel to the ground, he applies side strain. The fish slows down and the line sags. Winding as quickly as he can, tension is regained and the fish sets off again. More sidestrain; more winding frantically; not recovering line quickly enough, walking backwards, glancing behind for things which could trip him.

The battle is hard-fought, but bit by bit, the angler gets the feeling that he is now in charge. Taking his landing net from its ring on the back of his jacket, he flips it open, puts his foot on the rim and pulls the telescopic handle out to its full extent. Leaving the net ring in the water by his feet, he winds more line in until he judges that the fish can be netted without winding any more. Slowly the tip of the rod is drawn back, the fish comes quietly over the net and the net is lifted smoothly from the water with a glorious silver rainbow in the meshes. Turning around the net is laid down on the shingle, a priest is drawn from its usual pocket and with one smart rap on the head the fish lies still.

With shaking hands our angler takes the fish from the net, removes the hook from its jaw and lays it on the grass beside his fishing bag. He then sits down and pours himself a coffee with hands which still tremble, and admires the beautiful creature he has just killed, feeling the pang of sympathy mixed with elation at his success – the mark of all hunters when they succeed. Taking his priest, he unscrews the spoon in the handle and scoops out the stomach contents – as he thought – perch fry, mixed with midge pupae, but the midges are olive! He had expected them to be black, but no, a distinct olive.

Slowly he forces himself to relax again to nature's pace. His eyes roam the surface of the reservoir, now flat calm except for tiny catspaws out in the middle which die away almost as he notices them. Occasional fish rise here and there – feeding on something just under the surface. Thinking of the stomach contents of his fish, he decides that there has been a hatch of black midges during the night but that olive midges must now be hatching. Taking off the leader with the Baby Doll, he coils it carefully and puts it into a plastic envelope in his pocket – he could change to it very quickly if he saw another fry-feeding rainbow. Putting on a tapered leader, he adds a yard, leaves a dropper, and reaches for his flybox. Tying an olive midge pupa on the dropper and a small dry Grey Duster on the point, he oils the point fly carefully, then degreases the leader thoroughly. As he finishes, he looks up and sees the rings of a rise, off the point to his right.

Collecting his tackle, he wends his way through the trees along the bank. There is not much room on the point as the trees come right down to the water's edge. Wading out, very carefully and slowly, he pulls line off his reel, waggles the tip of the rod to work the loose line out of the tip ring and does a roll cast firmly along the bank to his left. The fly floats well and the leader nylon sinks. Good. Gently he does a Double-Spey cast out in front, the flies landing nicely 20 yards out, and as near as he can judge where the fish had risen. Nothing disturbs the calm surface. He remains motionless, watching his little Grey Duster sitting out there, looking for all the world like a little ball of fluff. He eases his feet gently in his waders, knowing that he dare not take his eyes off that fly, and he resists the temptation to look up as a jet screams overhead.

The minutes tick by. This is the hard part, he thinks, resisting the temptation to pull the line with the left hand in the mistaken impression that it would tweak the fly attractively and promote a take. No, do nothing, he decides, except stand there and concentrate. Suddenly, there is a wink of movement between the end of the fly line and his Grey Duster, and then the Duster is gone. Lifting the rod in a smooth tightening of the line, he starts to play another fish.

Ten minutes later, he is drinking another cup of coffee and admiring the two plump silvery two-pounders laid out side by side. Almost twins, he thinks, and checks that all the fins are perfect, the tails complete, and he sends a little thought of thanks to whoever it was in the Water Authority who decided to stock last September with one-pounders to grow on over the winter. Beautifully mended fish, they had both gone like trains when he hooked them. Then he remembers that he has not spooned the second fish, and does so. Yes, olive midge pupae, a close match for his dropper - but what's this? Some nymphs; half-a-dozen brownish ones mixed in with the midges. He studies them carefully. They are streamlined little things, about 10mm long, and he decides that they must be the nymph of some sort of olive dun. Probably a lake olive.

Nothing has moved in the bay since he landed the second fish. With a sigh, he heaves himself to his feet, collects his kit and trudges slowly back uphill to the car. There he puts the two fish into a coldbox in the boot, and gets out his binoculars. Nothing much is happening around the reservoir. Anglers are collecting in little bunches, with big gaps of empty shoreline between each bunch; hotspots, he thinks, always draw anglers like magnets.

There seems to be a steady ripple on the surface up in the North Arm. If there is going to be a hatch of olives, it will have to be from water no more than six feet deep, which is the sort of depth just where that ripple is. He moves again.

Two hours later, in the middle of the afternoon, he is fishing alone, with a steady warm breeze drifting his Light Pensioner dry fly enticingly along the surface. He's standing on the bank not wading, and so far - while the breeze lasted - he's caught three more trout, all over two pounds, by casting quickly to every rise within reach. He looks at the anglers asleep on the opposite bank, and feels a bit sorry for them. If they looked they might see him playing fish, and come around to the side where the breeze – warming the water – has encouraged that hatch of lake olives. But obviously they prefer to sleep and gather their strength for the evening rise.

As the sun sinks lower, he feels a chill in the air. The breeze drops and the surface of the reservoir takes on that glassy calm glaze – a bad omen. Not a rise mars the mirror of the opposite bank. Looking at his watch he realises that it is six o'clock; might as well pack up; that way he won't have to hurry on the way home and might even be a bit early – a nice surprise for his wife, she'd probably wonder if he was ill!

At twenty minutes to eight, he draws into the drive at home. Almost immediately the front door opens and his wife comes out.

'What's the matter with you?'

'Nothing,' he smiles, 'nothing at all. I had a great day, then it started to chill and the rise stopped so I came home. Now I can be late next time!' They grin.

'Come on in, it's freezing out here,' she says, as he realises that it is indeed bitterly cold.

'Pity the fruit growers,' he comments, 'having a ground frost at this time of the year.'

Later, he tells his wife all about his day as he eats and she smiles with that certain smile reserved for small children, fools and anglers, but is happy to listen. She's never seen a kingfisher, and half-wishes she had been there. After the meal has been cleared away, he cleans his fish, admires their solid pink flesh and carefully wipes down the draining board. As he takes the debris in its newspaper wrapping out to the dustbin, he shivers in the cold. That's some frost for May, he thinks. No wonder the fish switched off as they did. He turns indoors and spends the next hour happily writing up his fishing diary. He has had a marvellous day!

★ ★ ★

I would not like it to be thought that these two examples are true in every detail – they are not – but are both made up from various incidents I have experienced or seen, although not all on the same day. The stories were put together to illustrate as clearly as I can, that there are two distinct types of stillwater angler. I do *not* mean 'lure bashers' and non-'lure bashers': I do *not* mean dry fly purists and wet fly aficionados: I mean, simply, the *thinking* angler, and the *unthinking* angler.

The unthinking angler does something because he (or she) has always done it that way, or has been told once by some hero that this is the best way to do it. Or else he believes everything he reads in the more sensational fishing magazines and papers. On some days, the unthinking angler can catch a bagful – sometimes even achieving the apparently magical double bag limit – and has to go and get another ticket to make the slaughter legal. The unthinking angler is the man who, having been told that a fish has just been caught on a pink shrimp, proceeds to strip a pink shrimp in yard-long pulls on a sinking shooting head!

The thinking angler lets his powers of observation and his knowledge of fish and their food guide him into the best method. He is always prepared to listen to others, but likes to test theories for himself before adopting them as part of his armoury. He does what he can to increase his knowledge, trying to be a better countryman, and finds that he enjoys the ancillary aspects almost as much as he enjoys catching fish. And, averaging out fish per outing, he will always catch more fish than will an unthinking angler.

Which kind of angler do you want to be? Do not worry if you are about to go trout fishing for the first time, equally do not worry if you have been fishing for twenty years.

In this book I hope to be able to set out some of the immense amounts of knowledge which have been given to me so willingly – mostly in the form of casual fishing conversation – by a multitude of men and women who have been happy to talk of their successes and failures.

In writing this introduction to the revised 1994 edition, I am aware that there have been some significant developments in tackle and tactics since the first edition of this book was published in 1986. These developments are covered in the relevant chapters. If I do not mention your favourite new lure, please do not assume that I do not know of it. It is more likely that I have tried it and decided that it is not significantly better than a fly already in my armoury, as I am, too, a sucker for all the supposedly magic new patterns written about each month in the fishing magazines.

Not much of what follows is entirely new or original thought, but then very few authors can claim their work is a revelation. You might find yourself thinking that you know much of what I have to say – but do you never find yourself thinking, on the way home, 'Why didn't I try. . .?' If you had concentrated on being a more thinking angler, that thought would probably have occurred to you before the day was over and you would, perhaps, have caught more fish.

But you were too busy fishing to think . . . weren't you?

Tight lines and screaming reels to you.

Deer Springs Cottage
Wetherby
Yorkshire, England
1994

C·H·A·P·T·E·R

1

Clothing First

As this book is not intended for the absolute beginner, I must assume that the reader is already equipped in some way for fly fishing. So the best thing to do is for me to list the tackle which I suggest is correct for the thinking angler, and let you compare my suggestions with what you have. Not that you should rush out and replace all your kit – few of us can afford this drastic step anyway – but my ideas might point the way to a change of emphasis when you *do* have to replace something.

On the other hand, you might just have had your car broken into and all your tackle stolen! If you are lucky enough to be fully insured and with an insurance company which does not nitpick you into submission, then you can look forward to replacing some less-than-satisfactory tackle with something more in keeping with your improved level of expertise!

Let us start with the inner man. Unless he is comfortable, he will not think clearly. It is impossible to focus your mind on the detective work necessary for skilful fly fishing if, for example, you have hands so cold that they are one big hurt, if you are shivering and feeling thoroughly chilled, if you have sweat running into your eyes, or if you can feel a trickle of cold rainwater down between your shoulderblades. So a short mention of clothing and equipment to keep the inner man physically comfortable and able to think clearly seems appropriate, going from top to bottom in logical order.

First, a hat. Some incredible sights are seen around our stillwaters and reservoirs, from knitted bobble hats to tweed deerstalkers so covered in flies that they could strike you blind if you didn't peer at them through half-closed eyes. The snag is that no one hat will do a really good job for the whole of the fishing season – the weather varies too much from the frigid easterly winds of late March, to the occasional Costa-del-Sol heatwave of high summer.

In early spring, with the rain and sleet going horizontally past your nose, a hat must be waterproof and warm. Most waterproof hats I have seen are not warm, and most warm hats I have seen are not waterproof. There is an easy answer to this dilemma, however, but first let us choose a hat for cold weather.

It must have a good brim in front to keep rain and snow off your sunglasses. (At this early stage I can hear you saying to yourself that I must be a nut to wear sunglasses while it is snowing, but more of that later.) Next, and perhaps of slightly less importance, it should have a brim at the back to stop the rain running down your neck. If you do like wearing a hood then this rear brim will be nothing but a nuisance, but there are those - and I am one of them - who detest hoods as the rain makes a noise on them and stops you hearing fish rising. If the hood comes too far forward at the sides, it also acts as blinkers, cuts down your peripheral vision and prevents you seeing fish rising either side of you. As I regard it as most important that I am totally aware of my surroundings, I do not like hoods and thus I have a rear brim on my hat.

Basically, therefore, my cold-weather hat is a woollen or tweed deerstalker design. To keep the ears warm is sometimes a slight problem, but a good turn-up collar on a fishing jacket usually achieves this, providing the collar lies close to the neck so that the brim of the hat sheds the rain outside, not inside, the collar.

Wool or tweed is not waterproof. Some tightly-woven materials are nearly so, but not enough. The solution, once you have found a hat which suits you and fits well enough not to be blown off in a strong wind, is to waterproof it by spraying well with household furniture polish. The one I use is Pledge but any containing wax and silicones will do. Give it a good squirt all over and let it dry for a day or so. You will find that, once dry, the polish will not change the colour of the material and that from now on, the rain will run off in droplets and will not penetrate the surface. Having majored on the warmth of the hat, it is now waterproof as well and will keep your brains snug for clear thinking. Smelling of lavender, too!

In a heatwave, a woollen hat is too heavy, too hot and boils the brains. I have found that a German 'Afrika Korps' hat, made of lightweight cotton, is an excellent device. The British Army has copied this style for its tropical combat kit, and if you can find one in an ex-army store it makes an excellent hat for fishing in the heat of summer. Not only is it light in weight, with a good brim to protect eyes and sunglasses, it is camouflaged in greens and browns, helping you to get even nearer those trout you wish to stalk in the sunshine. Once again I proof mine with furniture polish, and then spray it well with midge repellent to prevent the little perishers from crawling around the hairline, driving me demented at times when I should be behaving like a cool calculating hunter of trout during the evening rise. So much for the headgear.

Around my neck I wear a towelling cravat. Some people advise looping a small towel round the neck, but I find this is too bulky at the back. Cotton towelling cravats do not cost much, and I have blessed mine dozens of times every season.

Tied in a simple half-hitch in front of the Adam's apple, the ends tucked down inside my pullover, the cravat makes a huge difference to my warmth and comfort on a cold day. It absorbs any slight amount of rainwater which finds its way down as far as the neck and prevents any from migrating down chest or back. On a very hot day I seldom wear one, but I always have it with me in case of a sudden chill wind which arises, particularly when in a boat. Because I hate anything restricting around my neck whilst fishing, I tend not to wear a tie or to fasten the top button of a shirt, but I wear my cravat on perhaps eight days out of ten.

Gloves, mittens or bare hands? Without a doubt, bare hands are the best. Not only can you tie knots, feel takes or remove hooks more easily, but they are the easiest to keep clean. On a bitterly cold day in early season it might pay to remember the old wildfowler's dodge; before starting to fish, stick your hands in the water until they feel really cold, then wave them around to dry them. I know it sounds daft to chill your hands right at the beginnng of a fishing day, but it works. Something to do with narrowing the blood vessels in the hands so that there is less heat loss for an hour or so. Try it – you will be surprised how your hands will feel warm for a considerable time.

Gloves with complete fingers are a disaster. Too much fumbling around altogether. Mitts which leave at least thumb and index finger exposed can be good, especially if you have a ghillie to change flies for you, and while I do own a pair I tend to wear them only when it is really frigidly sub-zero. After many years of stillwater fishing I think I have more-or-less decided that I shall carry them to wear when the line starts to freeze in the rings and I should be packing up anyway! Or when motoring the boat into the teeth of a blizzard to start another drift, but then I take them off for the actual fishing. One day, I suppose, I shall start to suffer from an old man's circulation and I might have to wear mitts for at least part of an early-season day, but I am aware that it will cost me fish either from a lack of sensitivity of touch, or from the extra time it will take me to change flies.

Now for the one item of equipment on which the majority of anglers spend most money – perhaps more than on their rod – and which causes most of the swearing. I refer to what is euphemistically called a 'fishing jacket'.

I am constantly amazed at the number of anglers who, perhaps unthinkingly, buy a jacket made from waxed cotton to wear for fishing. Waxed cotton is an invention of pre-First World War times. In those days they called rubber *gutta percha*, and plastics were unknown. Natural materials were all they had, and even in those days the best of the waterproof materials used for clothing was a thin layer of rubber bonded between two layers of cotton, invented by a Mr Charles Mackintosh (1766–1843). In various weights, this material was used for officers' trench coats, tarpaulins and gun covers. To this day a similar material is still used to make fishing bags.

'Oilskin' was invented around the same time, again using cotton as a basis, but in this case boiled linseed oil was applied to form a waterproof membrane. Because of cotton's tendency to rot, for linseed dressing to go tacky with age and for oilskin's liability to attack by mildew, the last use I can think of for this was for gas capes in the early days of the Second World War. In 1946, I think it was, I bought five of these gas capes for half-a-crown ($12\frac{1}{2}$p!) and managed to get perhaps two seasons of fishing and motorcycling out of them before they finally stuck together immovably or tore apart. I still hear anglers bemoaning the demise of the dressed-silk fly line. They must have short memories for the need to dry the line after every outing, polish it with French chalk and generally lavish lots of tender loving care on it. Modern plastic fly lines have entirely taken over and in the same way, oilskin-type material is now made with perhaps a nylon cloth base, laminated with one of the modern plastics.

The waxed cotton jacket has almost as many disadvantages as has oilskin. Like a suit of armour-plate in cold weather, restricting all but the most clumsy movements, it is heavy and unbreathing, it cooks you in hot weather; and must be removed every time you get into a car or public transport, or the wax will leave such a stain soaked into the back of the seat as to cause a scream of rage from the owner of the vehicle - probably the wearer himself! Even worse, if you are lucky enough to have one of those modern cars with a heated driver's seat, one trip with a waxed cotton jacket and you will have taken a couple of hundred pounds off the value of the car. But the biggest disadvantage of the waxed cotton jacket is that it is *not waterproof*. After a very few wearings, there is a creased effect at shoulders and elbows, and the water migrates through in a trickle which becomes a torrent once the jacket is a few months old. Re-proofing is then done, and the process starts again: and again, and again! Such is the power of advertising and tradition that anglers continue to buy jackets made from a material invented perhaps 100 years ago.

In the meantime, modern science has produced a multitude of much better answers. Materials which are *totally waterproof* in a monsoon, which breathe so that you do not parboil inside them, which need no re-proofing because they are always waterproof until they wear out after decades of hard use, and which can be cleaned by chucking them into a washing machine, provided it is set at cool wash and you do not spin dry. Marvellous materials, many of them no more expensive than waxed cotton, half the weight and just as resistant to thorns - and yet they seem to be catching on so very slowly. I am assured that the sales of waxed cotton jackets are as buoyant now as they have ever been: all I can assume is that the Sloane Rangers must number many thousands, as a waxed cotton jacket is - to them - a stamp of outdoor machismo, just as much as is walking down the main street of Ambleside in big boots with a coil of rope over the shoulders. Nowadays, to me, buying waxed cotton jackets is a sign of an unthinking angler.

Perhaps the best-known of the modern materials is Gore-Tex, but other similar materials are known by trade names such as Entrant or Cyclone. There are others, and there will be even more in time as competition hots up among the fabric makers of the world, who are all gunning for the huge outdoor market which covers not only fishing and shooting, but hiking, climbing, skiing and birdwatching (quite apart from the requirements of the armed forces). It is a huge and lucrative market. It is many decades since the skier or climber last wore waxed cotton – Sloane Rangers and unthinking anglers are the last stronghold!

Having discussed what material should be used, let us now talk about what a fishing jacket can be expected to do, apart from keeping you dry. Or dry and warm – not necessarily the same thing!

There are those who can remember the days when a well-dressed fly fisherman wore an old, well-loved sports jacket – the pockets of which held all his tackle – and had an ex-WD gas-mask bag slung over his shoulder to carry the fish he caught. These days it is not so simple, as magazine writers and advertisers have convinced us that it is vital to our hopes of success that we have lots of kit to carry around with us: the way we choose to carry this kit (and almost none of us can resist it all) is a matter of personal choice.

Some people prefer a fishing bag. This is soon so heavy that it tends to be dumped somewhere on the bank and, unfortunately to an increasing degree today, you are likely to find, when you next need it, that it has grown legs and walked away. I shall refer to fishing bags later.

Then there is the fishing vest, without which no American angler feels properly dressed, and which is finding a steady adherence in this country but is not yet widely popular. Fishing vests do not have sleeves, so even if the vest is made of waterproof material (and few of them are), your arms are going to get wet. If the vest is not made of waterproof material, the tackle in the pockets is going to get wet too. Unless, that is, you wear the vest under a fishing jacket, in which case the jacket has to be a couple of sizes larger than you would normally need.

Nowadays there are fishing jackets available with lots of pockets in which to carry tackle and this is the solution I personally favour. No longer do I find myself without some vital piece of kit. If I am wearing my jacket I know that everything I normally need in a day's fishing is in one of the pockets. Of course, not everything is in those pockets. I also take one of the recently-invented insulated shoulder bags containing, for a long fishing day, a flask of coffee, a flask of soup, sandwiches, my camera, a freeze-pack if the weather is hot and some bags for all the trout I hope to catch. So my fishing jacket not only keeps me warm and dry, it carries all my bits and pieces of tackle as well. Which means that if I do wade out 30 yards from shore (and I seldom do this, as we shall discuss later), I have everything in my pockets I need to change a fly or leader, to make flies float or sink, to net or kill fish (my landing net is hung on a ring on the jacket too), and I need to wade ashore only for coffee breaks or meals.

Below your fishing jacket you have another choice. Many of today's anglers do not think they are dressed to go fishing unless they are wearing thigh waders. Others, a minority, seem to think that knee-length boots with waterproof trousers will be adequate. Obviously, circumstances will be right for either waders or gumboots on their day, but for boat fishing I cannot stress too much that thigh waders should *not* be worn. Not only are they extremely difficult to swim in, but, if they are studded, a great deal of damage can be done to the floorboards of boats, and you are much more likely to slip on fibreglass or wooden boards if your boots do have studs. Life can be quite short if you fall overboard in the middle of Rutland Water, particularly if you are *not* wearing the lifejacket provided and you *are* wearing thigh waders.

Good thick socks to wear inside boots or waders are not a luxury. You may feel that thin nylon socks are correct inside Gucci shoes for the office or for a cocktail party, but they have no place on the banks of a stillwater. By all means have a mixture of nylon and wool, but the socks should be as thick and fluffy as possible. You then get the feeling of walking on a thick pile carpet, and this is very much less tiring than clammy feet which start to hurt after a few hours, as they assuredly will if you are wearing one or even two pairs of thin nylon socks. Finally, it is not an extravagance to put clean fishing socks on for each day's fishing. Clean socks are fluffier and more comfortable, are warmer and do not tend to slip down around the heel to nearly the same degree as socks which have been worn before. Many anglers I know do the same thing at the end of every fishing day; take their waders off, standing beside the open boot of the car and fling them in. Then they take off their wader socks, and tuck one inside each of the waders. Next time they go fishing, they are saddened to find that their socks are damp and uncomfortable from the very first pace they take. It is quite possible that these wader socks are washed only once in a year, in the close season! Not surprisingly these same men are often to be seen hobbling away from the water after a long fishing day.

Better still, of course, if you can afford two pairs of good thick socks for wearing inside waders, then you can have one pair on your feet and one pair in the car as part of your 'falling-in kit'. It does not take much mental discipline to remember to put your wader socks into the washing basket after every fishing trip, and to check that you have got them back among your fishing tackle before setting off on the next outing.

If you do forget those socks, you will always have a spare pair with you, if you do what I do and carry a 'falling-in kit'. This is an old ex-army haversack containing vest, underpants, ordinary socks, wader socks, trousers, shirt and a towel. None of these items would I care to be seen dead in, as they are all only one stage removed from the dustbin, but they sit there in the boot of the car from year to year, ready to be used in an emergency. I may be luckier than the average angler, but I have still had to use the kit on one occasion, one hundred and fifty miles from home, within ten minutes of starting to fish. At no time during that day did the temperature rise above 36°F (2.2°C) and without my falling-in kit there would have been the simple choice – go home or get pneumonia. I got three salmon that day, and ever since then my kit has been an old friend waiting in the corner for its moment of glory. Like insurance, you never need it until you need it badly.

Having now clothed and kitted out the angler so that he can function as a well-oiled hunting machine without the distractions of pain, cold, wet or discomfort, let us turn our attention to all the other kit which the thinking angler will carry and use on stillwaters.

C·H·A·P·T·E·R

2

Bits and Pieces

If we leave aside for the moment, the actual rod, reel and line, most anglers stagger down to the water's edge with a great weight of kit. Our coarse angling friends tend to use a set of wheels to make this transport easier, and at the other extreme is the elderly angler with a couple of old tobacco tins in the pocket of his old sports jacket. I refer of course to the bank angler. The boat angler has another problem in the transporting of anchors, chains, drogues and so on. If we ignore for a while the boat handling aspect we can confine ourselves to the bits and pieces we feel are necessary during a fishing day, all designed to help us present a fly to a fish at the right time and in the right way.

First, and absolutely essential, is a pair of polarised glasses. Whether you wear spectacles or not, you must have polarised glasses. If you do wear spectacles, find a good pair of clip-on polarised sunglasses to attach to them. If you can afford them, an even better solution is to have a pair of prescription spectacles made with polarised lenses. If, like me, you can still see a dry fly at fifty yards, but peer and poke to get nylon through the eye of a fly, then the best solution is to wear polarised sunglasses for fishing, and carry a pair of magnifying or reading glasses for changing a fly or tying knots. Remember also that to see modern nylon we have to see the shine of its surface – polarising removes the shine and makes it almost invisible, so remove your polarised glasses to tie knots. Why this strict emphasis on wearing polarised glasses anyway?

If you have ever, as I have, seen a man suddenly swear and clap his hand to his eye, turn to a companion and ask him to help, and when his hand is taken away see a small dry fly embedded in the eyeball with the jelly running down his cheek, you will realise that eyesight is very precious. The fly which blinds you does not have to be a large salmon double or treble – it can be size 18 dry fly. It is a sharp piece of steel, and if lashed into an eyeball it will blind you.

It is even possible to cut an eyeball with the end of a piece of nylon when trying out a rod or practising casting, the effect is the same as wiping a razorblade across the eyeball. So glasses or sunglasses at all times when you are waving a fly rod becomes rule number one. You have to forget only once, and you fit a glass eye into an empty socket every morning for the rest of your life.

Polarising, in removing the glare, works rather like the slats in a Venetian blind. For the sake of simplicity, imagine that the useful light is in horizontal bars and that this horizontal light can get through the slats in the blind. Glaring light or reflected dazzling light, on the other hand, is in vertical bars, which cannot get through gaps in the blind. Thus polarisation prevents glare from reaching the eye and makes it possible to see through the surface of the water much more clearly. It matters not whether the surface is reflecting strong sunlight - even the lightness of the sky on a dull day can make it difficult to see through the surface without polarised glasses. Even on very cloudy days it is incredible the difference which polarising makes. Wearing polarised glasses, you will have a much better chance of spotting fish, or seeing a rise in the ripple or of seeing that little wink under water which signals a take to a sunken fly. You will be able to watch the end of your flyline while nymphing, obtaining a much clearer picture of it even if it is lying there in a glittering ripple. How often have you watched your fly or line constantly for an hour or so, then looked up at the hillside opposite and seen the hill slide sideways for a second or so? That's eyestrain, which if not avoided, will give you a splitting headache at the end of the day. If you suffer from migraine, this glare must be avoided at all costs or you will spend a period in a darkened room suffering the tortures of the damned.

A word of caution is appropriate. There are polarised glasses and there are polarised glasses! They currently range from a couple of pounds to perhaps twenty five pounds, and it does pay handsomely to check for yourself that they suit you. A five second glance in the mirror is not good enough at all, in fact it matters not a jot what you look like in them! First of all, choose from the rack the pair which appear to have the lightest-coloured lenses. This is important as, if you buy a dark pair, you will tend to take them off at dawn and dusk, or not to wear them at all on very dull or overcast days. Then go to the door of the shop and look for something which has a glare or glint on it *on a horizontal surface*, like a puddle in the road or a reflection on the roof of a car. Look at that glare through the glasses, and tilt your head slowly sideways, first one way and then the other. You should notice the glare is at its least when your head is vertical. Do this with one eye at a time, to check that the lenses have been stamped out with the Venetian blind exactly horizontal. You will probably be surprised at the number of pairs of cheap sunglasses you have to try before you find a pair with horizontal polarising in both lenses. I cannot over-stress the importance of doing this test - if you get a pair with one lens out of horizontal you will get headaches for sure, and you will find yourself on the bank waggling your head from side to side like Noddy in order to see fish! Of course, this test should be done equally thoroughly with clip-ons. The higher the price you pay, ignoring the high cost of fancy frames, the less likely it is that there will be anything wrong with the polarising, and the better you will find them in day-to-day use.

Having gone to the trouble and expense of finding your ideal pair of polarising glasses, do realise that there are now two surfaces between you and the fish which will suffer from reflection or flare. There are four such surfaces if you wear specs and clip-ons. You must avoid direct light reflecting on those surfaces, or the flare will undo most of the good which the polarisation can do. The best way to do this is to wear a hat with a good large brim (such a hat was mentioned in the list of essential clothing). When Richard Walker wore his Australian bush hat for fishing he provoked amused comments from the unthinking, but if ever we wanted an example of a dedicated, thinking, fish hunter we need look no further.

Let me now consider – as representative of many experienced anglers – all the rest of the items (junk?) which *I* carry in the pockets of my fishing jacket, and which I think make an essential difference to my fish-catching ability.

There are four large pockets and four small pockets on the outside of my jacket. To eliminate the small ones first, let me say that I am an avid collector of insects. Thus three of the small pockets hold nothing except small plastic boxes with clear lids in which I carry specimens home for study and for photography. I also use one box for studying the stomach contents of almost every trout I catch. When tipped into a small white plastic box with a little water and gently shaken, the contents are no longer just mush, but become separated into recognisable food items. I shall return to this study of stomach contents later. The fourth small pocket carries a spare roll of film for my camera, wrapped in a resealable plastic bag just in case I fall in and have all my pockets fill with water!

First, the top pocket on the left breast. In there I carry several spare leaders, a nylon dispenser containing four spools of nylon, 25 metres/yards to a spool, of the various breaking strains which I shall need from time to time. When I am reservoir or stillwater fishing these would be 2½ lbs (but I take a risk when I use this – see *Numbers Rule*), 4 lbs, 6 lbs and 8 lbs breaking strain. If I were salmon fishing (with the chance of a seatrout), these would be 6 lbs, 8 lbs, 10 lbs and 15 lbs, but that is another story. The nylon dispenser is a most handy gadget. Invented by Jack Sheppard it carries small spools of nylon on spindles, with an end of each nylon sticking out of the side between small rubber jaws. To obtain a yard of nylon for a new tippet, just ease the lid slightly, pull the end of the nylon until you have enough, clamp the lid down and cut off the nylon an inch or so outside the rubber jaws. No longer do I have a birdsnest of nylon leaping off spools all mixed up in my pocket. Also in this pocket is the pair of magnifying half-spectacles which make me look like Mr Pickwick, but without which I can no longer tie reliable knots in fine nylon, or find the eye on a small fly.

Next, the large pocket on my left, at the bottom. Sometimes referred to as a 'cargo pocket', but as I am not a tramp steamer it is just the left-hand bottom pocket of my jacket! This contains two flyboxes only. They are Wheatley aluminium boxes measuring about 6 × 3½ × 1¼ in. thick. One is the dry fly box with a series of little lidded compartments on one side and Ethafoam on the other. In this box I keep all my dry flies, and some nymph and other beastie imitations. In the other box there is Ethafoam on both sides and on both sides of a centre leaf, in this I keep lures, wet flies and more nymphs. The two flyboxes sit neatly side by side in this bottom pocket.

In the top pocket on my right-hand side there is perhaps less organisation than in the others, and I confess that I do sometimes have to dig a bit before finding the item I want! Permagrease for re-greasing my fly line, or for greasing the leader (but I very seldom do this, as I shall discuss later). Dry and High powder for removing fish slime from a dry fly before oiling it. I regard this little plastic squeeze bottle as one of my best friends when I am dry fly fishing; take a small pea-sized heap of powder on the palm of the hand, grind the soggy fly in it, blow the powder off and you have a brand-new looking fly, ready to be dipped in the next bottle to be found in this pocket - dry fly oil. This is a mixture of solvents, waxes and silicones which waterproofs the fibres of a dry fly so that it will float for hours if necessary - not that it should get the chance! The next item is a small tub of Leadersink, a compound of Fuller's earth, detergent and glycerine with which I recharge from time to time the Flymate which hangs around my neck. Every single time I re-oil my dry fly, I stroke the tippet of the leader through the pads of the Flymate to make sure that the nylon sinks. I shall discuss this aspect later in the chapter on dry fly fishing.

Tucked away in the bottom of this same pocket are two more items - a hook-sharpening stone like a small triangular stick of carborundum, and a small smooth-jawed pair of pliers for flattening the barbs of hooks on those days when I know I shall be returning fish alive to the water.

Between the pockets on the right-hand side of the jacket is a triangular slot holding a pair of scissor pliers. These have a ratchet to hold the handles closed, and can double as forceps to remove hooks from tricky places inside a trout's mouth. The scissor blades forming the lower two-thirds of the jaws are serrated, so that nylon does not run away down the blades every time an attempt is made to cut it. The scissors are tied to a loop on the jacket by a piece of string so that I do not lose them every time I bend down.

Now, the lower right-hand pocket which contains only two items. Firstly a small bottle of midge repellent, which finds itself a comfortable corner at the bottom and stays there until I need it. And secondly, but by no means least, there is the priest. This is not just a priest, it is a combination priest and marrowspoon, and I use both ends every single time I kill a fish. We are in an era of social change in this country where every minority seeks to impose its will on the majority by shouting loudly, and one of these minority groups thinks it is cruel to kill anything. The way some anglers kill their fish I am sometimes tempted to agree. It really is providing ammunition to be fired at anglers if a fish is just thrown up the bank to gasp its life away, as I have seen done. On the last occasion on which I saw this, I was one of a group of five anglers who pounced on the perpetrator and turned the air blue as we told him what we thought of him. If you are going to kill something, you owe it at least a quick and as painless a death as possible, and this should happen before the fish is removed from the landing net. Grasp the fish through the mesh, draw your priest from where it is carried in a quick-draw position (in my case, the bottom right-hand pocket) and give it a swift crack across the top of the head. There is no need to pulverise it – all you are trying to do is to knock it unconscious so that by the time it would have woken up, it will have died quietly from lack of oxygen. But get your thumb out of the way or it will take a month for the bruising to go down sufficiently for you to be able to bend it again! This is not meant as flippancy – bashing your thumb instead of the fish brings tears to the eyes of even the toughest angler, and the colder the day the more it hurts.

Having killed the fish with one end of the priest, I then use the other end – the marrowspoon – and find out *why* I was lucky enough to catch it. Every single time I kill a fish I spoon it. I never cease to be amazed at what I see, as I shall discuss in a later chapter.

On the upper left sleeve of my jacket there is a pocket for sunglasses. As I am wearing glasses all the time I am fishing, this pocket usually contains only the empty case, but I have trained myself to put the glasses into their case every time I take them off my nose. Thus it is a long time since I lost a pair of sunglasses, or flattened a pair because I was careless in putting them down in a daft place – like the seat of the car!

In one of the two game pockets inside the jacket I carry some plastic freezer bags to put trout in and a small ball of string, not that I ever think I need it, but I know it will come in handy one day.

On the left rear waist of the jacket there is a ring on which I hang my landing net, but in the days before I got this all-singing and all-dancing jacket, I used to use a loop of thick twine over my shoulders in bandolier fashion and hung my net on that so it was suspended somewhere behind my left hip.

Supposing you do not have such a jacket, and prefer to carry all your kit in a fishing bag. Might I suggest that you put into the bag everything except the dry fly oil, leadersink and priest? Then at least you can leave the bag on the ground somewhere and fish a few yards away without having to walk backwards and forwards all the time for essential items. Sooner or later, though, you are going to slip a flybox into a pocket, followed by a pair of scissors, followed by some other small item and before you know where you are, you will be carrying just as much junk in your pockets as I do!

C·H·A·P·T·E·R

3

Rods

Such is the power of modern advertising, and its effect upon the psyche of anglers, that any angler today who is not waving a black stick tends to feel that he is underdressed, impoverished in the eyes of his fellows and incapable of catching as many fish as he should. This is all rubbish, really, as a good angler could catch fish with a garden cane, but perhaps 90 per cent of all the rods being used on our stillwaters today are made of carbon fibre. Why?

In my lifetime I have seen rods go from greenheart to cane to fibreglass to carbon fibre to boron. With a few minor diversions along the way, like tubular steel tank aerials, solid glass and an experimental solid carbon, the progression has been for only one purpose – to reduce the weight of a fly rod while not reducing the work it will do in casting or in playing a fish. Up to and including carbon fibre, this has been achieved to a remarkable degree. Boron was introduced to the market for, unfortunately, entirely another reason: to increase the price of a fly rod by launching a material which would cause the price of a fly rod to rise again to the level it had been before the Far-Eastern blank makers slashed the profit margins on carbon fibre. Boron is *heavier* than carbon fibre, and thus rods with any appreciable content of boron are heavier than carbon fibre ones. There have been fanciful advertising campaigns designed to reassure the customer that a boron rod is stiffer, recovers quicker from bending, does not break fine leaders on the strike and various other rubbish. This is all balderdash – designed to take more of your money from you. Any attribute of a rod can be designed in with almost any material – you want a rod which 'recovers more quickly from bending' (You mean stiffer, chum)? It can be designed, in either carbon or boron and the carbon blank will be lighter than the boron one. And a good deal cheaper.

Having said that, it should not be imagined that only carbon fibre will produce a good fly-rod blank. I have an old glass rod built on a Phillipson Gold Bank blank, and it is one of the sweetest-actioned rods I have ever owned, and is still a favourite. But it is brown in colour, and I have actually had fellow-anglers come up to me and ask if there was a special reason for painting my rod that colour!

Carbon fibre fly rods do not, of course, have to be black or dark charcoal grey. There are at least two makers I can think of who are using a dark red varnish on their blanks to give a burgundy or deep maroon colour – Fenwick of the USA and Century Composites of Britain, but this is just window-dressing to make the rod look different. In the early days of carbon fibre, Geoffrey Bucknall of Sundridge Tackle had some blanks painted heron-grey – presumably so that they were less visible against the sky – not a bad idea at all – but I do not think they were accepted by the majority of anglers, who, by some quirk of human nature, prefer their fly rods to be black and very shiny, so that others will be made aware of how much they paid for them!

There are so few cane rods being sold nowadays that it is often forgotten that there is one very great benefit in the material. It is not hollow (unlike glass or carbon rods, which are). Thus it can be trodden on with much less likelihood of breakage than can glass or carbon! Modern tubular rods are, to use a technical term, notch-sensitive, and thus a tiny nick in the surface caused by knocking the rod against something will cause a fracture to migrate from fibre to fibre, progressively weakening the rod until, perhaps hours, days or even weeks later, there is a sickening crack and a shower of bits around your ears. The average angler, faced with this occurrence, will blame the blank maker, forgetting all about hitting the rod with a fly on the backcast the previous Saturday. In short, modern tubular rods must be treated with a little more care than cane rods needed in their day, but given that care, they will outlast cane rods by generations of grandchildren. Carbon rods do not get old, fatigued and sloppy as cane rods did, and thus it is my advice that the modern stillwater angler should concentrate his rod-buying on carbon fibre. If he buys boron he is regretably being suckered into spending more than he needs to, and will end up with a rod which is heavier than it needs to be, if it has more than a tiny percentage of boron in it.

Having settled on the material, what sort of action should the rod have and how long should it be? Let me be a bit Irish and discuss the second question first.

It would be true to say that a single-handed fly rod can be any length from 6-12 feet (2-4 metres). At one end of the scale you have the little toothpicks, so beloved of American friends, and at the other extreme are the long wands used for wet fly fishing by the traditional Scottish boat angler. For the average stillwater angler, fishing from the bank, the best solution must lie between these two extremes.

First the very short rod, say from 6-8½ foot long. These short rods are hard work for casting further than a very few yards, as it is necessary to double-haul to get line speed through the air. The very shortness of the spring means that the line must be propelled faster by the arm muscles. While these short rods are excellent for fishing in brooks and streams, or for very small ponds, they cause much greater fatigue during a day's fishing than does a longer rod. Having said this, it must be noted that there is a great deal of pleasure to be gained from the occasional use of a short, very light rod; providing the rest of the outfit is also equally light. I get a lot of fun out of a day with a 7 ft rod, a Hardy LRH Lightweight reel, and a double-taper No.4 line. It is a lovely outfit for stalking trout with, using a little nymph or dry fly, and makes a one-pound trout feel like a monster. With good double-hauling technique it is possible to cast about twenty yards, and the trouble only starts when you stick the hook into a four-pound rainbow! Then it is quite likely that you will feel that the trout is playing you. Because I like to feel that I am in command of any fishing situation, I keep the little rod for fun days and not for occasions when I am doing some serious fishing.

At the other end of the scale, I often see very long rods recommended by some angling writers. Rods of over 10½ feet suffer from a leverage problem. The weight of the line is a long way from the wrist, and because in casting you move the weight of the line through the air, the weight becomes multiplied the further away it is from the grip. No great problem if you have arms like the branches of an oak tree, but for the average man or woman of sedentary occupation, casting all day with a long rod is very tiring indeed. To a certain extent this can be overcome by aerialising less line and shooting more, as this reduces the weight outside the tip of the rod, but this is no more than good casting technique anyway. It will be found that many rods on the market over 10½ feet are provided with an extension handle - another way of admitting that they should be used double-handed when the use of one hand becomes impossible through exhaustion! There are, of course, benefits to be gained from a long rod, mainly in boat fishing. The dibbling of a top dropper is possible at greater distances from the boat. The lazier action of hand and arm will lay out a short line during the fishing of a style known as 'show it to 'em and whip it off'. But on balance, the longer the rod the more tiring it is to fish with, and the older you become, the more critical this fatigue becomes.

Having discussed the two extremes of length, we come now to the main bracket - rods of between $8\frac{1}{2}$-$10\frac{1}{2}$ feet, and this is where the majority of single-handed fly rods belong. For utmost efficiency, one has to study the work done by the competition casters, and thanks must be extended for the great help, advice, friendship and courtesy shown to me by members of the British Casting Association. Attending their competitions at York and Scarborough, and watching people like the late Jack Martin, Peter Anderson, John Gibson, the late Brendan Mahone, Mike Weddell and many others, it became apparent that the one factor which governed the distance a fly could be cast was line speed. Line speed was governed by tip speed and the haul of the left hand, but mainly tip speed. So for distance casting, the tip of the rod has to move as fast as possible. Studying the ergonomics of casting with a fly rod, it seems that, for a man of average build, the tip of the rod moves fastest if the rod is no longer than 9½ feet. Any longer, and the leverage results in less tip speed - the muscles are just not capable of moving the tip fast enough. On the other hand, any shorter than nine feet, and there is a loss of line speed through *lack* of length in the rod. It is thus no accident that many reservoir rods, designed for distance casting, are 9¼ feet long, and thus designed for the average man, of average build and muscle power. It follows therefore that you can tailor this to your own circumstances, and if you are a young, fit version of Charles Atlas you can use a rod of perhaps 9½ or even 10 feet, but if you are over 40 years of age, you should opt for a rod of 9 feet. You can add a foot to each of these measurements if you are buying a rod to use solely from a boat, for shortish distances.

Before we discuss what sort of action a rod should have, may I just say that there is a peculiarity about British anglers. Each year, at the Game Fair, there are rods set up at the waterside by both makers and retailers, for anglers to try. The idea is that, if an angler finds a rod he likes, he will then go to that particular maker's stand and buy one. A typical scenario goes like this.

'Have you a little seven-foot brook rod?'

'Certainly, Sir, here you are. It has a double-taper four line on it.'

The rod is then handed to the angler, who marches onto the casting platform and proceeds to double-haul out of sight! After a moment or two, the maker turns to the angler and asks where he is going to fish with the little brook rod, only to be told that he is trying it out to see if it would be suitable for a little overgrown stream near his home, where little wild brown trout, about three to the pound, make fascinating fishing.

'Then why are you trying to cast the whole line out?'

'Because I read that article by so-and-so about short rods, and he says that he casts 30 yards with ease.'

After that the sale is lost, the rod and reel are smuggled back to the stand where, in private, six or seven yards are cut from the back end of the flyline, and the rod is then returned to the casting platform. The next angler comes along, picks up the little brook rod and proceeds to belt out a double-haul. With delighted surprise he is then told that he is an excellent caster, as he has got the whole of the fly line out! A sale is made, and both parties are happy with the outcome. The maker has sold a brook rod which he knows is of high quality, and good value for money. The angler has a tiny rod which he will use for many years of fun and pleasure on his tiny stream, telling his friends what a marvellous little rod it is – in emergency it is quite capable of casting out the whole of a fly line! As none of his friends are rude enough to ask him to prove it, the deception never comes to light. But the deception would not have been necessary if the rod had been tested for its proper purpose and not subjected to the craving for distance which infects so many of today's anglers.

The way a fly rod bends is a fertile source of verbosity on the part of an advertising man. I think there has been more rubbish written about rod actions in the past few years than on any other aspect of fishing. In the old days, say before the Second World War, rods were either 'dry-fly action', or 'wet-fly action'. This was a conveniently pleasant way of saying that they were stiff or soft. Let me explain by saying that a dry fly rod should be stiff enough to make the line go back in a backcast fast enough for the water to be flicked off the fly. Thus the fly is dry again when it lands on the water, will float well and will have a happy angler at one end and a deceived fish at the other. A wet fly rod, on the other hand, should be sloppy enough for the fly, wet when it comes out of the water, *not* to have the water flicked off at the extremity of the backcast, so it will still be wet when it lands in the target area and will sink quickly to the depth of the fish about to be deceived, again yielding a happy angler on the bank. Having once succumbed to the euphemisms of dry fly or wet fly actions, instead of just saying stiff or soft, or even stiffish or softish, we have today to be bombarded by long descriptions of parabolic actions (thank you, Charles Ritz), compound taper, modular taper, high modulus or low modulus and a host of other words which, for all the meaning they convey to the average angler, might as well be straight from the Dead Sea scrolls. What all these words do is to confuse. What they *try* to do is to show the potential customer that there is some magic property in this rod or that.

It all boils down to the fact that there are some lovely rods on the market, at a range of prices from bargain to indecent: and some lousy fly rods on the market, also at prices from bargain to indecent. And you can never tell which is which without casting a line with a few of them, comparing one with another or with your old rod, and letting your casting arm tell you which rod suits you. Only then should you look at the price tag, and you might get a very pleasant surprise, discovering that the rod which suits you is not going to cost an arm and a leg. Like factories making nylon, there are really very few blank makers in the world, and much of any price differential between two rods can be accounted for by the number of links in the distribution chain (thus the number of profit margins added on), by the quality of the fittings on the rod, and any possible little extras like ferrule stoppers, your name engraved on the butt, whether the rod comes in a case and any delivery charges which may be involved.

There is one other possibility. You might be one of those people who are never happy unless they buy the very best, and the most expensive must be the best. In which case you will spend a lot of money on your tackle anyway, and I wish you the best of luck, any advice given will be totally ignored, as your wallet knows better than anyone else what is good for you! As the average angler never dares to tell his wife what he spends on his hobby, you must have more secrets than most of us lesser mortals! It is a peculiar quirk of human nature that pride of ownership is in direct proportion to the cost, rather than the functionality, of an item.

How do you test a rod when looking for the kind of action which suits you? Of course you do not try to cast a DT 4 line 30 yards, at least to start with. You should attach the reel and line which you will use for most of your fishing, or for the kind of fishing you have in mind (whether this is delicate nymphing at 20 yards, or belting a lure on a sinking shooting head as far as you can, is up to you), but do test the rod for your kind of fishing. If you get an impression of sweetness of action, of a nice crisp feeling to your casting, then you have struck gold straight away and you can then look at the price tag.

It is very likely, however, that you will find the rod feels either too stiff or too soft for you. If it feels too stiff, it might be better with a heavier line. But do you want to buy a heavier line just to suit the rod? the answer is certainly that you do not. As I shall discuss later, you should have settled on the line first, and then be finding a rod which will cast it nicely. On the other hand, the rod might feel soft or spongy, and again a different line, this time a lighter one would perhaps suit it better. We now come to another benefit of the majority of carbon rods on the market today.

Fibreglass rods will normally handle lines of one AFTM number either side of their correct rating, but carbon rods will normally handle two AFTM numbers either side. Thus a rod correctly rated AFTM 7 will handle a No.7 line best but, if it is made of carbon fibre, it should handle a No.6 line very well and a No.5 line quite well. At the other end of the scale, the rod will take a No.8 line very well and a No.9 line quite well. If you want a rod to behave superbly for just one style of fishing, by all means choose a rod rated exactly for the line size in question. Thus, for sheer distance using a No.9 shooting head, choose a rod rated AFTM 9 or even 10 if you really want to set distance records. But for the average angler on a variety of stillwaters, fishing various methods depending on weather and time of the year, the following suggestion is sound.

Look at carbon rods rated AFTM 7 first. If you find one you like, you should then be able to fish with any of the following lines:

DT or WF 5, but the WF 5 might be too light for short distances.
DT or WF 6, but the WF 6 might seem a touch too light.
DT or WF 7, theoretically the best lines for the rod.
DT or WF 8, but the DT 8 might seem a touch too heavy on long casts.
A shooting head No 8, or a ten-yard head made of AFTM 8 line.
A DT 9, which will feel too heavy except for short distances.
A WF 9 or a shooting head 9, the only difference being that you will shoot more line with the shooting head, but the weight-forward is more pleasant to handle.

Remember too, that when makers rate a rod, they do so by personal opinion. A man will pick up a blank, bend the tip against the floor or ceiling, look thoughtful for a moment and then pronounce a number. This is, in theory, the line which that blank will handle best – *in his opinion*. If he is the boss, that is the number which will appear on the blank just above the handle! If he isn't the boss, somebody else will do the same thing, and if his verdict differs from that of the first man, they might decide to compromise by rating the rod with two numbers – like AFTM 7/8 – meaning that, *in their opinion*, the rod is equally good with either a 7 or an 8. There is just a possibility that, when you test the rod for yourself, you may decide that for your casting style the rod is best with a 6! So long as you use it with a 6, you can ignore what it says above the handle.

One last point, and this is most important, do remember that all rods are rated for 10 yards of line outside the rod tip, plus whatever level tip there is before the taper starts, plus the leader. Most fly lines today have a level tip of between one and two feet when they are new and before you have chewed away some of the level tip when changing leaders or tying fancy needle knots. The rod should feel exactly right, therefore, when you have outside the tip of the rod ten yards of fly line, say 2 ft of level tip of that fly line and, say, a 10 ft leader. Thus your fly should land 42 ft away from the tip of the rod. In other words, if you are using a nine foot rod, the fly should land 51 feet away from your hands and feet. That is not, I must stress, a ten yard cast: it is a 17 yard cast, and it is surprising how many fish are caught within that distance. If the truth were told, it is as far away as perhaps 25% of current reservoir fishermen can cast anyway, and on water it looks quite a long distance (see Appendix D).

Let me enlarge for a moment on the meaning of the rod 'feeling exactly right'. Let us assume that you are an averagely good caster, that you do not put too much effort into your casting, that you do not cock the wrist back too far and thus you normally achieve a nice high backcast, which flows out smoothly without waves along it, and that you can land a fly delicately at, say 15 or 20 yards. Thread the rod with the line of your choice and, for initial testing, it is my opinion that this should not be a shooting head (unless you are buying a rod only for shooting head work). Best of all the line should be a double-taper. Start by looking at the way the rod bends. Very gently, lay the tip ring on the ground, with the butt held up somewhere around shoulder-height. Have the reel upwards, so that when you press down, the rings are on top of the rod or on the inside of the curve. Do you get a nice smooth progressive curve? Or are there places where the amount of curve seems to change suddenly? (Any sudden change in the curve may indicate where there is a weakness in the rod, and the rod should be rejected right away.) Now turn the rod over, so that the rings are on the outside of the curve, reel downwards. Does it seem to need the same amount of effort to bend the rod by the same amount? It should. If it seems markedly easier to bend the rod one way, then you can assume that there is a pronounced 'spine' in the rod: carbon rods do not suffer from a pronounced spine unless the walls of the blank are perilously thin, and again the rod should be rejected then and there – you are aiming to buy a reliable rod, not one which is going to shatter when you are five miles from the car with no spare!

So far, you have only eliminated the 'Monday morning rod', and they do happen in even the best-run blank plants. I do not, however, mean that you should have bent the rod to an appalling curve to see what it will take. All you have done is to bend it gently, to see what sort of curve is built into the blank's design. If you are looking for a nice gentle nymphing rod, you should not have gained the impression that you were trying to bend a billiard cue: equally if you are looking for a rod to hurl a shooting head out of sight, it should certainly not feel like a thin sloppy reed.

Now you can go to the next step. Measure out ten yards of line outside the rod tip. Do not just pull lots of line off the reel, measure it by holding the tip ring in one hand beside your chin and pull, one yard at a time, with the other hand, to full-arm stretch. Do this ten times, and you can be sure that you have got ten yards of line, *plus leader*, outside the tip ring. Now you can try a cast, and judge whether the rod will handle your chosen line weight nicely.

Whatever you do, do not for at least the first few minutes pull any more line off the reel. Clamp the line to the corks with your rod hand, and forget all about shooting any line for the time being. Just cast with that ten yards. See how *nicely* you can cast that ten yards: try to land the fly gently, aiming a foot above the surface of the water or grass: see how the line goes out, is it straight? Turn your head to watch the backcast or, even better, have a friend watch the back-cast for you: does it flow out nicely, at least as high as the tip ring? Does the rod tip waggle around when you stop the backcast, or does it come gently to a stop? Now slacken your grip on the corks, and see just how *little* effort it requires to cast that ten yards. If, so far, you are delighted with the performance of the rod, you can proceed to the next step.

Pull exactly five yards of line from the reel, and dump it at your feet. Holding

Bending a fly rod against the floor. A nice smooth progressive curve, with no sudden variations in the curve. This rod will be pleasant to use all day for short and medium distances, and should handle a wide range of line weights.

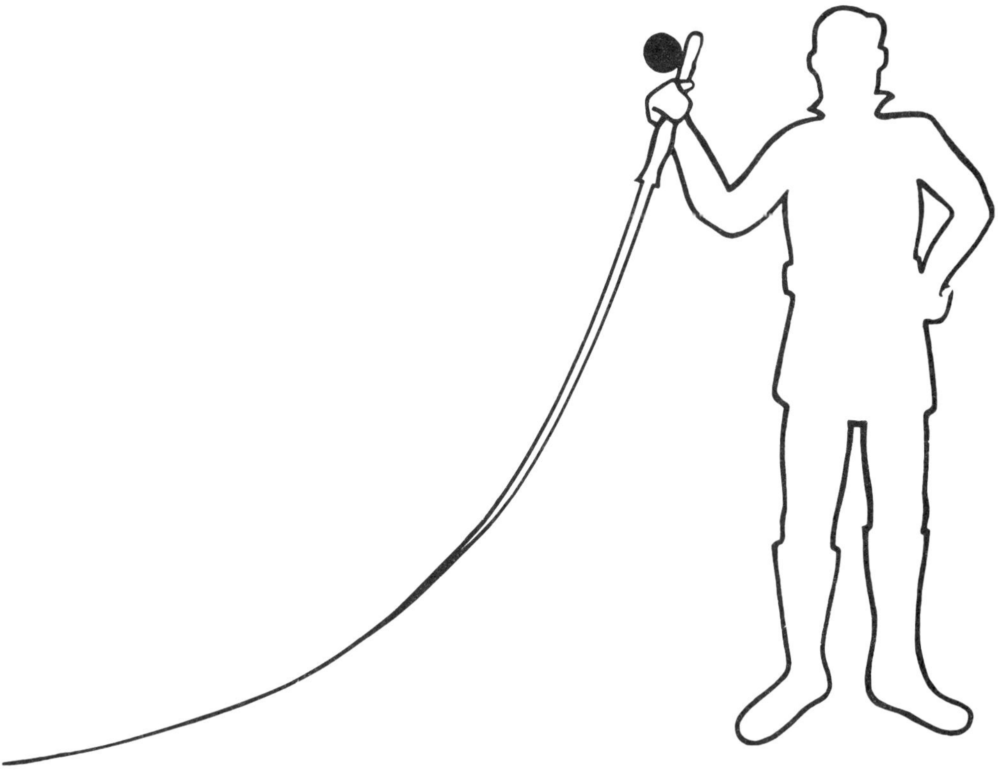

the line at the same point which gave you ten yards outside the tip ring (using the non-rod hand), try a cast. After only one backcast, try shooting that five yards. Did it all go out, or was there some loose line left between you and the butt ring? If there was, try again, and if it still fails to go out nicely, you should suspect that there is something wrong with the rings on the rod. Rings spaced too far apart allow the line to cone between the rings, with too much friction from line-slap on the blank. Too many rings, on the other hand, add friction on their own. In either case, it is not the rod for you. Assuming, however, that all five yards shoot well and that there is not that little zizz from the reel ratchet signifying that you put too much effort into the cast, you can then proceed to the next stage.

Pull lots more line from the reel and dump it at your feet. Now you can satisfy the primeval urge which you have so far kept under control – try to see just how far you can cast. Settle for the distance which gives a nice turnover to the leader, not the distance where the leader ends up in a heap. This is best done on grass, as you should now lay the rod down, and pace in nice long strides all the way to the

More of a tip action. There is hardly any curve in the butt half. This rod is more suitable for distance casting, but will be more tiring to use all day than one with a gentler curve.

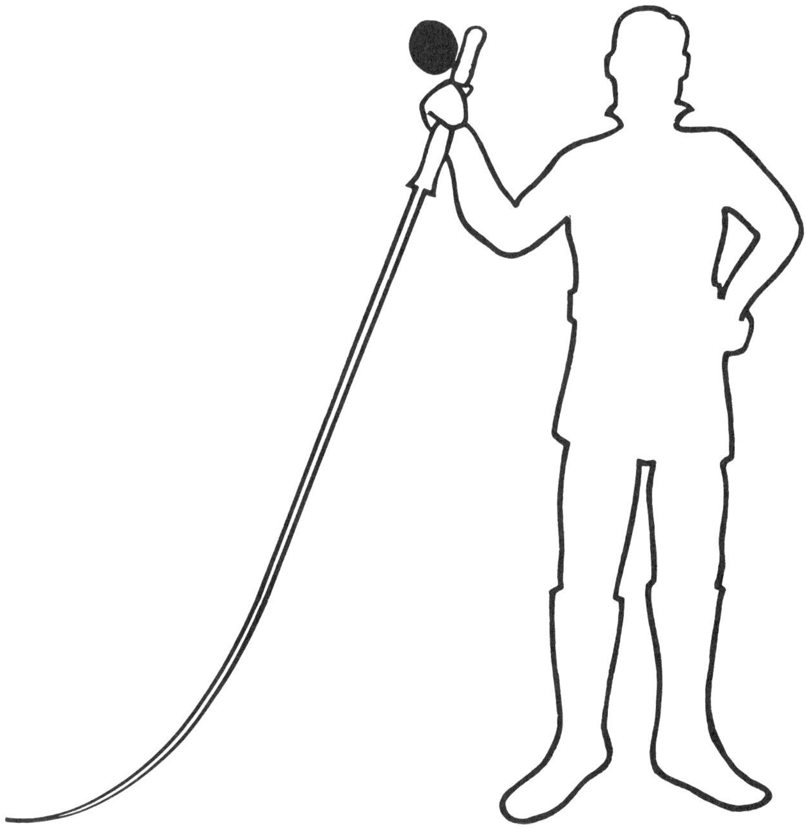

fly. When you have finished counting, you might look thoughtful if this is the first time you have ever measured your maximum casting distance! Please do not be depressed if it falls far short of the boastful 40 yards + so beloved of the writers of magazine articles and advertisements for the rod you are testing. If you have cast more than 25 yards with a double-taper, or 30 yards with a weight-forward, you are well above average, believe me, and you can rest assured that your casting standard will put plenty of fish in the bag. If, however, you have managed less than 18 yards with a double taper, or 24 yards with a weight-forward, you must decide whether the rod is at fault or whether you need a casting lessson! Many anglers do find it a sobering experience to measure their longest cast for the first time.

Equally, it must be emphasised that this last part – the sheer distance achievable – is the *least important* part of testing a rod for nymph, wet fly or dry fly fishing. It is of *major importance* only for a rod which you are going to use for belting a shooting head and, as we shall discuss later, this may well form a minor part only of a season's fishing.

You may, of course, be considering buying a blank and finishing it off yourself, and may I state quite categorically that there are more disasters around from this cause than any other. To buy a blank from somebody else's description of it, to put many hours of tender loving care into the whipping and varnishing, and then to find that the finished rod is a hellish casting instrument is an experience calculated to bring tears to the eyes of even the most hardened bank manager. Don't do it. If you are considering buying a blank, make sure that you follow exactly the steps I have outlined, using a made-up blank similar in all respects to the one you are considering. Any tackle shop which does not have a made-up rod for each blank it sells should be avoided like the plague, it is obvious that the blanks cannot have been tested by the retailer and that somebody else's word is being taken for the quality. There is a strong possibility that a batch of blanks have been bought from a wholesaler, using profitability as the sole guide to excellence (Buy 10 – get 2 free!). Don't touch these with a barge pole, or you will be sorree. . ..

If you do find a made-up blank to test and find it suits you, do not then rush home and start lashing rings on. Tape them on with adhesive tape, try the rod and look carefully at the way the line goes through. Could you improve on the suggested ring spacing? And here we come to only two really critical measurements. If the tip ring is more than 5 inches from the first intermediate ring you will, from time to time, get that annoying loop thrown over the tip – the one you look at and, if you are a beginner, take all the line back through the tip ring and re-thread it all! To avoid this irritating fault, make sure that the first intermediate ring is no more than 4-5 inches away from the tip ring. Now grip the rod normally and reach forward with the other hand to where you expect to grip the line immediately after casting. Funny how some rod makers think you have arms like a gorilla, isn't it? I have found that the butt ring should be no more than 15 inches from the thumb of the rod hand. Any further and you tend to be stretching for the line every time you cast. One last little dodge - on a rod intended to be used mainly with a shooting head - you will find that two identical butt rings, not too small, spaced only four inches apart, will cut out the coning of the running line, reduce the friction of the line up the rod and will add at least three yards to your distance. This *coning* is rather like the action of a skipping rope wielded by two enthusiastic small girls. But because two butt rings look odd and add to the cost, makers don't do it! We live in a funny world.

Now you have chosen a rod which your casting arm tells you is nice, and which you will feel happy with for hour after hour, day after day and year after year, we can move on to consider other aspects of tackle. But one final word, you will I hope appreciate that a rod should *never* be bought without first trying it out for yourself. Do not try a friend's rod, like it and march into a shop and demand one just like it - every rod varies to a certain extent; even if the model is apparently the same in every detail, *try it* and with your own reel and line. Your friend may have been using a heavier or lighter reel, and a different weight of line. I know this sounds elementary, but it does bear repeating as the same mistake is made by anglers almost every day.

C·H·A·P·T·E·R

4

Reels and Reel Fittings

There are those who refer to these as winches and winch fittings, but they are at least a hundred years out of date. Equally, it is many years since I heard a reel referred to as a pirn in Scotland.

When reels were first invented, their main function was to store all the line when the angler was not fishing, and to store the excess line when he was. All fine and dandy when fishing for little wild trout about 8 inches long, with a half-pounder being a fish to remember the season by. Nowadays we fish for stocked trout in stillwaters and they may well be as large as some salmon, so the reel has had to develop to fulfil another function, that of allowing the line to be pulled off under sufficient tension to avoid over-runs, and yet not enough tension to cause the leader to break under the strain. A much higher standard of engineering has, therefore, to be devoted to the reel than is commonly realised if reliability is to be achieved. But, basically, the reel is *still* there to store the line and backing while it is not needed.

However much or little you spend on a reel is not important. What is far more important is how you look after it. The key word is maintenance – preventive maintenance is the engineering term – the care which is given to a piece of machinery to make sure that it does not break down at a critical moment. I am reminded of the last service my car had, when a set of perfectly good spark plugs was discarded and new ones fitted. When I said that the old plugs looked OK to me, I was reminded that the service for which I was paying did not take into account the 10,000 miles the car had just done, but the next 10,000 miles it was going to do without breaking down. I took the point, paid up and tried to look cheerful, and remembered the conversation with some comfort the next time I set out on a long journey late at night. So the key to reliability is preventive maintenance – not ignoring one's reel from season to season, allowing grit and

Three types of reel fitting. At the right can be seen an up-locking fitting where the reel foot slides under the corks in a reinforced sleeve. This is best for an automatic reel, as the lever then ends up under the little finger.

In the centre is a down-locking fitting, for very long rods where it is best to bring the point of balance of the rod as far down as you can by taking the weight of the reel as far back as possible. The disadvantage is that if the rod is stood on its butt the reel goes straight into the grit or mud. Do not think my shooting head consists of the whole *of a DT9.*

At the left are two alloy rings and a cork bed. This type, which will loosen sooner or later and drop the reel off into fifty feet of water, should be avoided at all costs.

sand to accumulate inside the works, letting the spindle and pawls run dry and remembering to do something about it only when it starts to squeak when turned. Sod's Law says that if you do neglect your reel like this, it will cost you the biggest fish of your career when it shrieks into a solid state and the leader parts with a crack like a pistol shot. Or your rod breaks and the leader parts with a crack like a pistol shot!

It doesn't matter in the least whether your reel cost you an hour's pay or a week's, it will let you down sooner or later if you do not look after it. Actually, the more expensive it is, the tighter the tolerances on bearings and the easier will it jam solid with a few grains of grit and lack of lubrication. For the lack of a few minutes' work - all part of the fun of fishing, after all - you can easily wreck something which could, with care, still be purring smoothly when your grandchildren fish with it fifty years from now.

So what kind of reel to choose for those stillwater fish, which can weigh anything from half-a-pound to as much as perhaps fifteen pounds? Not in terms of money, as this is something you have to decide for yourself, but in terms of type and size.

Size first. If you have a large reel and then fit a light line to it, you will need a lot of backing line to fill it properly. It will then probably feel clumsy on the light rod which matches the line. So, to this extent, the reel should 'balance' the rod not, as some people think, bringing the point of balance of the rod to some mystical point on the rod when held over a finger as a fulcrum. It should just feel right when you are casting with it attached to the rod for which it is intended, and should hold a reasonable amount of backing. What is a reasonable amount of backing? Fifty yards of backing, a standard fly line and a nine foot leader, means that a fish can be 83 yards away from you when everything comes to an end. I confess that I have never seen a stillwater trout landed which took out as much as that. By the time the whole line is outside the tip ring there is so much resistance behind the fish that the hookhold usually tears out anyway: so fifty yards of backing is usually enough. There is, of course, no harm in putting lots of backing on a reel; any reel is best filled so that the maximum amount of line is retrieved for each turn of the spool.

As it is a mistake to have only one reel, consideration should be given to sticking to one design and make, and buying two reels the same. Then spare spools can be swopped from reel to reel. If you are a dedicated stillwater angler you will accumulate lines over the years, and having only one make and style of reel can be a great money-saver. Make sure, however, that the maker is not a fly-by-night outfit, just starting to take huge adverts in the angling magazines, or you may find spares and spare spools impossible to obtain in a couple of years. For my own reels I stick to Hardy and Shakespeare for reels with handles, and Mitchell for the automatics.

The reel you choose should therefore be capable of taking the bulkiest fly line you are likely to need (and that essential backing). I would suggest that this be a

DT 7, so any reel designed for a No.7 line will do. It will not be all that much heavier and bulkier than a No.5 reel, and by putting say 100 yards/metres of backing on, the No.5 line will go nicely on the No.7 reel. For a No.6 line you will have perhaps 75 yards/metres of backing. For heavier lines, a WF 8 or a shooting head 9 will go on easily. So for simplicity and economy it is my suggestion that you stick to reels designed for No.7 lines, buy two of them, plus spare spools and let your wallet dictate which model, from which maker, you buy.

If I may narrow down my suggestions still further, I would suggest any reel from the following list: Shakespeare Beaulite 3½in. wide; Shakespeare Speedex 3½in. wide; Hardy Marquis No.7; Hardy Marquis Multiplier No.7; Mitchell 710 Automatic.

Now the knotty problem of whether you choose a simple winding reel, a multiplying reel or an automatic, and here is a subject which tends to raise blood pressures among their respective aficionados. There are folk who would not be seen dead with a clockwork reel on a nice fly rod, and there are those who think that anybody who sticks to an old-fashioned winding reel is a fogey who isn't really keen on catching fish. Let me set out the pros and cons, and then tell you what I do!

The simple winding reel has fewest parts and therefore is, in theory, more reliable and gives least trouble. I have seen men winding like demented chimpanzees to get line in fast enough when a big fish runs straight at them: or else give up the attempt to wind fast enough, and hand-line in and dump it on the ground at their feet. When that big fish turns and runs away again, Sod's Law says that the line has caught around a stone or a thistle, or the angler has trodden on it, and there is a ping as the fish departs with a fly and a yard of leader. Such simple winding reels are usually referred to as 'single-action' reels.

Multiplying reels are geared to rotate between 1½ and 2½ turns of the spool for each turn of the handle. So line can be retrieved between 150 percent and 250 percent faster than with a single action reel. There is no doubt in my mind that a multiplying reel will cost you the loss of fewer big fish. There are, however, more working parts and they work under greater stress, and thus maintenance is much more essential than with a single-action reel. The gearing is a source of wear and tear, and unless the maker has taken great pains to see that all the parts are properly hardened and tempered, lack of maintenance will cause grief sooner rather than later.

Automatic reels work on a clockwork spring which, when fully wound, retrieves line with a whizz when a lever is pressed. This speed of retrieve is perhaps their greatest benefit. Pulling line off the reel without the lever pressed then rewinds the spring, but if a fish is allowed to do this then the effort required will be too much for leaders weaker than about 8lb breaking strain. As soon as a fish is hooked, therefore, the lever should be pressed and not released until the fish is ready for the net. Keep the lever pressed for too long, however, and you will have a long thin fish coming down through the rings at you! Apparently complicated, the mechanisms on most of the surviving makes of automatic reel have been developed to a stage of extreme reliability, but they are quite sensitive to being dropped in sand or grit and do require frequent cleaning and oiling if they are to remain trouble-free. Automatics tend to be heavy, are noticeably too heavy for rods of 8 feet or less. On rods of 9 feet or so they are only slightly cumbersome; and they can be a positive advantage on rods of over 10 feet, as they bring the point of balance further back to the hand, making the rod feel lighter and less fatiguing than it would with a lightweight reel. But the big advantage of an automatic reel *must* be the speed with which the loose line is buzzed back onto the spool, and the fish brought under almost instant control. Keep the lever pressed and the fish almost plays itself, and if the lever is pressed by the little finger of the rod hand, the other hand is free to reach for the net and land the fish.

To summarise, therefore, the single-action reel is best for the angler who neglects his or her tackle and wants to keep everything as simple as possible. The multiplier is best for the angler who is prepared to spend a little time in maintaining kit and who wants to get rid of loose line quite quickly when a fish is hooked, and the automatic is best for the angler who is prepared to regard the time spent on maintenance of tackle as part of the fun of fishing, and who wants to get a fish under control as fast as possible. I now use an automatic for all my trout fishing, and a single-action reel for salmon! (With one exception – I use a multiplier for my lead-core line.) All my other reels have now long been consigned to the top shelf of my wardrobe.

Having chosen the reel let us now consider how to attach it to the rod, a matter ignored by many anglers until it gives trouble. How often have you seen those little aluminium rings, sliding over a cork bed, on expensive rods? Too often in my opinion. They do not hold a reel firmly enough for a whole day's fishing and I regard them as an abomination, which allows a reel to fall off long before it has been noticed that it is becoming loose. It goes almost without saying that the reel will fall into fifty feet of water on the occasion when you omitted to tie the backing to the spindle, or that the reel will land on the only rock on fifty paces of grassy bank, and bash the rim enough to prevent the reel turning again until you have spent two hours in the workshop at home. Avoid sliding aluminium ring reel fittings. Many rod builders think that they are producing a nice-looking rod if they put a reel fitting on it which has both the male and female threads machined out of aluminium alloy. This alloy is soft, and threads made from it tend to bind. I believe that the technical term is that the aluminium 'rags'. At the end of a long day, you will find that you are unable to undo the fitting, and the reel has to stay on the butt until you can get home and attack it with a mole wrench or a big pair of pliers. So avoid those good-looking, highly-polished reel fittings where both male and female threads are made of alloy. (Unless you are prepared to take the trouble of melting candlewax on the threads every now and again, this helps but does not cure the problem.)

By far the most reliable reel fitting for today's angler is one where the female threads are made of steel or aluminium alloy, and run on male threads made from nylon, carbon fibre or similar plastic material. These will be found to grip well, screw together easily and yet will come apart at the end of the day when you want them to. They do not have the pure eye-appeal of the polished aluminium fittings, but then who needs eye appeal at the expense of reliability?

Too little attention is paid to the way the fitting screws tight. To use the American description, reel fittings can be either 'up-locking', or 'down-locking'. The up-locking fitting takes the reel closer to the corks, perhaps even with one foot under the corks: this is the best for an automatic reel, as the lever is then positioned close to the little finger of the rod hand. A down-locking fitting, on the other hand, takes the reel away from the corks when it is tightened, taking the weight further back and thus tends to balance the rod better. The disadvantage is that in many cases this allows the reel rim to be the first thing to touch the sand and grit when the rod is stood on its butt end. You pays your money and takes your choice, but at least you should think about which fitting is best for you.

So much of the design of our fishing tackle seems to happen by accident or by tradition - but at least a little thought can remove the minor irritations and make your fishing more pleasurable.

C·H·A·P·T·E·R

5

Lines

Logically, this should have been one of the first chapters, as the choice of fly line should come very early in the decision-making process, preceded only by the choice of fly and method to use. However, it seems tidy to do it in this order.

Firstly, may I say that I think far too many stillwater anglers use fly lines which are too heavy. They do so because they have succumbed to the craze for distance, and so need heavy lines to cast far enough to satisfy their egos. They also tend to use powerful rods, forgetting that no rod is powerful all by itself and that they supply the power needed to make a stiff rod flex. At the end of a day's fishing they must feel as if they have been put through a wringer, and by the end of the season they must have arm muscles well equipped for shovelling snow. Personally, I do not regard my fishing as a body building exercise, my object is to catch fish in as pleasant a way as possible, and with least effort. Perhaps I am lazy!

The heavier the line the more disturbance it makes when it lands on the water, however well it is cast. The more disturbance there is on the surface, the less likely the fish are to be left in an unfrightened, hungry state of mind. The fewer hungry fish there are left in front of you, the fewer fish will you catch. So this logic tells me, when taken to its conclusion, that the lighter the line I use the more fish will I catch. It cannot be proved, of course, as fishing is not a numbers game like golf or darts, all you know is the number of fish you catch and the number of blank days you have over a season. You will never know what you might have caught if you had done something different. and I learned long ago that whenever I make a definite statement about fishing, the fish will prove me a liar almost straight away. How often have you heard an angler, looking at another's fly, say 'You won't catch anything on that load of rubbish,' and within ten seconds the chap is playing a fish! Or watched a beginner thrashing a line out and thought that he didn't have a chance, poor fellow, if he couldn't cast better than that, and watched with fascinated horror as he proceeds to catch the only fish to be landed that day! So, to rephrase the categoric statement of a few moments ago, the lighter the line you use the more fish are you *likely* to catch! Logic tells me so, and I have nothing else to go on except experience, when I seem to have caught more fish than other good anglers who were using similar tackle but with heavier lines than I was using. It has happened often enough to be more than a series of coincidences, and casting distance does not seem to be a factor.

Numbers rule: this rule seems logical enough to me. An angler who is using a rod rated at AFTM 8, will use with it a line rated AFTM 8, and yet will then attach a leader tippet of 4 lb breaking strain. When he hooks a fish of any size, the line

The correct way to hold a fly rod, both for casting and for fishing. The thumb has a solid bump to push against, and the swell fits comfortably into the palm. The line under the little finger prevents loose line from tangling with the reel. The line under the forefinger gives a bite indication even if it is not seen. To pull line in, the loop is grasped by the left hand and slid over the forefinger. The line is taken off the forefinger to cast, but stays under the little finger at all times, except when playing fish.

immersed in the water has a high water-resistance due to its greater surface area, so the fish will have a lot of drag to overcome in just towing the line. Also the rod tip is not delicate enough to cope with the fish twisting and turning. The result is a broken tippet, a lost fish and an angler who sits down and has a good cry. The cure for this unbalanced tackle is what I call the numbers rule: the rod, the line and the leader tippet should all have the same number. If the rod is rated AFTM 8, the line should be an 8 and the tippet an 8 lb breaking strain. A rod rated at AFTM 5 should have a No.5 line and a 5 lb tippet. Vary these numbers by more than 2 downwards and you are in trouble with bigger than standard-sized stock fish: the man with his No.8 rod and line should not go below 6 lb nylon to avoid being broken by the first decent fish he hooks, however carefully he thinks he is going to play it. (The further the fish runs, the more line is drowned and the greater the risk of that leader breaking, however skilful the angler, however light the ratchet on the reel and however high the rod is held.)

Remember this rule as it will dictate the line and thus what rod you tackle up. To start even earlier in the chain of events – start with the size of fly. Decide what thickness of nylon that fly should be tied to, and that dictates the line to use and the rod. Simple, isn't it? Then why do so many people use a rod of AFTM 8 or 9, put an 8 or 9 line on it and then put on a nymph on a size 14 hook on 4 lb nylon? It can only be because they haven't used the numbers rule, and any fish which breaks their leader is an Act of God, punishing them for being late in the pub last night. Or they think that their particular brand of nylon is not what it used to be and change to another.

One dodge in some favour these days is to insert a foot or so of stretchy material, called High Power Gum, into the leader somewhere. Normally between the butt of the leader and the fly line. This is to cushion the strike of a powerful rod and avoid breakage of fine leader points. This it does but does nothing at all to prevent breakage when a big fish drowns lots of line and fights against the drag – the High Power Gum stretches and the fine tippet breaks anyway. But if you ever find yourself holding a rod rated AFTM 8 or 9, with an 8 or 9 line attached to it and you want to fish a 4 lb tippet for some reason, the High Power Gum will help. You won't get as many 'smash takes', but will still suffer from broken tippets from time to time. Far better to use a lighter, thinner line with less drag, and a gentler rod – balanced tackle in the first place. High Power Gum is a pliable material, and when inserted into the butt of a leader, that leader tends not to turn over as well, especially into a wind.

While a beginner is best advised to buy one line, and stick to it until he or she has mastered fishing with it, the more expert and dedicated angler will want to vary his approach by having a choice of fly lines. To save a lot of discussion, this list is my personal battery of lines, and reasons for them.

DT 5 F This is the lightweight floating line I use in calm conditions when I want sheer delicacy of presentation of a small nymph, dry fly or wet fly. Coloured brown it is spooled for my automatic fly reel and has 75 yards of fine backing.

DT 6 I An intermediate, or dual purpose line, this is *intended* to sink just below the surface and stay there, but is a very slow sinker. It was apple-green when bought but I have dyed it dark olive green by steeping it overnight in dark brown Dylon dye. It is almost brown, but the green still shows. It is almost the colour of many underwater weeds, but that was just a lucky coincidence. I use it for those days of flat calm when I wish to fish a nymph or small wet fly within a couple of feet of the surface, leaving no wake from line or knots. If ever caught without a lightweight floater, I grease this line with Permagrease and it will float. I think this has put more fish in the bag on really difficult days than any other.
DT 6 S The line I choose for fishing sub-surface when I need to be delicate. It is a slow-to-medium sinker, coloured brown and best for when I want to tweak a small fly along the bottom in shallowish water in calm weather. On a spool with about 75 yards of fine backing.
WF 7 F If there is a good ripple, or a wave in not too much wind, this is the line I reach for most often, as I can cast further with it than with the DT 5. It is brown in colour and fitted to the spool with about 75 yards of fine backing. I think over a season I use this line more often than the others, perhaps because British weather dictates windy conditions more often than a flat calm. After May the DT 5 comes into its own.
WF 8 S This is the line used when I have to fish a lure or go home fishless. It is a medium-to-fast sinker, brown in colour and fitted with 75 yards of fine backing. Used when the surface disturbance from the wind hides the slosh it makes when it lands, this line and the next, are my 'in case' lines. Comforting for an emergency, but not used often.
SH 9 S This is my 'despair' line, the one used when absolutely nothing else will do. It is a 10-yard head of dark charcoal grey fast-sinking line, backed by 50 yards of Cortland Cobra monofil (oval in section). This Cobra was red in colour when first bought but it has faded over a few seasons and is now a delicate pink. Still, it is seen on the ground more easily than clear monofil, and thus I tread on it less often. There is perhaps 100 yards of fine backing on the spool.
Lead core This is my trolling line for really deep fishing, and it is on a separate reel, a winding multiplier. I have three 10 yard lengths of lead core line looped together with spliced loops so that I can use ten yards, twenty yards or thirty yards at will. Backed by 100 yards of Cortland Cobra, it is not intended for casting, rather it is fed out over the stern of a boat when I want to troll deep. I can cast it if I use only ten yards, but any more overloads the rods I normally carry. If deep trolling formed a more important part of my season, I might indulge in a stiff, powerful rod but it is not justifiable on cost grounds at present.

Contrast my selection with that of the 'average' reservoir angler, who would have WF 8 or shooting head 9s in floating, slow sinking, fast sinking, ultra-fast sinking, and lead core and sink-tip. While he can fish at almost any depth, his lines land with a crash on the water without him being aware of how many fish he scares in the act of casting as far as possible!

All these lines except the last are on spools for my automatic fly reel, and all are cast with my favourite 9ft 3in. reservoir rod, rated at AFTM 7. (Or AFTM 5, or AFTM 9 depending on the line in use at the time!)

Nor do I tackle up two or three rods at a time; it only takes but a second or two to rethread the rod. The benefit is fewer broken rods, trodden on by other anglers marching along the bank, and when concentrating totally on the fly out there then I have no mental capacity left to worry about my spare rod. One rod in my hand and a spare in the car is enough for me. In a boat the spare comes too but stays firmly in its rigid plastic case. That way it doesn't get broken by having oars or an anchor dumped on it.

At this stage I can hear those cynics among you saying – but what about the rule of numbers – how can he use one rod and all those different fly lines? The answer is that the rod is happy with all the lines I have mentioned, so it can be regarded as being rated for the line in use. The rule of numbers does apply when I come to put a tippet on the leader. I never vary by more than one downwards.

When discussing reels I mentioned preventive maintenance. This applies to fly lines too, unless you are very rich and can afford to replace fly lines whenever you have to. The life of a fly line is in almost direct proportion to the care you devote to it. When new the plastic coating has been carefully judged to leave the factory with a certain suppleness. Too supple, and the coating tends to be soft, sometimes parting like a banana skin from the core. Too harsh and the line keeps its memory coils from the reel, and never straightens out in a whole day's fishing, and there is nothing more maddening than the wake this can cause. When a nice new, supple line is waved all day, some of the plasticiser will evaporate, leaving the coating stiffer. In time, this lack of plasticiser gets to the point where the dressing will crack, water enters the core and the line is no longer a floater. The answer is in preventive maintenance – the application of regular doses of plasticiser. There are liquid plasticisers on the market, but they tend to be a bit messy and, if over-done, turn the coating into goo and the line is ruined. For this reason, I use Permagrease, a nice firm mixture of waxes and plasticiser which, when rubbed on the line, will replace that lost suppleness, and the line floats better because of the waxes. It also shoots much better. There is a little felt pad in the Permagrease tin on which a small dab is scooped from the tin, the line pulled through the folded pad and back again to take off any excess. You could then take a tissue to polish the line to force the grease into the surface of the dressing although I do not normally bother: I only do so when putting the line away for the winter, as there is a risk of having a tacky line on opening day if too much Permagrease is left on the line.

How often should this be done? I suggest once every ten hours of fishing will double the life of your floating lines, and make them shoot and stay shooting, as well as, or even better than, they did when the lines were new.

Perhaps because they do not get waved around in the air as much, sinking lines need less maintenance. It is a mistake to apply Permagrease to a sinker but the line should be polished regularly with a tissue. It is amazing how dirty they become, and this does slow down the sink rate. Keep sinkers clean and polished, and they will last.

You can *hear* a neglected line, it grates its way back through the rings when the fly or lure is being retrieved. It's a horrible noise and tells you you are wasting money through neglect.

There has been much publicity lately on non-stretch fly lines. Apparently a non-stretch core to the line allows closer contact with the fish during striking and playing. Yet we also read adverts about braided leaders acting as shock absorbers. I suspect the poor angler is thoroughly confused by the technical jargon, all of which aims to make him happier to part with almost £40 for a fly line.

In my view there is much wrong with the supposed logic behind such adverts. Firstly, the amount of pull exerted by a fly rod is measured in ounces, and is certainly not enough to create much noticeable stretch during normal fishing. Nothing whatever to do with a 14 stone (196 lb) man pulling on a line tied to a fence post. He would certainly get the impression of considerable stretch before the line broke, which it will when the 35 lb breaking strain of the normal braided core is exceeded. It is, in my opinion, no accident that most world-renowned fly lines are made of a mixture of PVC and a form of buoyancy medium, either air bubbles or tiny hollow glass beads. Many years of careful development have brought fly lines to the current stage of perfection and durability, and now advertising begins to tell us how unsatisfactory they are. Highly reputable line makers world-wide have spent fortunes in slow, careful development and testing to get things right before selling to the public and suddenly they are all wrong!

A little analogy might help to explain my views on give or stretch in a fly line. Have you ever tied a weight to a piece of elastic and flicked it back and forth? See the way the elastic stretches and catapults the weight back fast? Tie the same weight to a piece of string and flick that back and forth: not nearly as fast. I think a fly line might catapult like that if there is a little give in it, rather than the dead feel of a completely non-stretch line.

As an old man, who has seen and heard it all before, and disbelieved most of it (or I would be considerably poorer than I am), my recommendation to the angler is to spend no more than £12 on a fly line. Maintain it properly, do not tread on it and see how long it lasts. Any line from a reputable maker, even from his economy range, will serve you well. I would rather have three £12 lines than one £36 line. Even if you use the savings to buy three floaters, one after the other, the total life of the three will far exceed the life of the single expensive one.

Equally, it is often impossible in normal fishing to tell the difference between two fly lines, even though laboratory tests might. If the line shoots well, feels pleasant to handle, floats in a straight line (instead of drawing slowly back to form a long coil spring with only the top of each helix actually on the surface!), and lasts for more than one season without showing signs of cracking, then you have a line with which you can fish confidently, regardless of cost. Do not believe all the advertising. Don't rush out and buy the most expensive fly line or you will find you are paying for the advertising and fishing with a line you cannot distinguish from a cheaper one.

Having bought your line and fished with it, do not hesitate to take it back to the shop if you find anything wrong with it. Under UK law a retailer must either replace it or give you your money back. Do not be fobbed off by offers to send it back to the manufacturers to see what they say, but insist upon instant replacement or refund. The retailer in turn will send it back to the maker and receive a replacement or credit; he will not lose money as a result of your action so stick to your guns and insist, politely of course, than you get a line which does what it should.

The one fly line I would caution against is the so-called Mill End. They are very cheap but tend to be sold in great jumbled boxfuls and whether you get the size you order is largely luck. Stay away from these unless your budget is so tight that you cannot afford anything else. The only guarantee you get with a Mill End is that there is something wrong with it.

C·H·A·P·T·E·R

6

Leaders

I think if I was asked for the quickest way to judge whether an angler was really good at his hobby, I would ask to be taken to his leader! Studying the variations on leaders seen around our stillwaters today, it is apparent that too many anglers believe all that they read and just do not think for themselves. Nor do they seem to experiment to find out what is best for their style of fishing. Not long ago I read a magazine article where the author recommended using 20 feet of 6 lb nylon to throw a leaded mayfly nymph. A couple of days later I saw two young anglers using this rig, and were they in trouble!

The leader is perhaps the most critical single part of the tackle. It is quite possible to catch fish on the wrong fly if it is presented well: it is nearly impossible to catch fish on the right fly if it is presented badly. And leaders are all about presentation. Not necessarily the art of landing a size 16 dry fly like thistledown, it is just as important to land well a huge lure at the end of a straight leader, as any coils of nylon dumped on the water around a fly can yield tangles, and trout will certainly refuse a fly buried in a birdsnest of nylon.

On a quiet calm evening, listening to a row of anglers fishing away, one can quite frequently *hear* tangled leaders being thrashed back and forth – they make whistling noises! Almost inevitably, you will find that those tangles have developed in leaders made of lengths of level nylon. Compounded, of course, by bad casting, but the main fault is in the make up of the leader. Such knots and tangles have a most serious weakening effect on nylon, and if you do not believe me then try tying a simple thumb knot in a length of nylon and seeing how strong it remains when jerked. You will find that 6 lb nylon will break like cotton. I suggest that the majority of 'smash takes' occur because there was a wind knot in the nylon. The knots we use have been carefully developed to yield the best residual strength in nylon, a material not very easy to join without weakening it. Extraneous knots *do* weaken it seriously.

A well-designed leader presents the fly well and will tangle less. This saves time spent fiddling with knots and tangles, and reduces the time your fly is not in the water catching fish. Most anglers go wrong at the point where the fly line ends. They have read the books and magazines which recommend putting a length of thick nylon permanently onto the fly line with a needle knot or a nail knot. At the end of this nylon they tie a loop allowing a quick change by simply threading loops into each other. In my view this is a mistake, particularly if using the usual advice of 20 lb nylon. I suggest you forget all about this nylon permanently attached to the fly line.

One also goes wrong when making a leader up out of one thickness of nylon, the straight 20ft of 6 lb nylon, for example. This was satisfactory in the old days when anglers followed the rule that the leader should be about the same length as the rod and they cast perhaps ten yards all day out of a boat. It worked fine, even with a three-fly cast, but today's stillwater angler doesn't feel he is fishing unless he is casting over 25 yards, and leaders made up of level nylon just do not turn over well enough for this kind of casting, however many or few flies are used.

Logic tells us that the flow of casting power should flow smoothly all the way from the hand to the fly. The rod tapers; the line tapers; so should the leader taper. Thus there are no sudden steps in diameter or in suppleness to prevent that smooth flow of power. Notice that I mention suppleness – if you attach flimsy nylon to the end of a relatively stiff fly line, you will get a hinge effect which will surely prevent the smooth flow of power. It is thus vital that any nylon, where it is joined to the fly line, should have about the same resistance to bending as the line has; and it will be found that nylon of perhaps half the diameter – no less – will have about the correct resistance to bending. If you measure this diameter of nylon (half the thickness of the average fly line at its tip) you will find about 35 lb breaking strain. So the suggestion for a yard of 20 lb nylon is understated by perhaps 50 percent, and the hinge effect will still take place. The right idea but not carried to the proper conclusion. You may now say that obviously you will add, not a yard of 20 lb nylon, but a yard of 35 lb nylon! Wrong again. You will have too many knots in your leader, knots cause wake, have an inherent weakness and contribute to tangles. The idea is to have as few knots as possible.

The solution which I have come to rely upon is to use a ready-made tapered leader. Not the kind which is a slow taper for the whole of its 5 metre length, as I do not think the butt is nearly thick enough on these, even though they seem conveniently packaged with a cutting list giving the breaking strains you achieve when you cut off a length; nor the kind called a tapered leader, is nine feet long, but has a butt section only about 0.015 in. ('fifteen thou') thick, as these are not thick enough either: the kind of leader you want to find is one which has a butt section about 0.022 in. ('twenty-two thou') thick. This is about 35 lb breaking strain, as I mentioned above and *that* leader will allow the flow of power in an

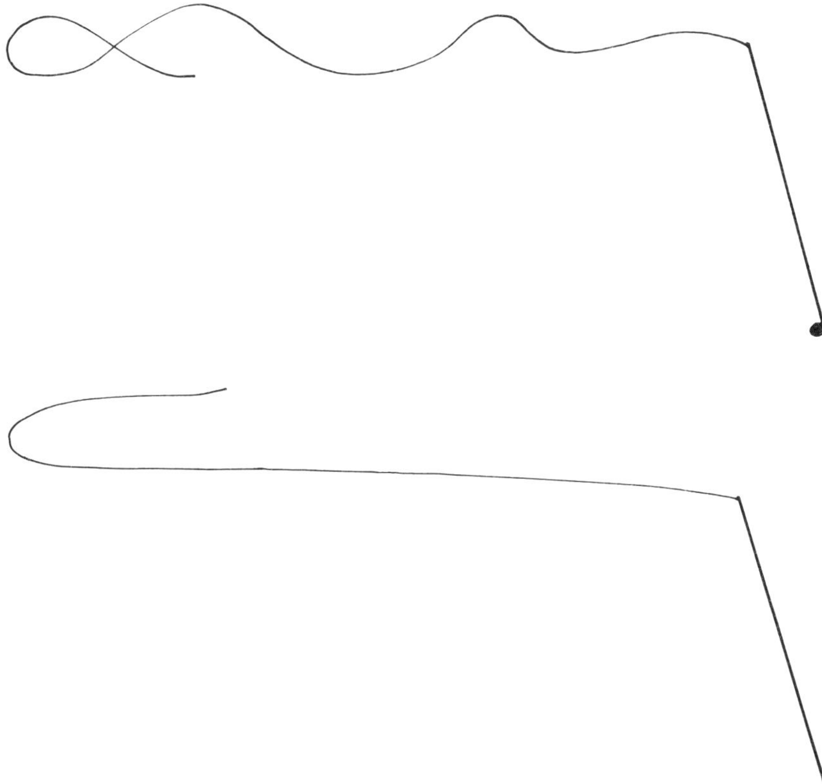

The cause of wind knots

Two forward casts. The top one shows all the signs of too much effort in the cast. When the excess power is stopped, the tip of the rod vibrates, sending a wave along the line. When the wave gets to the end, the fly flips back and hooks onto the line, or goes through the loop it formed when 'tailing'. This is then called a wind knot, though the wind didn't do it, the angler did!

This is very common when a leader is made up of a length of thin nylon - the 20 feet of 6lb nylon syndrome - as the power cannot be transmitted smoothly if there is a sudden change in diameter or stiffness between fly line and leader. Such excess power can happen in the backcast also, but the fault is more common when an angler delivers a final huge effort on delivery.

The cast should have a smooth flowing loop as in the bottom drawing, both in the back cast and the forward cast.

uninterrupted progression along the fly line and into the leader itself. This leader is known as a 'Big Butt leader' in the trade, and I use no other.

Now for the bad news. I have spent hours trying to tie needle knots with these Big Butt leaders and have found eventually that the nylon is too thick for the core of most fly lines. Needle knots, therefore, are out, except that . . ..

James Armstrong, of East Horsley, gave me a useful tip. He favours a needle knot, even with a Big Butt leader, using this method. Start the hole in the fly line core with a fine needle. Leave needle in and lay line aside for a few hours. Remove needle and insert thicker needle, following track of thin one. Lay aside overnight. When thick needle is removed the plastic coating of the line will have settled, and the hole stays open. Insert thin end of leader into hole in side of fly line, and pull whole leader through (much easier than trying to thread thick butt up core). Hold thick end of leader under a hot tap for a few minutes to soften nylon, and tie knot before it cools. Persuade friend to hold line and leader-tip while you tie knot: you have two hands to lay coils up snug in a neat, strong knot. When I prepare my tackle properly, I use this method.

Nail knots are not too difficult, but because of the thickness of the nylon they are pigs to persuade to lay nicely as the coils tighten. I may be clumsy and lack manual dexterity (I do not think so), but I gave up nail knots after a couple of months of trying. And now for the heretical part – I use a loop on the end of the leader and a figure of eight knot to attach the fly line! Just what our forefathers used when they attached their silkworm gut cast to the end of their dressed silk fly line: if it was good enough for them, it should be good enough for me, especially as I have tried all the magic new knots and found they just do not work with the thickness of butt I want.

The Big Butt leader is usually obtainable in a 9 foot length. The butt section ('twenty-two thou' thick) remember, is 5 feet long. The next 3 feet is a steep taper, going from that 'twenty-two thou', down to whatever breaking strain forms the tip. The tip is then one foot long. To keep my personal stockholding simple, I have standardised on 6 lb breaking strain Big Butt leaders – when I want an 8 lb tippet, I cut the tip off to where the taper starts and knot on my level 8 lb point around where I judge that the leader nylon is about the same diameter as the tippet.

To judge thicknesses of nylon, it will be found easiest if the pieces to be compared are held at right-angles to each other. It is very difficult to see minor differences in thickness if the pieces are laid parallel. At right-angles, even differences of one thousandth of an inch can be spotted without the need for a micrometer or kite-hawk's eyes.

The level tip I add to my leader usually starts off about a yard long, and is attached by one of two knots. If I am fishing a single fly, which I do perhaps 75 percent of the time, I will use a four-turn water knot because it is quick and easy to tie with cold, wet hands and has not yet let me down. The snag is that the ends lie parallel with the leader, and thus are no good for tying a dropper fly onto, so if a dropper is needed, I use Richard Walker's grinner/half blood knot and ensure that the fly is tied to the waste end of the Big Butt leader, never to the waste end of the tippet. (In other words the fly goes on the waste end of the half-blood knot, not on the waste end of the grinner.)

When I want a fine point on the leader, and the finest I usually use is 4 lb nylon, it is a simple matter to use a four, or five turn water knot to attach the tippet to the end of the Big Butt leader. So I step down by 2 lb in breaking strain from the leader to the tippet. Most of the time I would be using a 6 lb point, so there is no step in diameter, and when I want an 8 lb point I cut the tip off and try to find an equal diameter on the leader at the knotting point.

Having started with a tippet 3 feet long this obviously becomes shorter each time I change a fly. By the time it has been eroded away to about a foot, I cut it off and put on another tippet. I have never counted, but I must be able to go through perhaps ten tippets before the level tip of the Big Butt leader is used up. This would normally take several fishing days to do, and thus a Big Butt leader will last me for quite a long time, and I would venture to suggest that this would be perhaps three fishing days. Three days fishing from one leader currently costing less than £1 is, in my opinion, reasonably economical fishing.

I can see the cogs turning in your mind as you deduce that my standard leader is a total of 12 feet long. You are quite correct. By using the dull-coloured fly lines, by casting gently and by using a bit of fieldcraft in approaching fish, I have never felt the need to use great long leaders as some anglers do. And I get fewer wind knots and tangles than they do, I see more takes to my nymphs than they do, I see those takes more quickly than they do too and thus I hook more of them. That puts more fish in the bag and to hell with 20 foot leaders! I shall come back to this subject in the chapter on nymph fishing.

There are times when I want a leader shorter than 12 foot, like 9 foot when I am fishing a daddy-longlegs or a big mayfly in a wind. In the teeth of a good breeze, these big bulky flies do require a shorter leader to obtain good presentation - it is no good if the leader lands in a heap, the fly is taken as soon as it lands and all the strike does is to straighten out part of the leader. If the leader does not land straight, many fish will be missed on the strike. When I want a 9 foot leader, I cut back the Big Butt leader by 3 feet at the butt end, giving me the thick butt which is essential to good turnover, but now it is only 2 foot long. I still have that vital taper too.

So let me summarise my thoughts on leaders. I use a commercially tapered leader nine feet long, and I add a yard of level nylon to the tip. That level yard will be of the breaking strain I want in order to fish the fly properly. I will have whatever knots I use to join the leader to the line, and the tippet to the fly, and only one other - where the tippet joins the leader. Couldn't be simpler, could it? Surely much better than all the fandangle undertaken by those who favour knotting all those bits of nylon together to get the same basic taper as I have? All those knots collecting weed while fishing, and leaving wakes like motor torpedo boats on the surface. Ugh! No wonder you can hear the fish laughing sometimes. . .

Big Butt leaders are available from several sources. Those I have tried include the Hardy Knotless Tapered Leader, the Shakespeare International Leader, the

Big Butt Leader sold by Fishermen's Feathers and the Scorpion Leader sold by Fulling Mill Tackle. In every case I use the 6 lb breaking strain, 9 foot version. All suffer from one slight problem – how to get them straight for a day's fishing. The answer is to pull the leader slowly but very firmly through warm hands. Be warned – pull quickly and the nylon will cut you to the bone; slowly does it.

There is a current campaign on the subject of braided leaders; one of the advertisements actually shows a twisted leader, yet calls it a braided leader. I have tested perhaps four or five makes of braided leader and have formed only one conclusion, that the man who invented the idea fished only with the wind at his back. (When any damned leader will turn over anyway!) I find that the braided bit, supposedly the thick butt section, being made up of many thin strands of nylon, is very pliable, far too pliable in fact to allow that smooth flow of power from the fly line. (In the same issues of the fishing magazines I read ads for *stiffer* fly lines, saying that they go into a wind better!) Braided leaders do not straighten out well when cast into a wind and, for that reason alone, I would not use a braided leader: quite apart from the cost which is horrific, at least five times that of a commercial Big Butt leader. Yet another example, I am afraid, of an idea designed to make money for the tackle trade, not to help the angler catch fish. Leaders have also been made with a flattened butt section – disasters, every one. It is merely making the nylon stiffer on one plane, but more supple in the other, and the leader will always seek the more supple side when being cast, and will blow back in a heap when cast into a wind. Do not fall for these either.

Apart from being a bit cynical, I suppose I am a bit old-fashioned in my outlook. If a new idea comes up, I will leap to test it and if it is genuinely better than the old method it replaces I will adopt it with pleasure. Cyanoacrylate glue was such an idea. The prospect of being able to glue the end of the leader into the braided core of the fly line, leaving no lumps or waste ends, seemed almost too good to be true. I glued a leader into a line and tried to pull it apart – I couldn't. . .So then I soaked it for 24 hours in a glass of water and tried again – still I couldn't pull it apart. I sat back and looked at it and pondered. . . Would I be happy if I had my biggest-ever trout tearing around while I relied on a dab of some Superglue to keep me connected with it? And the reluctant answer was that I would be terrified of losing it, far more so than if I was relying upon a good solid knot. The cynicism won, and I do not use glued joints between leader and fly line. Old-fashioned I may be, but this was one marvellous new scientific invention I was not going to adopt. There are those who swear by the whole idea of glueing leader to line, and good luck to them. But ask one of them which he would use, glue or a knot, when he stuck his hook into the only salmon of a fortnight's Scottish fishing holiday, knowing it was a thirty-pounder, and see what he says!

No mention of my favourite brand of nylon? No, because I do not think it is all that important, despite the arguments one hears, usually accompanied by liberal amounts of Billingsgate language. The short answer is that there is a lot of conning on the subject of nylon. There are only about twelve factories in the world making the stuff, and most of it is intended for use in coarse or sea fishing, for making fishing nets, for stringing tennis racquets and for ladies stockings and undies. Fly fishing forms a tiny part of the nylon market. The conning takes place when the bulk nylon is re-spooled for sale to the unsuspecting fly fisherman. There are so many trade names on labels – far more than there are brands on bulk spools – and I have heard anglers arguing heatedly the merits of two brands of nylon both of which, I knew, came off the same bulk spools, from the same factory at the same price. The anglers did not pay the same price, of course, as nylon is subject to heavy advertising overheads and offers to the trade of high profit margins, and 'buy ten get two free' gimmicks. The two spools of nylon owned by those men may well have been different, however, because there is an old dodge frequently used by the packers of bulk nylon onto those attractive small spools. If you spool 8 lb nylon onto a spool, label it as 6 lb nylon and sell it to anglers as 6 lb nylon, it will soon get the reputation of being an excellent, extremely strong 6 lb nylon! The honest man who spools 6 lb nylon and calls it 6 lb nylon is often told he is selling bloody rubbish, not nearly as reliable as Brand X! So it pays to compare the thickness of the nylon you buy with a micrometer, checking the thickness stated on the spools with what you read on the dial. But find a brand you like and stick to it, and if you get unaccountable breakages, test it against a spring balance – it might have been contaminated with suntan oil, petrol, fly repellant, the vapours inside a new car or other solvent which has weakened it (see Appendix C).

Don't leave spools of nylon in sunlight, put them away in the shade every single time you use them, and at the end of the season put all spools of less than 15 lb breaking strain into the dustbin. Buy fresh nylon a week before the next season starts. The cost of three or four spools of nylon is not high enough to risk losing the fish of a lifetime on. But before you leave the shop, pull a yard of nylon from each spool and test it in front of the shopkeeper. If it breaks like cotton, thank him and leave it on the counter. If it seems to break at the poundage you expect, pay for it whatever it costs, and fish with confidence knowing that, if you do your part in tying good knots, it will not let you down in practical fishing.

The brand of nylon I favour for the tippet (and I have had more queries on this subject, since this book was first published, than on any other), is Drennan Double-Strength. I have this nylon tippet material in strengths from 10 lb BS down to 2 lb BS. You may suggest that 2 lb breaking strain nylon surely has no place in stillwater fishing, and I would agree that up to a year ago the finest nylon I possessed was 4 lb BS. However, I had an experience which altered my attitude to very fine nylon.

I was fishing Farmire, near Knaresborough, Yorkshire on a baking hot, glaring bright day in August. There was not a breath of wind, the water was clear as crystal, and lots of large fish proceeded to drive me nearly mad. I would cast out a little dry fly, similar to the flies which were being taken in a steady rise. Fish after fish would rise from the depths, confidently aiming for my fly, but at the last second would turn away. Frequently there would be a swirl at the fly which looked just like a rise, but the fly would still be sitting untouched in the rings. Standing on my casting platform well above the water, with the sun shining straight down, my polarised glasses well shaded by the brim of my hat, I could almost count the scales on these fish.

I sat down to have a cup of coffee and ponder. While I was doing this, I decided to try a change of fly, but fumbled and dropped the fly I had just removed. It fell into the water right below me, and before I could try and retrieve it, a fish rose and took the fly with total confidence. The water was so clear that I even saw the fish spit the fly out about two feet below the surface, and immediately another fish appeared from under my platform and took the fly, spitting it out after a second. So two fish had taken a fly which had previously been rejected by perhaps six fish – the fault cannot have been in the fly. It must have been the nylon!

None of the other anglers there that day had any nylon finer than the one I had been using, so I packed up my tackle, got into my car and headed for a local tackle shop. Half an hour later I was tying on a tippet from a spool which said 1 lb 8 oz breaking strain. Putting on the same pattern of dry fly, I cast out, and was promptly taken by a large rainbow which sucked the fly in with total confidence. I do not think I have ever played a fish more carefully, but eventually it was netted and returned.

For the rest of that hot afternoon I rose fish steadily, hooked most of them, landed all that I hooked, and thoroughly enjoyed myself. Not a single fish refused the fly after eyeballing it, as so many had before I changed the tippet nylon. The largest fish I caught that day was about five pounds in weight.

I am not suggesting that all dry fly fishing on stillwaters should be done with 1½ lb nylon on the tippet. This would undoubtedly cause a lot of fish to be swimming around with hooks stuck in them. What I *am* saying is that sometimes, in bright calm conditions, fish will be put off by the thickness of nylon we normally use, and *on these occasions only* it can pay to go down in nylon thickness, providing one remembers to strike and play fish with the greatest of delicacy.

Consider what happens when a fish sees an insect. It does *not* charge at it with its mouth open. It swims towards it with its mouth opening and closing normally for breathing, which is not very wide. At the last split second it opens its mouth wide, sucking in water, air if the insect is on the surface, and the insect. The water goes out through the gills, and the food goes to the back of the throat, to be swallowed after the mouth has shut.

If, on the other hand, the fish decides at the last instant that there is something wrong with the target food, it cannot stop – it has no brakes. So the typical rise form of swirl is seen, but the fish does not open its mouth to suck in food. Such fish are sometimes hooked in a fin, or on the side of the face, or the side of the body. These unlucky ones are, however, the exception. Most fish swirl at the fly, do not take it, and cause the angler to say to his friends – 'They are rising short today'. If that angler changed to finer nylon, or maybe less glittery nylon, for his tippet, he would find that the fish stopped 'rising short'.

Having discussed rods, reels, lines and leaders, logic dictates that the next chapter will be on flies! It isn't! We shall discuss flies later on, after we get to the waterside. Meanwhile, there is a lot to do before we get there, if we are all to be thinking anglers.

C·H·A·P·T·E·R

7

Time Spent In Reconnaissance. . .

. . .Is seldom wasted. So says the old army adage, and it is very true. In this context we could substitute the word 'homework' for reconnaissance.

There are those to whom the word homework conjures up visions of sweat and effort on some detested subject like Shakespeare, Algebra or Calculus. Thinking about one's sport is different. There is more to fishing than just catching fish. Fishing can include cleaning and oiling a fly reel, or re-whipping rings on a favourite rod, or even leaning on a bar on a winter's night *talking* about fishing. It is all part of one's hobby – not perhaps an essential part, but an enjoyable part all the same – and the men who never do all these ancillary things cannot get as much fun out of fishing as those who do. On all 365 days of the year there is *something* you can do which is connected with fishing, even if it is only to dream about it! You can close your eyes anywhere – in a crowded bus or a busy airport – and visualise the wink of a rising trout, the selection of a fly, the stalk to casting position and the thrill as you see your fly being taken. People sitting opposite you in that bus or airport might wonder how you can sit there with half-closed eyes and a serene smile on your face, and if they knew what you were thinking about they might well think you were some kind of a nut, but you will remain sane while they fume their hurried lives away.

Not all time spent in thinking about fishing is unproductive or just calculated to keep you sane in moments of boredom or stress. Quite a lot of the thinking can be productive in terms of more fish in the bag on the next trip. Most of us have to plan when we will go fishing next, as we are not lucky enough to have a stillwater at the bottom of the garden ready for the moment we choose to grab a rod and go. We will normally know at least a week beforehand when the next fishing trip will occur. Yet how many of us will wake up on that long-awaited morning and leap to the window to see what the weather is like? We should *know* what the weather is going to be, because on the previous Sunday there was an excellent weather forecast at the end of the Countryside Programme on television. The night before, after the news programme there were more, and even more reliable, weather forecasts. We should have watched them, or at least had another kind member of the family watch them, to give us a report of the sort of wind and temperature we can expect, the kind of cloud cover and the barometric pressure likely. We will know what the weather has been like for the past week, and thus how warm or cold the water is likely to be. So on the morning of our longed-for fishing day, our look out of the window should merely confirm what we expected the weather to be like, and be more of an eyeball-clearing exercise than a first clue about what sort of day it is going to be! If we have failed to do our homework, of course, our planning for the day will start only a couple of hours before we cast the first fly, but with the reconnaissance done thoroughly, the planning should have been progressing towards its logical conclusion for almost a week. I know which I would rather have, don't you?

If, for example, we have watched the farming forecast the Sunday before, and it has told us that there is a warm front moving in from the Atlantic, that there will be mild south-westerly winds and it will be cloudy with intermittent sunny spells, we can look forward to that fishing day in the hope that there will be hatches of fly and that dry fly or wet fly or nymph should be the choice of the day. If the weather has been cool for a week, but now it is going to be warmer, the first choice will be the eastern shore, and a boat may well not be necessary for good fishing. So not only can you visualise what the conditions will be like, you can save money on unnecessary boat hire too. Just by doing a bit of homework on the weather forecast.

Let us now discuss one of the most important aspects of the effect of weather on a stillwater. The larger the stillwater, the more important the effect of wind and temperature on our fishing. This chapter – if read carefully – will help to remove some of the agony of indecision on the approach to a huge water like Rutland, Grafham or Kielder. For too many anglers such a water is an inland sea, thousands of acres of damn all, daunting in its vastness, and the problem of where to start fishing is an initial hurdle to overcome. A little forethought, a little knowledge and this decision becomes easy.

What we are talking about is the interaction between wind and water, which can be vital to everyone's fishing success, as this interaction will dictate where the insects will hatch, where the fish will be feeding and thus where you should be fishing for them. Knowledge of this interaction will, for a start, prevent you fishing in empty water.

When a wind blows across the surface of a body of water it has two main effects. The first effect is to cause a surface current to flow with the wind, from the weather shore (where the weather is coming *from*, in other words, the upwind shore) to the lee shore (where the weather is going *to*, the downwind shore). Do not confuse the lee shore with the place where the water is in the *lee of the shore*, these are on opposite sides of the lake! Perhaps it would be better to keep it nice and simple and refer to the *upwind* shore and the *downwind* shore. I have seen articles which have managed to confuse me thoroughly until I realised that the writer did not know what a lee shore was! So we shall stick to *upwind* and *downwind*, and forget nautical terms which might not be understood by someone living a hundred miles from the sea.

Having caused a surface current to flow, the wind will have one other main effect. It will cause the water to warm up or cool down, to nearer the temperature of the wind. This is, after all, exactly what we do when we blow on a hot cup of coffee to cool it – we cause a surface current across the top of the cup and we cool the coffee down a bit. Great, but how does this affect the fishing?

Imagine a large body of water. (If it helps, think of Rutland as an example.) In early season, the water temperature is pretty cold – there might even have been ice around the margins at times, and the water temperature in early April will certainly be below 40°F (4.4°C). That is only 8°F above freezing, and only the hardiest of midges will find it desirable to hatch (But they will!). The fish, which are always at the same temperature as their surroundings, will feel sluggish and not inclined to dash around looking for food which isn't there anyway. Their whole metabolism will be slowed down and they will take a long time to digest whatever food they do eat. For this reason, fish which have endured a hard winter are often in better condition than fish which have lived through a mild winter – torpid fish do not use up their reserves of body tissue to nearly the same extent as do fish in warmer temperatures. In a mild winter, fish feel hungrier and are constantly looking for food which isn't there, thus they use up their reserves more, and are skinnier on opening day.

Now consider what happens to a torpid, cold fish when the water suddenly warms up by a couple of degrees. The stomach will suddenly start to raise its acidity level as digestive juices are generated, and the fish will feel pangs of hunger. In other words, the fish will start thinking about *food*. So, with a bold eye, the fish will start swimming around, having a go at anything which moves. At this stage he will be a sucker for the first lure of the season which flashes past his nose. Given reasonable weather on opening day, fish should be caught fairly easily on black lures, brown lures or on any fly which looks more or less like a recognisable food item.

A few days after opening day, however, any fish which is still uncaught will have learned that everything which moves is not necessarily an item of food. The fish may well have followed a few flies or lures, taken them tentatively into his mouth, felt the prick of the hook and learned caution. In some waters the fish may even have been caught and put back a couple of times, in which case will be well 'wised-up' and will take a jaundiced view of every artificial before finally accepting or rejecting it. But another rise in water temperature will cause the metabolism to accelerate again, and as hunger takes over from caution the fish again becomes easier to catch for a while.

This process will continue until we reach the stage in high summer when the water is *too hot* – perhaps over 65 or 70°F (18-21°C) in some small waters, and warm water does not carry the amount of oxygen needed for the fish to be really active. It is then that the angler will look for cooler water to fish in, as happens anyway when the evening rise starts. The evening rise is not caused by the light level going down; it is caused by the temperature going down, from a level which was too high for comfort for both insects and fish. On those evenings when the temperature drops too far, there isn't an evening rise of any consequence; so if you detect a chilly evening, it is likely that there won't be a good hatch of fly or a good evening rise.

What we are talking about really is a temperature band within which insects and fish are at their most active. Not air temperatures, but water temperatures.

To return to the effect of wind on water. Imagine cold water, with a warm wind blowing across it. The current caused by the wind is flowing from the upwind side to the downwind side. As the wind travels across the surface, it warms the water so that the warmest water is piled up on the downwind side of the lake. The coldest water is welling up from below to replace the water taken away by the surface current, and is on the upwind side of the lake. If the wind is warmer than the water, therefore, as it often is in the early season, for best results you should fish on the downwind shore, where the wind is blowing in your face. Yet so many anglers on opening day tend to stand with the wind behind them so that they can cast further. The likelihood is that there are no fish there, so they really do need to cast far!

In the height of summer – on the other hand – particularly after a couple of weeks of heatwave, the body of water might be too warm for the happiness of both fish and insects. If the wind is *cooler* than the water, the coolest water will again be on the downwind shore, and it will be warm water which is welling up on the upwind side.

The surface current is warmed up as it travels across the lake. The warmest surface water is therefore on the downwind shore. If the wind is warmer than the water you should fish facing the wind. This is where the insects and fish will be most active.

If you fish with your back to the wind, you will be fishing in the cold water welling up from deeper down, and there is much less chance that there will be insect or fish activity in front of you.

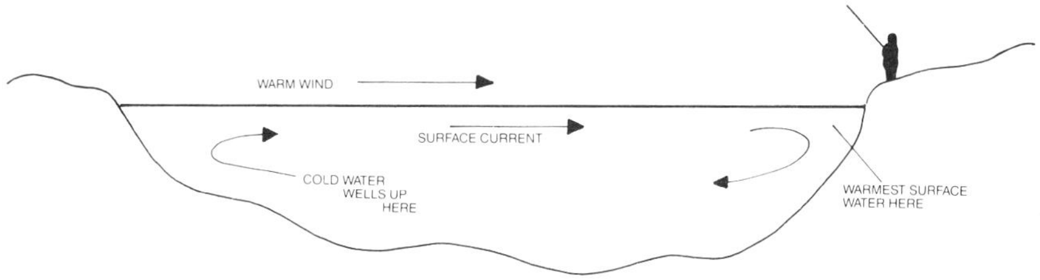

It is very seldom in Britain that we get a heatwave of such intensity that fish in large bodies of water start to suffer distress from high water temperatures or their associated lack of available oxygen. This problem is more or less confined to small shallow lakes. If you arrive on a hot summer's day on the banks of a small lake and find fish swimming aimlessly about with their noses out of the water, you should not bother to put your rod together – you will not catch anything.

On large bodies of water, however, it is quite possible for the downwind surface water temperature to be too warm for feeding activity: yet for the upwind shore to have water welling up which is too cool for maximum activity. In this case try a spot half-way along the wind current. The temperature there might be just right for maximum activity, and if you fish there you might have a ball while anglers at either upwind or downwind sides fish all day and never even see a fish.

If we are fishing one of the larger bodies of water, therefore, we can (almost) ignore the possibility that all the water will be too warm for fish and insects. Even in the height of summer, there will be enough cold water in deep spots to keep fish at maximum feeding activity, as they will move around to find the temperature which suits them best. Actually they will not – they will move around to find the temperature which suits their food supply best – a chicken and egg situation, but one of which we can take advantage.

We can therefore summarise by formulating a simple rule to help us to decide where to start fishing:

If the wind is warmer than the water, fish facing the wind
If the wind is colder than the water, fish with your back to the wind
(Only at the height of a heatwave might this rule be reversed)

Thus we can eliminate half of the shoreline of a stillwater from our initial agony of indecision. Look at the weather of the last week or ten days, judge how warm or cool the water is likely to be and, on the day itself, you will know whether you should head for the upwind or downwind half of the reservoir, just by feeling the wind on your face or by listening to yesterday's weather forecast!

If the wind is colder than the water, fish with your back to the wind. This is where the warmest water is welling up, and where there is the greatest possibility of insect and fish activity.

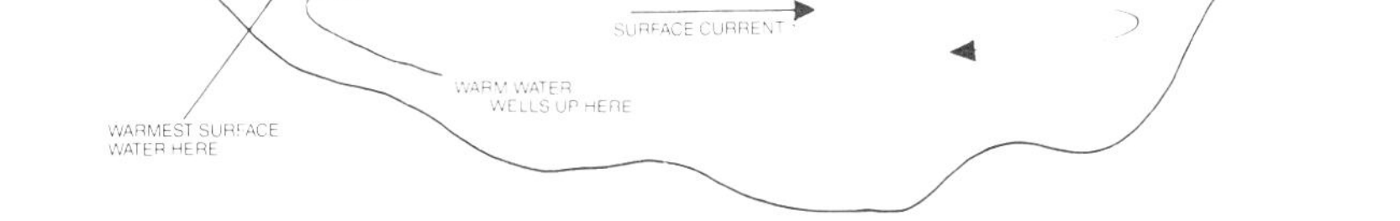

One caution. While rules in fishing are formulated by men, intending them to be applicable to fish and insects, they are never infallible. They should be regarded as an initial guide only. If you try it and it doesn't work, try something else. If that something else then works, you can have a lot of fun in doing the detective work to find out why. You might then be able to formulate a different rule for yourself, which will give you great satisfaction. But if you find an infallible version of the simple rule I have outlined above, then please *do* tell me! All I can say is that the rule has worked for me nearly all the time, and on the occasions when it failed, nobody else caught anything anyway, so I did not feel left out of the action.

There are those who advocate telephoning the bailiff on the evening before a fishing trip, checking if re-stocking has been done recently, are catches good, what fly is best at the moment and so on. I am not sure that this is a suggestion which I can support, as it does depend on the bailiff. Too many bailiffs have to work long hours starting in the early morning and finishing late at night. To have the telephone ringing non-stop every evening while tomorrow's anglers ask all sorts of damn silly questions puts a severe strain on any bailiff's patience, and if his wife has to answer the telephone while he is out at all hours on an anti-poacher patrol, his marriage will also come under strain; and the result will be a surly reception for anglers in the morning. If you are certain that Charlie is always in the lodge at 6.30 and is happy to give advice for the morrow, then fine. But unless you are sure, I think it better to leave the poor bailiff to his hard-earned rest in the evenings and turn up on your chosen morning with an open mind and your wits about you.

By all means quiz the bailiff when you arrive on what fly is catching fish? He will normally be delighted to tell you, and to give any other help he can. After all, he is there to keep the paying customers happy, just as much as to keep non-paying customers out. If anglers become unhappy at that particular stillwater then they will go elsewhere and his job will be in jeopardy. So the average bailiff is only too pleased to answer sensible questions from new arrivals. A variation of the usual question about what fly to use, ask him what flies have been hatching from the water at different times of the day recently. This could be even more instructive.

Too many anglers will be told, for instance, that an Invicta is working well, and when they look into their flybox they haven't got an Invicta. Then they go quietly mad all day worrying that they might be catching more fish if only they had an Invicta. Better to be told that there are largish sedges hatching, and then to fish with a fair amount of confident ignorance, using a sedge imitation of some kind! This situation becomes worse when one travels a long distance to a strange water, and is told that the only lure to use is called the Cat's Pyjamas, and you haven't even heard of it, let alone got one. The mental stress thus invoked is best done without; you are there, after all, to enjoy yourself!

What else can you do before you actually set off on the morning of your fishing day? Quite a lot. You can check over your tackle, making sure that rings are firm on the rod, varnish does not need touching up and that the reel fitting is clean (if it is an alloy one, you can drip a little candlewax on it). Are your waders dry inside, or are they still a bit damp from the last trip? Stuff some newspaper well down into the toes to make sure they are dry and comfortable in the morning. Check that you have got your clean wader socks packed, and that your 'falling-in' kit is complete. Check your flybox, or the flybox you are taking with you. Glance at the bottle of dry fly oil – got enough? Check your leadersink – has it dried out? A little water puddled on top will soften it for the morning. If you smoke, have you got a packet of cigarettes and matches or lighter? Nothing worse than gasping for a cigarette when you are supposed to be concentrating on fish. (If you do smoke, have you got a small tin in the pocket of your fishing jacket for spent matches and cigarette ends? To dump these at the waterside creates litter – the curse of our countryside.)

Having checked all your tackle, do you then leave it in the car and leave the car outside all night? You are asking to have it all pinched if you do. Far better if you do not have a securely locked garage, to pile the tackle inside the front door and load up in the morning. Have you made your sandwiches? If you make them the evening before, wrap them well in Cling Film or aluminium foil and they will still be moist and edible when you want them. I have not found the secret, if there is one, of drinkable coffee the following day, and I fill flasks at the last possible moment before leaving; but because I am most forgetful I put a piece of paper on top of the tackle saying 'FLASKS', and that reminds me that I have this job to do before I rush off.

Last of all, get a good night's sleep. There is nothing more tiring than a day in the fresh air, and lack of sleep can turn you into a road accident statistic waiting to happen on the way home. If you normally get seven hours sleep before a day's work, try to get eight hours sleep before a day's fishing. Not only will you feel better, you will think more clearly and thus should catch more.

A day's fishing, if you are really keen, *is* more tiring than a normal day's work. You will tend to get up earlier than normal, rush breakfast, drive some distance and then spend the whole day on your feet staring at rippling water. The eyestrain can be considerable, even with polarised glasses on. Then, much later than the end of a normal working day, you point the car home and turn the heater on. Most anglers know exactly what leaden eyelids feel like at 70 miles per hour, they have them on the way home from every fishing trip. You owe it to your family to start such a day as relaxed and fresh as possible, that way your safe return home is more likely.

C·H·A·P·T·E·R

8

On Arrival

Anglers are dedicated to their hobby. There is a natural inclination, if I may use a good Glasgow expression, to 'get tore in' as soon as you arrive. This is a mistake, and those who do this are typical of the unthinking angler, tackling up with the latest lure in the car park, rushing straight into the water and starting to double-haul out of sight at fish they have already frightened away.

You have planned your day. You know that there will be a wind blowing in a certain direction, that the wind will be warmer or cooler than the water, and that your best chance of fish *should* be on a particular bank of the reservoir. By all means head for that chosen spot after you have signed in and got your ticket, but a little time spent looking at the water might save you a fruitless hour or so. At this stage, a pair of binoculars can save miles of walking. Find a vantage point, where you chosen shoreline can be searched with binoculars. On opening day you might find that there is an angler every three yards, flogging the water into foam. If there is, go somewhere else, the fish will be seeing flies of all kinds being dragged past their noses and, unless they are all poor ignorant stockies dumped in during the last 48 hours, your chances of catching anything are reduced by angler pressure. If the fish are recently-introduced stock fish, you don't want to catch them anyway. They give little satisfaction to the dedicated angler, and taste like blotting paper when cooked.

You may be lucky enough to discover that you have the shore to yourself, which is quite likely if you have opted to fish into the teeth of a wind. Do not rush off yet. Spend at least ten minutes studying the shoreline with those binoculars. Watch, of course, for rising fish; but watch also for swallows hawking on the surface, picking flies off the water. If there are terns around (they look like a small seagull, with skinny wings and a hesitant wingbeat!) watch for these taking flies off the surface too. Beware of thinking that a lovely confident rise-form in a distant calm bay is necessarily caused by a trout, as careful study through the glasses may reveal a dabchick or little grebe busy diving for weed. I have, in the past, spent fruitless hours walking to such a scene of activity, only to discover these little birds with their fascinating little hop into the air before they plonk below the surface. They are lovely to watch, but that is not what you are here for.

Study the shoreline and study the way the wind-lanes flow. Can you find a spot where a promontory funnels the surface drift in such a way that a trout only has to stay put to have its food brought to it? Study the calm water in the lee of any promontories, are there signs of land-born insects being blown onto the water or telltale signs of fish rising just where the ripple first strikes the water surface? Are there any daddy-longlegs in the grass at your feet?

The surface of the main body of water may be lashed by a strong wind into a good wave. If so, are there any calm bays showing rising fish?

If you can see any fish rising, you can do some more detective work. Is the rise-form a quiet swirl, or a hurried slosh? How deep is the water where that fish rose? If you can see some fish rising, you can deduce what method will give you the best chance of a fish or two in the next hour or so, by remembering some of the following simple rules (remembering also that rules apply only when the fish want them to).

1) A trout will never use up more energy eating something than it will gain from the food. So a tiny insect will deserve only the minimum amount of energy expended in catching it. The smaller the insect, the quieter the rise-form therefore. While something large, containing lots of calories and hormones will justify a fast, slashing rise in order to capture it. So a tiny midge pupa will cause a tiny sipping rise, whereas daddy-longlegs or large sedge, or even a juicy minnow, will justify a fast, slashing rise.

2) Insects hatch in different ways out of the water. Midge pupae will hang for hours in the surface film, and, in calm oily water will often have a deadly struggle to get out of that final skin, stand on the surface and dry the wings, and finally take off on their first flight. Trout know that midges do not hatch in a hurry, so they do not have to hurry to eat them. Rises to midges, therefore, are quiet, confident and sometimes hard to see in a wave, often with the dorsal fin and tail showing in a porpoise-like roll.

Upwinged flies of the Ephemerid family tend to hatch more easily than do midges, but their wings seem to take longer to dry. So they sit there, looking like little yachts facing into the wind, and trout have to hurry slightly more than they do for midges. Thus rises to lake olives and, of course, any other upwinged fly tend to be more of a swirling action, the kind where the rings spread out like the scoring rings of a target, and are noticeably more determined than the rise to a hatching midge.

The fastest hatchers of all are the sedges. It matters not whether it is a tiny sedge like a silverhorns, or a large red sedge the size of a large moth, they hatch out of their skins like lightning, and start running along the surface even before their wings are thoroughly dry. I have timed a great red sedge from first appearing before my fascinated eyes an inch below the surface, swimming upwards fast, getting out of that skin and starting a running takeoff, and it took about four seconds! No wonder the fish have to hurry, and show a typical slashing rise-form which – to the experienced angler, seeing it after mid-day – announces sedge just as surely as if one had been found in the stomach contents.

3) Insects lay their eggs over different kinds of bottom. Ephemerids lay their eggs over weedbeds, as they know that their nymphs thrive best around vegetation. Nymphs which spend their lives in a weedbed for a year will hatch on the surface over that same weedbed. And as weedbeds in stillwaters normally do not grow in water more than a few feet deep, it follows that flies hatching over weedbeds in fairly shallow water are most likely to be of the upwinged variety. (Damselflies climb up a stem of some kind to hatch, and can be ignored for the purpose of this exercise.) Sedges, whose larvae build themselves little tubes of reed, sand or other debris from the bottom, seem to need a high level of oxygen and light, and are thus found in fairly shallow water, probably not more than ten feet deep. Insects seen hatching therefore in fairly shallow water devoid of weedbeds are thus likely to be sedges. Midges, on the other hand, because of the haemoglobin in their blood, can tolerate very low levels of oxygen and still thrive: and the bloodworms (midge larvae) and the chrysalis stage (midge pupae) need mud to bury themselves in. Such conditions of soft mud are found most often in deeper water, where currents have carried the sediment downhill. So insects seen hatching over deep water, usually devoid of weedbeds, will tend to be midges.

You do not, of course, have to see the actual insects as they hatch in order to be able to tell what they are. Swallows or terns feeding on the surface will tell you, *a)* that there is a hatch in progress and *b)* depending on the kind of bottom they are feeding over, what those insects are most likely to be. Binoculars, too, can help you to identify insects on the surface of the water.

There is one other possibility. You arrive, perhaps very early in the season, and stare at a frigid, wind-blasted surface on which there is not the slightest sign of activity. At the lodge you are told that nobody caught anything yesterday, but that the fish were stocked before the season opened. It is likely that you will see other anglers fishing where the fishing is easiest, either with the wind at their backs or where there is a nice left-to-right breeze along the shore. Left-handed anglers will all be on the opposite shore! Your preliminary detective work may well tell you that, in these circumstances, that you should be fishing where the fishing is most difficult, in the teeth of the wind with waves lashing the shore. Go there. If other anglers are fishing where your homework says they shouldn't, that could explain the poor catch rate yesterday. Nature is logical, deadly logical and all wildlife is engaged in a battle for survival. Use the same logic and you will find the fish, and if the conditions are difficult to fish in when you do find the fish, then bad luck, you didn't expect it to be too easy, did you! What you must never do is to fish somewhere just because the fishing conditions are pleasant for you as a human being, you are not trying to catch other human beings, you are trying to catch fish and must think like one, so that you can detect where they are most likely to be. Fish need three things to make life pleasant for them. A water temperature which makes them most active and which causes insect activity, a good level of available oxygen in the water (so not too high a water temperature) and food, lots of food. All you have to do on any particular day is to find where these three conditions are most likely to be met *underwater*. And they have nothing whatever to do with the conditions for casting a fly line from the bank!

Simple, isn't it? Not infallible, of course, but good enough as a guide to start you off for the day with a lot more confidence than you would have had if you had just ploughed in and started fishing. Having done your ten minutes or so of spying around with your binoculars, you can collect your tackle and start walking to your chosen starting point. Having first checked that the car is thoroughly locked, with no temptations left in view on seats, dashboard or parcel shelf. Put the keys in a safe inside pocket where they are not likely to drop out during the day!

Personally, I prefer to put the rod together, attach the reel and thread the line through the rings before I leave the car. Usually I put a fly on too, based on the detective work I have done so far, as I can immediately cover a rising fish with a fly which gives me a good chance of a take. Nothing more maddening than to be walking along the shore towards your chosen spot, see a fish rise and by the time you have tackled up it has moved on! For this reason I am ready for instant action while I am walking along the bank.

One little dodge which will save valuable time. I tend to get my tackle ready the night before. So, for instance, the spool carrying the DT 5 floating line will also have the Big Butt leader and a tippet of 4 lb nylon all ready attached. Put the spool in the reel, pull off the whole of the leader and some of the fly line. Double the leader back so that you are holding the doubled-back leader where it joins the fly line. Thread that doubled bit through the rod rings, all the way to the tip ring and out. Then if the line slips out of your fingers (as Sod's Law says it will when you get near the tip), you will not watch the tippet leap all the way back down the rod to the reel, you will watch it stick at the last ring you threaded, ready to be grabbed again to continue the threading. A silly little dodge, but I am often surprised to see intelligent anglers struggling to thread a tippet end – made of fine nylon, which is hard to see anyway – up through the rings of the rod, pulling off the reel as they go, just asking for aggro.

Take out your flybox and using your detective work, and perhaps a touch of intuition, choose a fly. Tie the knot carefully and check it. Leave only a short end on the knot which attaches the fly to the tippet, a waste end of nylon here over perhaps an ⅛ in. long can act as a hook-guard, and bounce the fly out of a fish's mouth before the point contacts flesh. Cut that waste end as short as you can, then take a minute or so to de-grease the leader. Do it now, not when you see a fish rise, or the temptation to cast at that fish without degreasing the leader will be overpowering, and you may frighten the fish instead of catching it. Remember that the first cast of the day is the most important. If you catch a fish with it you boost your confidence for the whole of the day. If you just frighten a fish with it, you are wasting your time being there.

So now you are all ready with tackle prepared, you check that you have got everything you will need. Got your landing net? Sandwiches? Coffee? You put your flybox back in your pocket and it's not lying on the roof of the car? Good, then you can start walking away from the car park.

At this stage, beware of succumbing to the temptation to go to the nearest bit of water and have a quick cast or two, just to limber up. You made a decision to go to a certain place along the shore, stick to it and go there. . .with only one exception. If you see a fish rise within reasonable casting distance from the shore, regard it as a sign from heaven and have a go at it. The easiest fish to catch is one which has just enjoyed a mouthful of food, and which then sees another similar mouthful in the same place. Like the small boy offered a second chocolate biscuit by an Aunt, he is likely to grab first and wonder what Mum would think of his manners second!

While you are walking you should not be idle. Keep your eyes open, not just to admire the view but to look for insects in the grass, they could be another piece of the jigsaw puzzle. If you pass trees or bushes, look under the leaves for flies which have already hatched and flown to cover. Notice I said look under the leaves. Flies, or most flies, apart from the housefly, damselfly and mosquito types cannot drink once they have reached the dun stage. They therefore have to seek cover from the heat of the sun or the last skin covering will dry and become too stiff to shed. If they cannot shed that last skin, they cannot turn into spinners, mate and lay eggs. Thus, they try to keep cool and moist, so look for them *under* the leaves. And if you do find a mass of flies under the leaves, all of a certain type, it is likely that they hatched either early that day or during yesterday afternoon or evening. Unless the weather has changed considerably, you can expect a similar hatch sometime today – you now have another piece of the jigsaw.

You now arrive at your chosen fishing spot. Again there is a great temptation to wade straight in and start fishing. Don't. You have chosen this spot for a reason, and the reason is likely to be that you have seen fish feeding here. If you hurry now you will frighten them off, and all the work and patience you have shown till now will have been wasted. Stand at least two rod-lengths back from the water, and get the rod ready to cast. Pull some line off the reel, point the tip of the rod downwards to within a foot of the ground, and waggle the tip gently back and forth. If you hold the loose line in your left hand higher than the butt ring, this waggling will cause the fly line to slide down through the rings and out through the tip ring. Holding the fly in your left hand, you now have several yards of line outside the tip of the rod, ready to do a quick roll cast. As the tension is felt on the fly, let it go and the leader will land on the water in front of you. At last you are fishing!

Just one word about how you hooked the fly on the rod, and how you held it for that first roll-cast. I never use the keeper ring on a rod. I hook the tail fly on one of the intermediate rings, well up the rod as far as I can comfortably reach. Then I bring the leader back around the reel. When I wind the line up snug, I have the end of the fly line, not a piece of the leader, passing through the tip ring. This avoids the kink in the nylon often caused by the leader being doubled back through the tip ring. The kink in the supple fly line is much less likely to stay there for long. When I grasp a fly ready to cast it, I always hold it by the tail, or by the body or by the bend of the hook, with the point of the hook well away from the skin of my fingers. That way when it is flipped out of my grasp in that first roll cast it does not sink deep into my finger! It is a waste of blood and fishing time, both equally precious, to have to remove hooks from one's person.

You should still be standing two rod-lengths back from the edge of the water, with your fly perhaps 10-12 feet out from the edge. Any trout in that water now has a chance to see the fly and take it, as the fish should not have been frightened by your quiet approach. What would have happened if you had started by wading? The chances are that you would have frightened the fish, and greatly reduced your chances of catching one.

Imagine that you have seen a fish rise fifteen yards from the shore. Most anglers would cast straight away to that fish. Their fly line lands on the water, assuming they are using a 12 foot leader, for eleven yards. That eleven yards of fly line will frighten any fish over an area of 66 square yards. There is an excellent probability that there will be a fish in that 66 square yards, and when it flees it will also panic the target fish. Panic is infectious among fish, they know enough to realise that another fish fleeing in panic knows something that they don't, and prudence dictates that they had better flee too or they might get eaten by some predator. It cannot be stressed strongly enough that you should never ignore the water between you and a target fish. And the further away that target fish is, the more important this rule becomes.

Consider two typical anglers, one fishing from the shore and the other fishing from a boat. The angler on the shore tries to cast out as far as possible. The one in the boat tries to land his fly a yard from the shore. One of them must be wrong! To put this another way, a trout in shallow water is not there for fun. The fish is conscious that he is a long way from the security of deep water, and so tends to be more edgy and more alert than a trout in the murky depths. He is there for only one purpose – food. Therefore he is a feeding fish and feeding fish can be caught much more easily than soporific fish. To follow this argument to its logical conclusion, therefore, fish found in shallow water can be caught more easily, and so should be fished for before casting at those fish further away from the bank.

To return to our situation on arrival at our chosen fishing spot. The first few casts should land only the leader and fly on the water, with the angler standing well back from the water's edge, at least two rod lengths. Perhaps, if you are really keen, kneeling down to lower your skyline silhouette. The first few casts should cover a fan shape in front of you, starting with a cast along the bank to your left and finishing with a cast along the bank to your right. Having done this, and risen nothing, there are two possibilities – you have the wrong fly on or there are no fish within the distance covered. But you have done your detective work on the type of fly most likely to succeed, and three or four casts do not provide enough evidence to condemn as totally wrong all the brainpower you have used.

In case you start to feel depressed, consider that a feeding trout will have a go at anything which looks like food, whether it is exactly what it sees in profusion around it or not. As we shall discuss later under autopsies, trout very seldom become locked on to only one food form, ignoring all others. No, the strongest possibility is that there were no trout in your target area, and you can lengthen your line and search further out. Without moving your feet!

Pull another two yards of line off the reel, and cast in that fan shape again. Now you are searching an arc with a radius of 18 feet; then you pull another two yards off the reel and search an arc with a radius of 24 feet; then 30 feet; then 36 feet; then 42 feet; and then 48 feet. Each time you search that arc in front of you. By the time you have covered the 40 foot arc, you have got twelve yards of fly line off the reel. Now, if you must, you can stand up and advance to the edge of the water and get your toes wet. But *do not wade*!

This 'approach drill', as I call it, applies every single time I approach the water. It matters not in the slightest that the water may shelve out from half-an-inch deep at the edge to perhaps only a couple of feet deep ten yards out, or whether the shore drops off straight away into several feet of water. Trout do feed in very shallow water at times, most frequently in the evenings, during the night and at dawn, but they can be found in water only just deep enough to cover their backs at any time of the day. Remember – trout in shallow water are feeding trout.

Once you have carried out the approach drill, you are now standing at the water's edge and have satisfied yourself that there are no catchable trout within 16 yards of your feet. What to do now? Simply keep lengthening line by two yards at a time, and cover that arc again and again, until you are casting as far as is comfortable for your casting ability. By all means do a double-haul to increase distance if you want to, but stop before you are casting beyond your own personal 'distance of delicate presentation'. However far you can cast, there will be the time when a fish is rising one yard further out that you can reach. Learn to live with this – it happens to everybody sooner or later. One way round this problem, of course, is to change lines. A weight-forward line will add perhaps five yards to your casting distance and just might put that fish in the bag, and it takes only a couple of minutes to change the line. It can be worth the effort. Whatever you do, do not be tempted to wade out to the tops of your thigh waders just to gain a few yards – wading will reduce the height of your rod tip above the water and above the bank behind you, so your backcast will be nearer to the vegetation which is reaching up to grab that backcast anyway! At best you will have to wade ashore to untangle the fly from a thistle. At worst, you will break the hook on a stone, rise the fish and, after a bump or two, feel the fish come off the hook which didn't have a point on it! One scared fish which will not rise again for a long time, if you had not tried so hard and had been just a little more patient that fish might well have worked its way nearer the shore and been caught with a delicate cast at a reasonable distance.

During the approach drill, you should avoid at all costs the habit of many anglers – false casting. Flickering a fly line over a fish is one sure way of putting it down for an hour. It matters not that the line is white, brown, red, or green, it will frighten fish. Wet fly lines flash in the sun whatever colour they may be, so, as a basic rule avoid false casting if at all possible.

Don't walk boldly up to the edge of the water and then kneel down. I have seen it done, by anglers who then think that they have become invisible to fish. They may well be but the fish have already gone, scared off by the sight of that tall predator which clumped up to the edge of the water. If you want to remain invisible, start kneeling when you are a couple of rod lengths back from the edge, and creep forward on your knees.

Wading carries another penalty. It kills fish food. Let me explain by illustrating that every big boot landing on a lake bed will flatten the eggs, larvae or pupae, of insects. Those insects are fish food. Weeds, too, are killed when big feet crush them, so cover for insects is also reduced. On all our stillwaters where wading is allowed, by the end of the season there is a sterile band of water along the shore, perhaps ten paces wide in which no insect survives. If there are no insects there is no fish food, as without insects there will not even be minnows. So the trout will not come close to shore, and anglers will have condemned themselves to long-distance casting in order to reach them. If I can leave no other message with readers of this book, it is *do not wade.* For those who run stillwaters the message would be – *do not allow wading* – it would also be my suggestion that you do not allow waders to be worn at all, as anglers have this strange lemming-like instinct to walk into the water, even where they know wading is not allowed. They seem incapable of stopping themselves!

As a caring, devoted angler, would you deliberately kill on every fishing trip perhaps several hundred olives, several thousand caddis flies and another thousand assorted items of trout food like waterboatmen, midges, beetles and damselflies? Of course you wouldn't. But you do, every time you spend a day standing up to the limit of your waders. Think about it and then stop wading, I beg you, all anglers not just stillwater anglers. River anglers too do just as much damage to the environment by wading, crushing insects under the stones of the stream. If insects had nice kind faces like seals, otters, badgers or foxes, the anti-hunting brigade would have been at the throats of anglers long ago. The damage is insidious, it is not noticed until an elderly man happens to remark that the hatches of fly are not as prolific as they were in his youth, and we then tend to smile and put his remarks down to the 'things are not what they used to be' syndrome. But he is probably correct, and the fault cannot be laid entirely at the door of agricultural sprays or land drainage. Until anglers put their own house in order and remember that wading kills food, we cannot blame anybody else. . .

C·H·A·P·T·E·R

9

Casting

In the first few editions of this book, I devoted several pages to talking about casting. Since then I have written a book on casting: *The Flycasting Handbook* (Ward Lock, 1991). In revising this edition of this present book, it became apparent to me that I could not do justice to the subject of casting in one chapter, and so I decided to do two things. First, to concentrate upon enabling you to judge your own casting; second, to entreat you to have a casting lesson from a qualified instructor. If you also want to read my book on casting then all well and good; most libraries have it, or will be able to get it for you, or you can add it to your Christmas present list.

If the truth is told, most men feel that it is more important to perform well at their hobby than to perform well at their job! Then why do so many anglers starting the sport just borrow a rod from Uncle Joe and go fishing? They thrash and bash in their efforts to get a line out there, and catch nothing. Slowly the penny drops, and they start to achieve a little distance, but they have adopted many of Uncle Joe's faults as well as their own. When they see some really smooth casting being done, they tend to feel jealous of the man performing it, and a feeling of inferiority tends to creep into their fishing. If they have not caught some fish by this stage, they will join the great band of men who decided that fishing was not a sport they could take to, and who now watch football on television instead. Such a tragic loss of so much pleasure over so many years, and all because they were too mean, or too pigheaded, to take a professional lesson to start them off on the road to smooth, effortless casting.

Notice that I say a professional lesson. I cannot stress enough that, at present, there is only one qualification which is worth considering. The Association of Profesional Game Angling Instructors (APGAI) is the only body that examines candidates for their knowledge of teaching skills and their ability to spot and correct faults. I suggest most earnestly that you have your lesson from a member of APGAI, and no other. The Association advertises in some of the fishing magazines, and so do many of the members, and your local tackle shop may well know of a member living locally.

So how can you tell if you need a lesson? I could tell you by watching you make one cast, but here is how to decide for yourself. Raise your right hand from the book, pretend you have a fly rod gripped in it, and go through the motions of one cast. Now you have the idea, do another cast, but this time freeze your hand half-way through, having done the back cast, and while the line is rolling out behind you. Look at your frozen hand and arm. Go on, turn your head and look at them. If your thumb is within eight inches of your right ear, and that thumb is pointing upwards, you are perhaps a reasonable caster. But now study the pictures which form the rest of this chapter, and see if you recognise some of your faults. If you do, you will be doing yourself the greatest possible favour if you pick up the telephone and book that casting lesson from a member of APGAI.

On the other hand you might have fished all your life, and feel that you are a reasonably competent caster, but you would love to be able to roll cast, or cast safely with the wind blowing on your 'wrong' shoulder, or while sitting at the 'wrong' end of the boat. Book that lesson.

A common casting fault. The hand is raised high above the head while making the backcast. Much greater effort is therefore required to overcome all that adverse leverage and drive the rod forward – the muscles which are used to do this are much smaller than the muscles which drive the hand forward when the hand is at ear height.

Another common casting fault. The hand is out to the side, at the extremity of the backcast, which lowers the backcast by several feet, resulting in loss of flies or hook-points. Again the leverage is all wrong, as the pulling muscles are smaller than the pushing muscles, and in this fault the hand has to be pulled forward to drive the rod.

A very common casting fault. The wrist is cocked back at the extremity of the back cast, dropping the line down behind. An angler suffering from this fault often has great difficulty in casting into wind, as he will automatically aim too high in front and, while the line may land straight, the leader will be blown back in a heap.

This man is a good angler, catching his share of fish. He is left-handed and the wind is coming from his left: so he turns around and casts facing the shore, delivers the line on a backcast, and then turns around again to fish the cast out! In the meantime he is screwing his feet into the bottom, and is in grave danger of falling over when he does decide to wade out! If only he could develop the habit of bringing his left-hand casting arm to his right ear, so that the line stays on the downwind side of him (and safe). That way he could then stay facing the fish, instead of pirouetting all day. Remember, with an adverse wind blowing onto the casting arm, take the rod hand to the opposite ear – it's easy!

Now a sequence of photographs showing good, effortless casting with the right arm. The haul with the left hand is not shown. Ignore the positions of the feet – they moved between shots! The start of the cast. The rod is low, there is no slack under the rod tip, and the rod is now glided upwards.

The line is being lifted off the water in a gentle draw, until it reaches about ten o'clock, leaving no foam to scare fish. At this stage the power comes in, in the form of a flick upwards and backwards, done entirely with the bicep.

The power is in for the backcast, the rod is starting to load and the line is now all off the water, accelerating backwards, to roll over the top of the rod.

The rod stops here. The position is critical for a nice high backcast. The thumb blocks any further movement of the rod, and the wrist does not cock backwards. If you have trouble in controlling this cocking of the wrist, try tucking the butt up the sleeve of your jacket. It will, at first, feel most awkward but your backcast will be much higher. The moment the line is straightened behind, the forward cast starts.

The forward cast in progress. The thumb is driven straight forwards at an aiming point on the opposite bank.

The extremity of the forward cast, 'stick your thumb in his eye'. The line is now rolling out in front of the angler, the rod has a slight droop as the line starts to drop towards the surface, and all power is now eased off gently. Do not thrash the rod to a stop, or the tip will vibrate and cause wind knots.

As the line drops gently to the surface, the rod follows it down until – as the line lands – the rod tip is low: so low, it can almost touch the surface. This results in a nice straight line from rod to fly with no slack under the rod tip.

If you stand square-on to the target, and then turn your head to watch your backcast, it is inevitable that your arm goes out to the side. . .

So if you do want to watch your backcast in the air behind you, stand sideways to the target. Then your casting arm can travel back and forth along the 'curtain rail' (which is fastened at one end to your ear or shoulder), and does not wave around sideways. Therefore the forward push of the rod uses the largest muscles possible, and the forward cast is thus as easy as can be, simply a dab forward with the thumb to full arm stretch in front.

C·H·A·P·T·E·R

10

Dry Fly Fishing

After the approach to the waterside and all that should precede it, and the actual casting, I had thought of a single chapter entitled – *what to do with the fly once you have put it out there*, but at this stage there are so many variables – depending on what fly is on the end of the leader – that several chapters are necessary.

I shall start with dry fly fishing, not for any silly reasons of purism but because it seems logical to start at the surface and work downwards into the depths. While I do admit that I like dry fly fishing more than any other method, this is simply because I get a greater thrill out of seeing the fish come up and take the fly than I do from getting a tug underwater at the end of a sinking shooting head. And I do think that dry fly fishing is an under-rated method on stillwaters.

The eyes of a fish are near the top of the head (a trout's eyes are anyway). Thus it looks upwards for much of the time. It is far, far better to be fishing a little too shallow than it is to be fishing a little too deep: a fish may well not see a fly below it at all, particularly a dark fly against a dark bottom. Any fly shows up well against a light sky. So it can be stated with some certainty that a floating fly will be seen by more fish than will a deeply sunk one, unless the fish are lying very deep indeed. So, in theory a dry fly can be seen by more fish than a deep nymph, therefore it *should* catch more fish. Remember also that if you see fish rising, those fish are feeding on something very near the surface. . . It might not be a food form which is entirely on the surface. It might be a fly in the act of struggling out of its shuck in the film, or a nymph or pupa a couple of inches under the surface but, as a basic rule, if fish are to be seen rising, they can be caught on a dry fly.

You will not need many dry flies for stillwater fishing in this country, perhaps half a dozen patterns will do, but as you gain experience you will find yourself using them more and more, and ignoring the lures in the flybox. Dry flies will work at any time of day, and all that is needed is a water temperature which is conducive to insects hatching. On the cold blasted surface on opening day, you are probably wasting your time with a dry fly, but once the balmy days of late spring arrive and the underwater life starts to become more active the angler who is skilled with a dry fly can catch fish, and get a lot of fun doing it.

Obviously it helps if you have a target fish. If there are no target fish then there are no fish feeding on the surface, and you are wasting your time anyway. Let us assume that you do have a target fish, one which you have seen rise. The essential detective work on the type of rise will tell you what kind of insect is being eaten by that fish. Go to your flybox and choose a fly as near to an exact imitation as you can. Nothing there? Then choose something nice and big which will float well, and put that out there. If the fish is hungry, it may well take the fly anyway. As an example, think of the fish happily eating lake olives. . .the fish will be chomping nymphs as they swim up past his nose as they head for the surface with a desperate energy. He will be grabbing them as they stick for a moment in the film, struggling to cast that last skin and get their wings out and dried. He will be slurping them down as they sit on the water, head into wind as they dry their wings off. He may well be slashing at them a split second after they have managed to take off into wind and are flittering an inch above the surface. Now you put a daddy-longlegs over his nose, and *bang*, there is almost no way he will refuse such a juicy mouthful. So do not worry too much if you have not got an exact imitation of the current food form – put on something larger and pray.

I have often been told that it seems to take me an age to get ready to cast a dry fly. It does take a long time, and all the time I am probably quivering with eagerness to get that fly out there. But I must not hurry. Skimp any of the preparatory work and you might as well sit and drink coffee for all the good that fly will do. It is essential that the presentation is perfect, first time. If everything is done right, the fish should take the fly almost as soon as it lands, so let us now go through the drill I follow before I cast the fly.

To start with I check the leader for wind knots. It must be perfect. Then I check the knot at the eye of the fly. That must be perfect too. If you neglect either of these simple steps, you will leave that target fish swimming away with the fly and perhaps a yard of tippet. Somebody else might catch that fish later and recover your fly, but it won't end up on *your* breakfast plate.

Then I oil the fly. No matter if it was oiled twenty minutes ago, I oil it again. You might think that this is being hyper-fussy, and it probably is, but I do oil the fly very often. Then I *know* the fly will sit perked up on the surface and not sink half-way into the film like a half-drowned water rat. (Just occasionally the fish want a half-sunk fly, but that is another story.) Having oiled the fly, I blow it dry with several good explosive puffs of breath, holding the fly in such a way as to result in the blown spray of oil being carried *away* from the leader. I regard it vital that I avoid getting any fly oil on the nylon of the tippet. Now I wipe my fingers on the seat of my trousers or on the rump of my fishing jacket, which gets the oil off my fingers before I handle the tippet nylon. The next step is to get the

Leadersink out of my pocket, and thoroughly degrease that vital last yard of nylon up to the fly. Having put the Leadersink back in my pocket, I am at last ready to make that critical first cast. I have been told that it takes me far longer to get ready than it takes me to catch the fish, and that may well be true. All I know is that when that fly goes out there into the target area, I have done everything possible to ensure that all is perfection. The nylon will be sunk for that last yard at least, not leaving a tramline of *meniscus* pointing like an arrow at the hook. (I am not sure that I am technically correct in using the word meniscus, but I refer to the little lip of water surface which rises on both sides of a floating line or nylon.) This tramline causes a prominent shadow in shallow water which scares the living daylights out of any fish it passes over: in deeper water it causes a refraction along the surface much more visible than a wisp of sunk nylon against the light from the sky. I also know that the fly, if I put it down gently enough, will sit perked up on its hackles in what I believe is an attractive manner. I also know that there were, before I started this final cast, no wind knots in the leader to cause that sickening ping when I strike.

I can hear you thinking that I must have the patience of Job not to dive in and cast straight away. Why waste time with all that mucking about? Firstly I am not there on a time-and-motion exercise, having to hurry or lose a bonus. For me it is all part of the fun and the bonus is a fish in the bag and that is most likely if I do not hurry. What if the fish goes away? That can happen, but if you are patient it will come back again. A fish, once it locates a supply of food, does not wander away from it. It tends to stay there eating until either it has eaten its fill, or the food supply dries up. Brown trout are quite territorial in their habits, so if it is a brownie, it should be rising thereabouts for some time. A rainbow is more likely to wander, but it will have a patrol beat which will bring it back in a short time. There is therefore no need for haste.

The only time I hurry is when, having got everything ready I look up and try to see the fish rise again. I am all set. All I need is a target to fire at. When the fish rises again, I keep remembering the comment of an old friend of mine, when he said that he was sure that the secret of my success was my ability to land my fly in the rise rings within one and a half seconds of seeing the rise. I think he hit the nail on the head and he was, of course, referring to the speed with which I actually delivered the fly from an 'all-set' position. This speed does not allow for much false casting. I drop the fly out of my left hand, pull enough line off the reel, do one false cast and then put the fly in the rings before they fade away.

I watched one young man once on our lakes at Deer Springs. There was a good rise going on and we had suggested the correct fly to him. I counted seventeen false casts over one fish before he finally put the fly on the surface, and then stood there like a heron waiting for a frog. The fish had gone, terrified by the constant flickering of line and leader in the sunlight over its head. I put up with this constant false casting for perhaps half-an-hour and then I went out to speak to him.

'Caught anything?'

The expected reply was given, 'No, I think I have the wrong fly on!'

'May I borrow your rod for a moment?' I then went through my pre-casting drill of checking the leader. There were about six wind knots so a new tippet was attached, the old nylon rolled around my fingers and cut through with the scissors to leave a hank of two-inch lengths which were dropped in the long grass. The fly was attached and oiled. The leader was degreased. I then did only one false cast to my left, changed direction in the backcast and put the fly down over a fish to the right. As the fly settled like thistledown on the surface, the fish gulped it down. I struck, and handed the rod to the young man who thought I was some kind of magician! Nothing magic about it, of course, just applied common sense.

So much for aiming at a target fish which has just risen to give us an up-to-the-second picture of where it is. In this case it is obvious that speed of presentaton is of the essence. But supposing we have approached the area of a rising fish, done all our preparatory work, and then looked up at a blank surface with not a sign of a rise? My first thought would be to wonder what I had done wrong. Why had that fish been scared into stopping its feeding? Had I frightened it by wading? Had I

This is the result of stopping the rod too soon when the line lands. Two yards of slack will sag back under the rod tip, ready to be blown around by the slightest breeze, which moves the fly in an uncontrolled way. If the fly is taken now, those two yards of slack have to be heaved out of the way before the hook sticks in. Put another way, the rod tip has to move perhaps six feet to move the point of the hook that vital quarter of an inch! Lower the rod right down to the surface as in the photograph on page 84.

been skylined like a multi-storey block of flats on its horizon? No? Then it must just have wandered away a bit or gone into a sulk where it was. The answer then is to put your fly out into the best guess of a target area, and let it sit there. And I mean sit there, dead still. Without a single movement at all.

Too many anglers - brought up on lure fishing - are mentally incapable of leaving their left hand still. They have this compulsive pulling motion of the left hand, and do it all the time they are fishing, no matter what kind of fly they have on the end. They move every single fly with yard-long pulls. Sometimes very gentle yard-long pulls, but pulls all the same. *Don't do it.* A fish feeding on real flies is accustomed to seeing them sitting still. Lake olives do not glide in one-yard pulls; midge pupae do not glide in one-yard pulls; stunned minnows do not glide in one-yard pulls. Cast that dry fly out, *and let it sit there.* Do nothing, nothing at all, except concentrate like mad on that little speck of human ingenuity which you have placed out there. Sooner or later a fish will come along and take it.

There is one sure way of making that fish rise to your fly. Look away, just for a moment! It is as though the fish is sitting there, watching you, and as soon as you turn your head to look at an aeroplane or talk to a friend it will seize the opportunity to catch you unawares. You will look back at your fly and see nothing but a spreading ring. It is no good striking - the fish has gone! This has happened to me so often that I am almost convinced that fish *do* watch me to see when I am not paying attention to the job in hand. So concentrate, hard, and don't look away for an instant.

Wind, of course, will have an influence on our desire to leave the fly floating exactly where it is. In a breeze along the shore, a belly will form in the line and cause the fly to skate. In a head-wind, the fly will be drifted back to our feet. Only in the case of a wind directly on our backs will the fly stay where we put it - with one exception, which involves a little bit of animal cunning.

Imagine standing on the upwind shore, with the wind on your back. The flies hatching from the water in front of you are drifting with the wind, away from you. You now cast your dry fly out. If you pull line in, your fly will come towards you, against the wind. It will therefore be the only fly travelling in the wrong direction! It will be facing the right way, into wind, but it will be apparently achieving the impossible, drifting straight into the wind. Trout tend to notice these things.

The solution is simple. Cast out, allow the line to drift with the wind until it is all straight, then pay off some line from the reel. Waggle the rod tip gently from side to side to feed the loose line through the rings, and allow the fly and line to drift further away from you. Repeat as often as may be necessary. By doing this you can end up with your dry fly perhaps 50 yards away, drifting in the same direction as the naturals. But there is a penalty, hooking fish at that distance is not easy, but it is fun to try.

Having got your fly as far away as you dare, give a sharp jerk on the line to sink the fly, and work it slowly back towards you as a wet fly. This is getting the best of both worlds and is the little bit of animal cunning I mentioned, and when you catch a fish either on the dry fly or its returning wet version, it is the cause of great satisfaction!

One word of caution. When doing this trick, do not move your feet. If you have recovered all thirty yards of fly line and perhaps twenty yards of backing and dumped it all in a heap beside you, you will get the birdsnest of all time if you then tread on it. Don't move your feet at all, until all the line is back out there on the water, or is safely wound back on the reel.

Let us consider the breeze or wind along the shore. If we cast a line dead straight, lying like a ruler on the surface when it touches down, it will not be long before the fly starts to drag. Fish do not, as a general rule, like a dragging fly. Particularly if it is dragging fast enough to leave a wake. The answer is to cast, and immediately *mend* line upwind to give the wind a belly of line to work on before the fly starts to move. The result is that the fly will give a little skate when the mend is done, but will then sit still for much longer. I do not use this technique when I am aiming for a fish which has just risen, as the little twitch of the fly when I mend will often prevent the fish taking it. In this case, I cast and pray that the fish will rise to the fly before drag sets in, and it has to be a strong wind or a lazy fish for this not to work. If I am casting into an area of previous activity and prospecting with the fly, then I do mend line hoping that drag will not set in before the fish eventually finds the fly. Sod's Law says that both will happen at the same instant, but luckily not often!

Drag can occasionally be a positive advantage. I found this out one evening on a lake holding wild brown trout. They were most difficult, ignoring my offerings on a glassy surface, yet rising all round my fly sipping naturals steadily. There was one fish which rose a yard on my side of my fly, and without thinking I lifted the rod to put the fly down nearer. The fly disappeared under the surface and was gliding towards me at high speed ready to accelerate into the backwards flick of the rod when everything stopped with a bang. I had a fish on! The fly was a Light Pensioner, a fly I shall describe in more detail later, but the fish took it an inch under the surface at about five miles an hour. For the rest of that evening I had great fun casting my 'dry' fly a yard beyond the rings of a rise, and pulling the fly gently towards me. They took it skating on the surface and they took it an inch below, it did not seem to matter. They took it, that was the thing. Why, I do not know, as I could not see any naturals moving at that pace.

There are some flies, of course, which fish see skating along the surface. Sedges, when they hatch out, take off like little flying boats and an artificial sedge, dragged, will often promote a savage take. Daddy-longlegs too, can often be seen flying half-an-inch above the surface trailing their legs in the film, and trout slash at them. They often miss, but if the daddy-longlegs was walloped onto the water in the process, the fish will often circle around and take it properly and quite gently. Egg-laying midges skate along the surface, I think washing the eggs off their rear ends, and trout can be seen trying to intercept them. Not very successfully, but they try if they are hungry and there are no easier pickings to be had. Mating damselflies have the habit of flying very low over the surface, linked together, one blue and one khaki, looking for a suitable blade of weed on which to dunk the female below the surface to lay her eggs, and trout make a great show of trying to catch these. As far as I know, there is no successful pattern for an adult pair of damsels. I have often tried to dress one, but without significant success.

So there are some natural flies which do move on the surface, and they will all be betrayed to the observant angler by the slashing rise of the trout in its attempt to catch them. In the case of imitations of these, it *can* pay to drag the fly.

Fish rising with an air of calm confidence, however, are not feeding on moving insects, and thus your artificial cast to a calmly rising fish must not drag. Do everything you can to make that fly just sit there, doing nothing except waiting for the moment, the best moment in all fishing in my view, when that great nose rolls over the fly, followed by the wave of the dorsal fin and a wag of the tail, and then you strike gently and the fireworks start. . .

If you actually see the fly disappear in the rise rings, you can strike, with some confidence that your fly is in the fish's mouth. If, on the other hand, you are fishing a dragged dry fly I beg you not to strike until you see the leader, or the end of the flyline, move. It is highly likely that the fish has slashed at a big moving fly just to drown it, and will then come back to swallow it. Strike when the leader moves, not when the fish slashes at your fly. If you were wrong and he took it first time, he will probably hook himself and the leader will move anyway. If you whip the fly away after he has only drowned it, there is not a high percentage of probability that he will have it when you put it back there, he will have been frightened away by the strike and will have been put down for a while. But I never can resist putting the fly back just in case!

I used the word 'strike' a moment ago. To many reservoir anglers a strike is a multi-faceted operation. They do several things all at once. They heave line towards them with the left hand, they whip the rod back over their right shoulder and they take two running paces backwards. All very well if you are using a huge hook on the end of a 10lb leader and the fish is a 1lb stockie, but disaster if you have a size 14 dry fly and a 4lb tippet. The usual result of this typical stillwater strike it that there is a 'pinging' noise, a fish thrashes briefly on the surface and then the angler turns to his pal along the bank and says – 'See that, smashed me rotten, it did!' It didn't, he did all by himself.

A strike when a dry fly is taken before your very eyes should consist of no more than a swift but gentle lift of the rod tip. Nothing more. The fish should be pointing at the bottom, going down. The leader and line were lying straight along the surface. The fish should almost hook itself! All you have to do is to tighten gently into the fish so that it hooks itself, preferably in the scissors. Nothing to it, but if you are all eager and keyed up and suddenly your fly isn't there anymore, there is a great temptation to snatch the rod upwards. Fatal, especially with a fine tippet and a big fish. Look at a typical dry fly. Imagine how far that hook has to move to stick into a fish. A quarter of an inch perhaps? How far should you have to move the tip of the rod in order to move the hook a quarter of an inch? The answer – if the line and leader are quite straight, and there is no slack under the rod tip – is exactly a quarter of an inch! So please, no great heave backwards next time, that way you will have fewer broken tippets and more fish in the bag.

Finally, may I discuss the best places to fish a dry fly. It would be facile to say – where the fish are rising, but that's the simple answer – too simple.

If you have done your homework with the binoculars, you will see exactly where the activity is. It will be most likely where food is channelled to a waiting fish. On the upwind shore, food in the form of land-born insects will be blown onto the water. They will be most concentrated at the point where the breeze first strikes the water, where the ripple starts, not in the calm water inshore. The problem of fishing here is that your line will land on the calmest water, and might scare fish lying on the edge of the ripple before they can take the fly. Better to look for somewhere else if you can. If there is a point or promontory sticking out into the ripple, especially with an along-shore wind, this will channel floating food into a line directly downwind from the tip of the point. Stand on the point and cast downwind along the shore, and you will cover those fish which are feeding on an easy food supply. They are likely to be the bigger, more cunning fish, who have been in the water long enough to get wise and grow a bit. It will be the stock trout feeding in the calm bays, and you don't want them if you can aim for bigger fish.

To summarise my suggestions for dry fly fishing. Prepare well before casting at all. Do not move the fly. Concentrate like mad. Do not strike hard. Dry fly fishing is easy!

C·H·A·P·T·E·R

11

Wet Fly Fishing From The Bank

There are two basic kinds of wet fly fishing. The traditional method uses a team of flies while the modern reservoir angler tends to stick to one fly at a time. Let us discuss the differences between these two methods first.

Wet fly fishing goes back into the mists of time, and during the past three hundred years or so has developed in Scotland and Wales into a tried and tested method. Usually a cast is made up of a point fly, and one or two droppers. Thus the fish are given a choice of three patterns at a time, and this is probably the key to much of the success of the method. Usually, in a Scottish loch, the fish have in the past been small, perhaps the standard 'three-to-a-pound', with a one-pound fish being the pride of the season. It was not a recipe for disaster to hook two fish at once, but the cause of a little extra excitement. All this is changing fast, with the huge increases in fishing pressure in the last fifty years, the demand for stocking of trout, the advent of the rainbow trout and the urge to catch bigger fish - often straight out of a fish farm.

Today, in many places in Scotland, the traditional methods are still used and anglers happily fish for wild trout with a team of three flies. They sometimes have more, and I recall many years ago when I tried to take the choice offered to the fish to its seemingly logical conclusion and had eight flies on a cast. I gave it up pretty quickly when it dawned on me that I was spending more time in untangling bird's nests than I was in fishing! Nowadays the usual cast is of perhaps nine feet, with a fly every yard, a total of three flies.

Wet fly fishing using the traditional cast of three flies allows one very great benefit over dry fly fishing, and that is mobility. Let me explain.

Imagine a Scottish loch. By virtue of the geology, it is likely to be long and narrow, and the wild trout tend to keep fairly close to the edges, as there is no food in the deep acid water. Land-born insects form a considerable part of the diet. The shoreline will be a mixture of shingle beaches, rocky clumps, stunted trees and perhaps a background of heather-clad hillsides. Trout are not densely stocked here and, being browns, tend to be territorial. If you catch a trout, therefore, it is pointless to cast again in the same place, hence the method evolved over the generations of 'cast-and-pace'. The angler casts out, and immediately takes a pace forward along the shoreline. Then he works his flies in by lifting the rod tip, casts again and takes another pace. In this way he can cover miles of shoreline in a day, showing his team of flies to lots of trout, some of which are almost bound to be hungry enough, or unwise enough, to try to grab a meal. It is important to cast first, then take the pace. If the pace is taken first, it is likely that one will tread on any loose line hanging from the reel. With sharp shingle this is asking for trouble, you only do it once!

Equally, the flies are not usually left lying on the water for long. There is a school of thought which feels that the most successful way to induce a take is to 'show-it-to-em-and-whip-it-off', and the flies are laid out on the water, left for perhaps three seconds then accelerated into a backcast. Takes come quite frequently as soon as the flies start to move, and the fish is hooked by the backcast rather than by a conscious effort to strike. This is a fascinating method, enabling the angler to cover miles of shoreline, working his way slowly along, a pace at a time, with always the thought that a particular spot up ahead is bound to produce a whopper. Certainly it is a way of removing the mind-bending tedium of standing in one spot all day flogging away into the blue, as so many anglers seem to do. It is of great benefit to travel light when fishing in this way, and everything needed for the day should be easily transportable in pockets or a fishing bag.

The flies used for this method tend to be the old favourite classic flies, and examples which come to mind are as follows:

Butcher	Greenwells Glory	Soldier Palmer
Peter Ross	Black Pennell	Invicta
Mallard & Claret	March Brown	Blue Zulu

If I was to be restricted to just a few flies for Scottish loch fishing for wild brown trout, it would be these, with perhaps the addition of a couple, one dry fly and one lure, which I shall come to later.

Make no mistake about it, this is not an old-fashioned fuddy-duddy method. It involves delicate casting and complete concentration, and it works well. It would work just as well on a modern English stillwater if only the courage to try was there, even on rainbow trout.

One of the keys to success is not to wade. The trout are close in – in the shallows if they are in a feeding mood – and they are in a feeding mood most of the time, driven by the lack of underwater insect life into an almost permanent state of hunger. And they are well aware that much of their provender comes off the bank

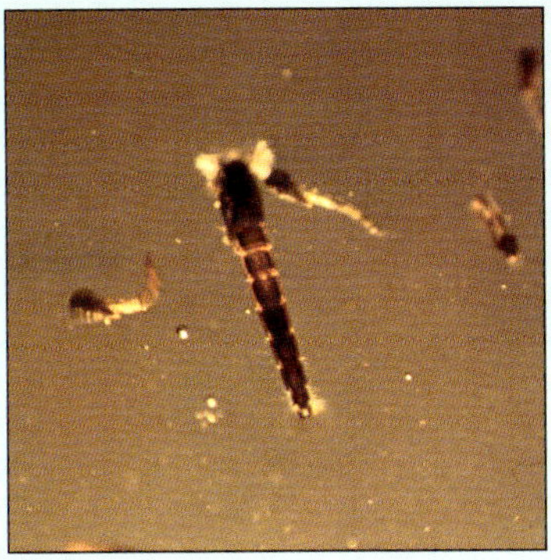

Midge Pupa

Artificial Midge Pupa

Mallard & Claret

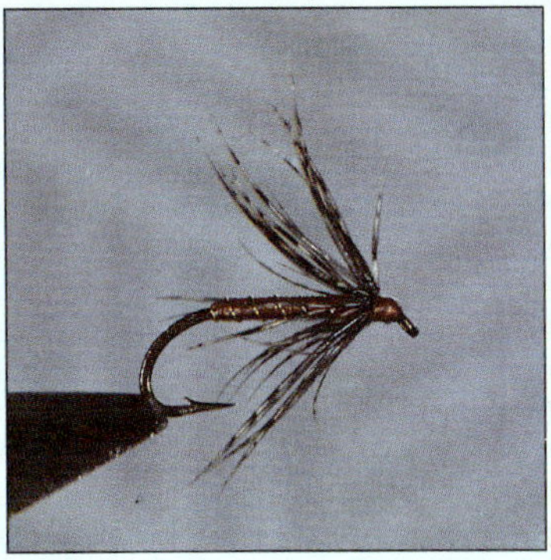

Partridge & Orange

Cove Pheasant Tail Nymph

ADULT MIDGES

Adult Midge

Artificial Adult Midge, Carnill-style

Black Pensioner

Grey Duster, without tail

NYMPHS OF UPWINGED FLIES

Olive Nymphs

Sawyer's Pheasant Tail Nymph

Artificial Olive Nymph

Olive Dun

Hare's Ear Nymph

UPWINGED FLIES

(scale in millimetres)

Light Pensioner

Spinner of an Olive

Greenwell's Glory, with tail

Blue Dun

Damsel Nymphs

Empty Damsel Skins

Artificial Damsel Nymph

Male Damsel

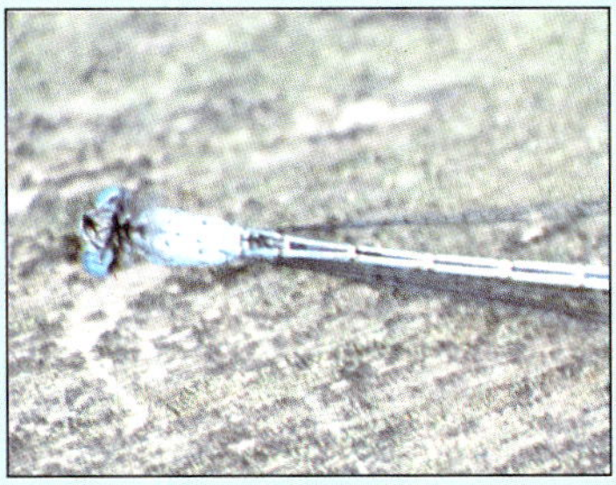

Underview of Damsel

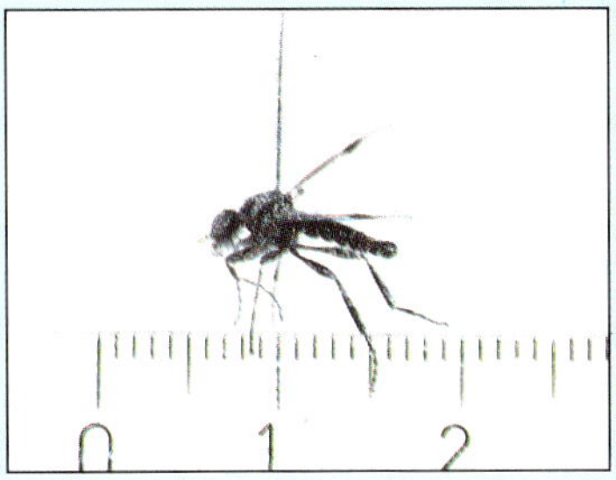

Hawthorn Fly

Artificial Hawthorn Fly

Anglers' Curse

Hare's Ear Nymph

Grey Duster, with tail

Artificial Daddy, with legs spread

Daddy Longlegs

Artificial Daddy, legs trailing

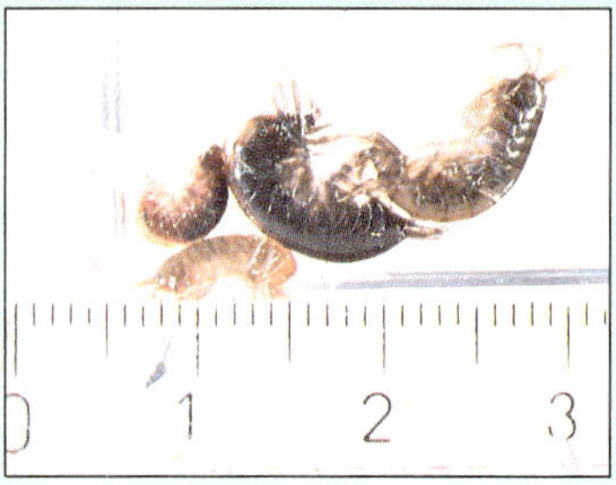

Shrimps, various sizes and colours

Pink Shrimp

Invicta

March Brown

Shredge

Waterboatman

Chomper

Black & Peacock Spider

MAYFLIES

Mayfly

Artificial Mayfly Nymph

Dry Mayfly

Light Pensioner

'addis Grub in Case

Stick Fly

Small Sedge Pupa

'addis on the bottom

Shaggy Sedge

Shredge

EDGES

Empty Skin of a Large Red Sedge Pupa

Dry Sedge

Soldier Palmer

Small Light-Coloured Sedge

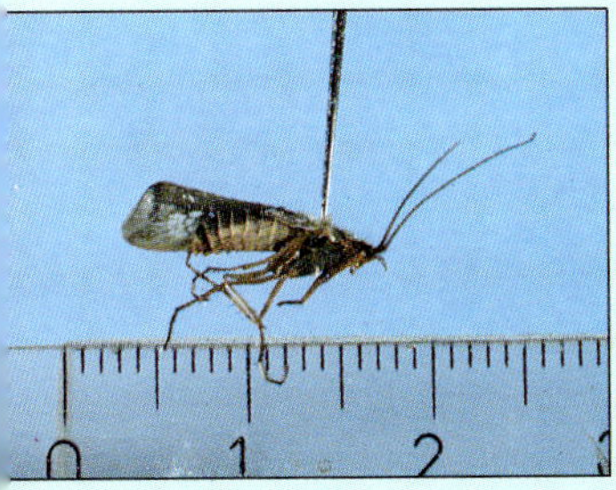

'arge Red Sedge (near wing removed to
'how body)

Muddler Minnow

Invicta

FAVOURITE FANCY FLIES

Coachman

Peter Ross

Butcher

Zulu

Blue Zulu

J P Special

Black Pennell

Cinnamon & Gold

Black Spider, Williams' Favourite

Greenwell's Glory, Wet

FAVOURITE LURES

Church Pheasant Tail Nymph, Red

Church Pheasant Tail Nymph, Lime

Dog Nobbler (Lead Headed Lure)

Yorkshire Flasher

Leprechaun

Whisky Fly, Variant

Black Lure

Bowler Hat

Abbot

White Lure

Pink Baby Doll

Orange Ear

Pink Dog Nobbler

Goldhead

Falklands Flasher

Two lovely wild brown trout. Twelve inches long with tails like shovels, these fish fight better than two pound stock rainbows, and tastê better too. Fish like these can be caught in lakes and lochs throughout Britain, if you take the trouble to search for the wilder places in which to fish.

in the form of flies blown in by the wind. Casting, therefore, should be along the shore, not straight out at right-angles, and extra attention should be paid to the ripple where the breeze first strikes the water. Other favoured spots are where streams enter the loch, carrying a delta of shingle which can support some forms of underwater life.

One of the great benefits of a multi-fly cast is its ability to dibble the top dropper on the surface. For some reason the impression of a fly struggling in the surface is attractive to trout, and takes can be quite determined. There is a secret to successful dibbling of this top dropper which is not appreciated by many anglers.

First of all, a heavy line will sag low if the tip of the rod is lifted. This drags the flies towards you too quickly for successful dibbling, and does not hold the top dropper on, or in, the surface film. The secret is to use the lightest line possible, as light as a double taper No. 4 will work far better than will either a heavier double-taper or a heavier weight-forward line. However long the rod it is almost impossible successfully to dibble the bob fly with a WF 8.

The other key to success is to use a heavy fly, or a bulky water-resistant fly, on the point of the leader. This causes more tension in the leader, allowing the bob fly to be lifted onto the surface and to stay there. As bob flies are usually bushy ones it pays to put something like a weighted lure on the point, not perhaps as heavy as some lead-headed lures, but you do want a bit of weight at the tip of the leader. Dibbling is not usually successful if the other two flies are sleek wet flies of traditional style, on small hooks. The key to success is to use three flies – a heavy one on the point, a sleek traditional on the middle dropper and a bushy bob fly on the top dropper. Then when the tip of the rod is raised, the leader comes under tension, and the bob fly will trickle attractively on the surface.

A longer rod will be found to be an advantage for this style of fishing, over 10 feet if you can manage it all day. And, of course, a light line will reduce the leverage on your wrist and make a long rod easier to sustain all day. Remember that frequent casting is used and a rod built for a light line will be much less fatiguing than a stiff, powerful reservoir rod. A loch rod is traditionally 10½ or 11 feet built for a DT 4 or 5, and this is manageable all day without your wrist killing you all evening.

If, therefore, you are a Scottish angler of this traditional school, do not despair if your job takes you south of the border. There are many reservoirs of all sizes, well stocked and your methods will work on them. Perhaps not quite as well as some of the stillwater styles evolved over the past twenty years, but well enough.

The angler born and bred on the stillwaters of the English midlands is of a different breed. He tends to fish a wet fly as a single fly on the point of his leader, for the simple reason that if he hooks two fish at once their combined weight will almost certainly result in a broken leader. One fish at a time is enough if it weighs over two pounds!

With the normal reservoir tackle of a powerful rod, a weight-forward line of AFTM 7 or heavier and a level leader of 6lb nylon, the stillwater unthinking

Bank anglers at Rutland, on the first cool breezy day after a long hot spell. There was a line of muddly water along the shore, and the fish were feeding along the outer edge of the cloudy water. The young man nearest the camera was casting a nice line, but his backcast was six feet lower than it might have been if his arm had not come out to the side. They both waded ashore to land fish and gained only two rod lengths by wading at all. And what about glasses? He would be a long time blind if he lashed a hook into an eye.

angler cannot in my view fish a wet fly properly. What he is doing is to fish a wet fly as he would a small lure, and the methods should not be the same.

Even with a single fly on the end you should start off with the lightest line possible for the conditions and it should be a floater. In English stillwaters the water is usually much less acid than elsewhere and therefore there is more underwater fly life available as fish food, and the fish will be more spread out over the acreage of the reservoir – not stuck in the shallows hoping for the bonus of a land-borne insect. Therefore the fish can be found at any depth, and anywhere. It does not matter that the water is 50 feet deep at that point, there is likely to be some form of insect or animal life available at one depth or another. (Remember the midges – they can hatch out of 100 feet of water, and the pupae have to float up through the whole of that distance to do so. Some of the big brown trout caught at Rutland by trolling at the bottom of 40 feet of water have been found to be stuffed with big midge pupae. They were not caught on wet flies, but more of that later.)

By intent, wet flies are designed to imitate food forms, even though there is much argument about the insect represented by a Butcher or a Peter Ross! So it follows that wet flies should be used for imitative fishing intended to fool the fish into thinking that it is eating an insect of some kind. Alright, some of the things which trout eat are not truly insects, but you know what I mean! Wet flies are sometimes classed as 'attractors' by those who cannot think of any insect resembling, say, a Dunkeld. I still think that trout take such flies because the fish think they are food. I think fish take many lures out of sheer curiosity, but the general reason for the taking of a wet fly is because it appears edible.

It follows, therefore, that to be really successful with a wet fly, that wet fly should be moved as if it were a food item, and the average insect underwater does not move in yard-long pulls. (Yet how many anglers have you seen, even nymphing, who have that compulsive left-hand pull?) This is where, if you must move the fly with other than a gentle lift of the rod tip, the figure-of-eight movement of the left hand is so useful. It moves the fly in four inch pulls, and not quickly. The fly underwater thus is moving in a similar way to a little insect swimming along, all the while looking fearfully over its shoulder thinking about the onrush of those huge jaws! Insects may well live a terrified life underwater, but they are not capable of huge leaps, a yard at a time! A steady twitch, twitch, twitch is a much more lifelike motion to imitate. Another way to convey this movement is to use the rod tip to impart it. A tiny twitching of the rod tip as the line is retrieved slowly will be found to give better results, and this is the habit of the traditional stream and river wet fly angler. If it is correct for the insects of a stream the same drill will work on stillwaters, they are similar insects. So forget the yard-long pulls! Leave them for the lures, which we shall come to later.

If you have done your detective work beforehand, you will know roughly what flies should stand the best chance and you will have made up your team accordingly. Remember to put the heaviest fly on the point and the bushiest on the top dropper, so that it can be dibbled on the surface if you want to. I have never found the argument really valid that one puts on the point the fly which one wants to fish deepest, and the top dropper the fly which should fish shallowest, as the difference in depth along a 9 foot leader is really negligible, unless it is left sitting there allowing the whole lot to sink at the end of a floating line. Then there is a possibility that the leader will incline down through the water with the point fly at the deepest part. But this is not usually how a team of wet flies is fished. It *can* be done this way if you have a particular reason for so doing, but it is more usual to do this with nymphs, not with wet flies. We shall cover this aspect in more detail in the chapter on nymphing.

There is one other reason for putting the sleekest fly on the point and the bushiest on the top dropper, and that is for ease of casting. If you reverse the system and put the bushiest on the tip, it may well not turn over into a wind. Then you have the classic problem of the line going out straight, and the leader blowing back to land in a heap somewhere near the end of the fly line. It could be said that this is just poor casting and it may well be, but a bushy fly on the point of a leader made up of level nylon will compound the problem. For nice smooth turnover, put the most streamlined fly on the point, every time.

Assuming you opt for the classic three-fly cast, which flies do you choose? I am a great believer in offering a choice, certainly until I know that one particular fly, or one particular colour, is favoured on that day. It is not a bad rule to follow to put, say, one bright one, one black one and one of another colour. The bright one could be a Butcher, Peter Ross or even a Mallard & Claret; the black one could be a Black Pennell or a Butcher or even a Blue Zulu; and the other fly a choice between a Greenwell, a March Brown or an Invicta. In the chapter on flies we shall discuss this choice in more detail. The bushiest flies in the short list of a couple of pages ago would be the Zulu or the Soldier Palmer, and these inevitably go on the bob fly position, or top dropper. I do not always stick to the traditional flies, of course, as I might well have a Pink Baby Doll on the point to give weight! Heresy, I can hear you say, but it works for me.

Inevitably, if you do want to dibble the top dropper, or bob it on the surface, you have to be moving the flies and sometimes quite rapidly. I know that I have just said that insects move slowly, and therefore imitations of those insects should also be moved slowly. True enough, but just to be difficult about it, I will now say that sometimes - not all the time - fish want flies which *are* moved fast. I shall return to this when I discuss boat fishing, but as a guide if wet flies do not work when moved slowly, be prepared to experiment with speed, it can sometimes trigger a fish into grabbing a fly. I do not mean that if tiny twitches do not work you should go to yard-long pulls, but I remember a friend of mine who turned to me with a grin and asked if I thought that the fish had ever heard of Victor Sylvester, as he got takes when he moved his flies in 'slow, slow, quick, quick, slow' time! So be prepared to change from tiny twitches, to four-inch pulls to foot-long pulls, done slowly or quickly. Sooner or later you will discover a speed which the fish like that day. The worst you can do is then to think that this is the speed you should use for the rest of the season, tomorrow it may be completely different! Wet flies seem to come into their own in a good wave: those days when there is a stiff breeze and a nice rolling wave along, or onto, the shore. The days when a rise is signalled by a glint of gold in a wave and a shattering of the wave pattern for an instant. Some people say they cannot see these rises but if you watch long enough you will see them. These conditions seem to be the time when bushy flies are best, and I feel that this is because in all that turmoil near the surface they are also the most easily seen by the fish. The extreme example is the Daddy-Longlegs, dressed with a bushy hackle and fished as a wet fly in a rolling wave. In calmish conditions a Daddy-Longlegs seems to work best as a floater and when you think about it, this is entirely logical. A good wave will drown the fly under the surface while in calm conditions it will remain buoyant on top. So we can deduce another rule to follow: the bigger the wave, the bigger the fly can be. In a flat calm, the flies need to be as close to the size of the natural as we can dress them. Bigger flies use bigger hooks, and bigger hooks give better hooking ability, so we should, in rough conditions, land a higher proportion of rises. I confess that I am filled with a great glee when I wake in the morning and hear a good roaring wind blowing.

Providing it is a warm wind in the summer, I know I am going to have a ball with a wet fly, or a team of wet flies, fished from the shore into the teeth of the wind, with the spray lashing into my face. I am not a masochist, believe me, I just like catching fish!

It also seems to me that in England a high proportion of the Midlands reservoirs have the dam at the Eastern end, as the river flows eastwards. A warm wind in the summer is likely to be westerly, and that means fishing off the dam. Some stillwaters have the rule that the dam may not be fished from and that is a pity, as in conditions like these the best of the fishing is likely to be just there. It is usually impossible to fish the face of the dam from a boat, as the water is too deep for the normal length of anchor rope to reach bottom and, in a good wind such as I am describing, boats might well be withdrawn as being too dangerous. The solution is to search the map of the reservoir for another downwind shore and to fish there; or try to cast along the face of the dam from an allowed spot on the bank. But while you may pick up a couple of fish doing this, it will be nowhere near as many as you might have got if you could have fished the whole of the dam wall.

In conditions of strong wind, there is sometimes a problem of line control after the cast has been made. Either the surface wind blows the floating line into a belly or the wind catches the slack line under the rod tip and bellies that. If the flies are moving too fast by being dragged by the line on the surface, you can change lines and use a neutral density fly line which goes just below the surface and does not sink far below. Most useful in conditions like these, and I would put on one of these dual-purpose lines rather than a floater right at the beginning of a windy day when I was to fish in a wave. The removal of wind effect on the slack line under the rod tip is even easier. Remove the slack altogether by sticking the tip of the rod under the surface. You are now in complete control of what the flies do, and the wind can do what it likes! But put the tip of the rod under the water immediately you have cast, not when a belly has blown under the rod tip, or you will miss the fish because you have unwanted slack to move before you can stick the hook in. A line under total control has no slack in it right from the beginning.

Mobility is really the key to success with a team of wet flies in rough conditions. Keep moving, showing your flies to fish after fish. If you stand in one spot all day, you may catch a fish or two to start with, but after a while the fish in front of you will have seen and rejected your flies, and your chances of catching are almost nil. The other possibility is that you are hoping for a shoal of rainbows to swim into your sphere of influence. Again, you might catch one from the shoal on the first or second time they pass, but they will quite quickly begin to associate your flies with the sudden disappearance of Charlie and Willie, and not be fooled. I feel it is a golden rule that the longer you stay in one spot, the slower will your catch rate become. How often have you chosen a spot, caught a fish with the second cast, another one ten minutes later and then nothing for hours? We keep thinking that fish are poor ignorant creatures, but they stay alive by learning fast. Most of them make only one mistake, and they end up in your freezer. So move. Constantly.

Become a roving angler, but have a reason for going somewhere by doing detective work.

Just occasionally, you will see a fish rising and a dry fly will not work. I have had this happen quite often on Gowthwaite reservoir where the trout are all cunning wild browns, usually in conditions of flat calm. The fish are rising, sure, but their food is being taken from just under the film. My fly perched up beautifully on its hackle points - perhaps with nylon showing up clearly on the calm surface - is totally ignored much to the detriment of my blood pressure. I can be heard talking to fish that I have just covered with a dry fly, telling them how tasty it is and urging them to 'have a go, blast you'. Nothing. In circumstances like these the single wet fly, on the end of a fine-pointed leader, will often fool even highly educated trout. A wet version of the fly seen hatching is a useful starting point. I am lazy and make it even easier. I have a chew at my dry fly, giving it a good wet with saliva. The dry fly oil tastes hellish, so I do not swallow it but spit it out, but once the dry fly is well masticated it will sink. The leader is again degreased, and I cover the rising fish with what is now a wet fly. It has worked so often that it is now one of my favourite methods, and the favourite fly for it is a Light Pensioner. A small wet Greenwell would be my first choice if I was to attach a fly which had been designed as a wet fly in the first place, in similar circumstances. If the fly is not taken as soon as it lands, it is left there for a second or two, and then given a very slow draw away. Why the fish should be feeding on immobile hatching lake olives, and take a drowned one moving away I cannot imagine, but they do, very, very often.

I can hear the purists swearing - doesn't the fellow know the difference between a dry fly and a wet fly? Of course I do. A dry fly is one which is floating at the time, and a wet fly is one which is sunk at the time. How simple-minded can you get? The pundits can rave as long as they like about the difference in stiff or soft hackles, up-eyed or down-eyed hooks and so on, but all this mumbo-jumbo can be ignored. If it will float when you want it to, it can be a dry fly: if you spit on it and it sinks, it is a wet fly. The same fly can be used for both, and that saves a lot of aggro when you are hunting through your flybox for an imitation of a particular insect.

Almost as an aside - but on the same lines of using one thing for several purposes - I did once have a man walk fifty paces to ask me if I could please lend him a pin, as the eye of the fly he wanted to tie on was bunged up with varnish. When I said I had no pin but that I used the point of the hook of any other fly, he thought for a moment and then started laughing. He went redder and redder, until I thought he might be ill, and then he said that for forty years he had carried a pin, and never would again! A silly little example of how we can all become hidebound by an idea or method, often when we are too busy fishing to think! I have been just as guilty of this syndrome, until perhaps a chance remark or a flash of inspiration has brought me up short and made me use my brains for a change.

Using a dry fly as a wet fly, as I have just mentioned is, of course, an example of using a single wet fly on a leader. This is best done with a tapered leader to achieve good presentation and turnover, and I use this system most often when I have a target fish in calm conditions. But where to aim? The rise rings are seen, but which way was the fish travelling when it made them? There is no point in putting the fly down behind the fish, is there?

I have been lucky enough to have had the opportunity to study fish behaviour in our own small lake for seven years now, and one thing which I have seen happen with unfailing regularity is that a fish will turn towards something which goes into the water with a plop. No matter that it is four feet behind the fish, if it makes a little plop the fish will whip round and look at it. I have tried to ascribe different motives to this instinctive reaction, but I think it is simply that the fish wants to see what it is and the fish sees better when the object of its attention is straight in front of it.

Many anglers talk for hours on how to detect which way a fish is going when you have only the rise-form to study, and then only for a fleeting moment or two. I do not think it really matters too much. I have also heard some anglers say they always cast to the upwind side of a rise, as that is the way the fish will be travelling. Not always so. I have seen too many fish cruising in totally random patterns to think that they follow a beaten path like a sentry outside Buckingham Palace. In my experience, they behave like a small boy on a beach looking for a lost coin – wandering along in small circles, looking hard and diverting every now and again to investigate something which catches the eye. So I do not despair when I have no clue as to which way the fish was going when it rose.

Equally I have heard the argument that you should always over-cast a rise, so that you then pull the fly back through the rings. But what about the fish which was travelling towards you – all you do is to land the line over it (unless you have a very long leader indeed) and put the fish down. I tend not to do this if I can help it.

It can be said with a fair measure of confidence that fish do sometimes travel in straight lines. Particularly if they are feeding up a wind-lane, or a line of foam which traps their current food item. But in the absence of any clue like this, I try to land my fly – if it is a dry fly or a single wet fly – bang in the middle of the rings. Such a bull's eye narrows the odds a bit, I think. The fish might not have gone far, in which case I am giving it the best chance of seeing the fly. If I guess the fish is going left and it was, in fact, going right I double the error if I cast to the left, whereas I halve the error if I land slap in the rings. If I land the fly with a tiny plop, the fish is almost certain to whip round, wherever it is and look at my fly. The fish will then either tell itself that another item of food has suddenly appeared and take it, or decide to ignore it as a suspicious fraud. If I then draw away slowly, the fish might think that it had better grab the fly or it will get away. So I have evolved my own method of fishing a wet fly to a rising fish; plop the fly in the rings as soon as possible, count three slowly and then draw very slowly away. It works often enough to keep me fat and complacent that I have discovered the key to successful wet fly fishing, but I do have the little niggle at the back of my mind that the method could be improved upon, as I have about all my fishing. And if I ever lose that little niggle, I shall stop being a thinking angler.

Sometimes you will see a fish rise in a lovely slow porpoise-like roll, with the dorsal fin going over and the tail following in a gentle curve. You can then be reasonably certain which way the fish was facing when it rose. Ignoring the strong possibility that the fish then changed direction underwater, you might find that you do want to put the fly in a position ahead of the fish so that it intercepts it. This situation also applies to wind-lane fish. The problem is, how far ahead should you aim?

The further ahead you aim, the more likely it will be that he changes direction before he gets there, and never sees it. Ten yards is too far: one foot is perhaps not enough! Somewhere in between the answer must lie, and this depends on two factors. How fast was the fish swimming when you saw it, and how deep below the surface do you think the insect was when the fish took it? Both must be allowed for, and a study of how fast your fly will sink is obviously an essential. At the beginning of the day, and every time you change a fly, try dropping it into the water at your feet - *after* you have tied it onto the leader, of course! - to see whether it sinks like a brick, or just drifts down through the water. Bushy flies have more water resistance, and sink more slowly. Sleek flies will sink more quickly. Big hooks will sink faster than will small fine-wire hooks. Make sure you know how fast your fly will sink.

There is no point in casting so far ahead that your fly will sink below the level of the fish - trout tend not to look downwards when they are feeding near the surface and your fly will not be seen at all. The best level, I have found, is right in front of the fish's nose, then when you draw the fly away, the fly will tend to rise in front of the fish in exactly the same way as nymphs and other hatching insects tend to rise.

Please do not think I am ignoring the possibility of a fly being taken on the drop. This does happen, but usually the fish has seen the fly when it was above and taken the fly as the fly passed its nose. Not at all the same thing as a fish going deeper to take a fly and this, I think I can say with some assurance, I have never seen with a wet fly. I have with something on the bottom, but in that case the fish was grubbing there anyway, and merely tilted his head downwards to take it. The secret, I am convinced, is for the fish to see your fly at the same depth as - or less than - the fish is feeding in. Only you can judge this, on the day, by using your powers of observation.

So far we have talked about casting to rising fish. It pays perhaps to bear in mind that if you saw the fish rise it was no deeper than, say, two feet. Probably only a few inches below the surface, otherwise you would not have detected the rise at all. Fishing to rising fish, therefore, is an occupation which takes place in the film, or in the first foot or so below. It follows that if you can see fish rising, you should be using a floating line. The negative buoyancy of the flies takes care of all the depth you are likely to need.

But supposing you can see no fish rising whatever? It is perhaps a day in early season, with a frigid easterly wind blowing, sleet stinging in your eyes and not a sign of activity on the surface. The answer is simple, do not use a wet fly at all: and there lies one of the keys to modern stillwater fishing, the method can be varied to take account of weather and water conditions. The traditional Scottish loch angler would be defeated by these conditions, and would go home empty-handed. The modern reservoir angler knows that fish can be caught in these, heretofore, impossible conditions and still expects his bag limit. He has paid for six fish, and is going to get them or else he is going to complain about the stocking policy!

Wet fly fishing, therefore, is normally used in conditions when you can see fish rising to sub-surface food of some kind, and usually with a floating line. You can occasionally catch fish on a wet fly if you use a sinking line to get those flies down to the depth where the fish are sheltering from the cold surface water, or where there are insects living in a temperature they favour (take your pick of reasons), but even if you do have a wet fly on the end when you are sunk-line fishing, we shall cover that method in discussing lure fishing.

How about wet fly fishing from a boat? I have found that it pays to regard a boat as a moveable casting platform, and fish a wet fly in exactly the same way as I would from the bank. The rest is boat-handling, which is a skill all to itself and I shall devote a chapter to that alone.

C·H·A·P·T·E·R

12

Nymph Fishing

We could now get into an argument about the difference between a wet fly and a nymph, but we won't. A nymph, for the purpose of this chapter, is an imitation of an underwater food form. So is a wet fly, so let's start again!

A nymph is an imitation of an underwater food form, where some attempt has been made to copy the shape of an insect which lives underwater. . .is that better?

Nymphs can include the imitations of the larvae of flies like lake olives, damsel flies, alder flies, the pupae of midges and sedges, and adults of beasties like waterboatmen and shrimps. Any artificial, in other words, which imitates in a deliberate way an insect which, at the moment, is spending its life underwater and is available as fish food.

Nymphs are relatively new to fly fishing, having been entirely developed over the last hundred years. If you look at flies from the mid-eighteen hundreds, there are no recognisable nymph forms in any of them. Pictures of old flies all show dry or wet flies, but no nymphs. Flies in the old days had to have bodies and hackles, and often wings, or bodies and wings without hackles. It had not been realised that much more accurate imitations were possible for many underwater food forms. Whoever was the man who invented the Partridge and Orange, he did a great job – he invented a wet fly which the fish think is a nymph! And my tongue is firmly in my cheek when I say that.

Starting, perhaps, with Skues and Ogden, and developed by thinking anglers like Frank Sawyer and Oliver Kite, the development of the nymph has involved many millons of hours of human brainpower. Yet I am sure that we have not yet found the key to absolute success. How often has a fly dresser slaved for hours at his or her vice to produce a fly which is so lifelike to human eyes that it seems it could walk off your hand and find a mate? Yet the fish are not deceived. At the other extreme, we have all seen the horrible concoction of fur and feather produced by a beginner; frequently drawing such sarcastic remarks as 'You must be joking, you won't catch anything on that.' Shown to trout, every one wallops it!

Examples like these have slowly but surely formed a picture in my mind, and many years of experiment have reinforced my view that a nymph, fished near the surface, is better at catching fish if it is shaggy and apparently carelessly tied. Every now and again there is a surprise when a sleek nymph is taken, but then it might be said that the ignorance of recently stocked trout makes a mockery of any rule anyway. I have found that a *general* rule is that nymphs fished near the surface should be shaggier than nymphs to be fished deep.

Let us examine, for a moment, why this might be. Imagine a nymph ascending to hatch. When it leaves the bottom and starts to swim up through the layers of water it is a sleek, slim, agile insect. As the water pressure decreases the nearer the surface it gets, it can bulk out its body inside that last skin (the skin it will shed when it gets to the surface) as gas expands inside its shuck, and it will look bigger. At the same time, legs, tails, gills and breathers will all swell as the constriction of water pressure reduces. As it swells, its legs will tend to stick out at right angles to its body as joints are no longer capable of being bent. The whole effect is that the real insect will look bulkier than it did on the bottom before starting its journey. In other words it no longer looks sleek.

When it arrives at the surface film it may pop through into the air, or it may have – as in the case of midges in a flat oily calm – a deadly struggle to penetrate the surface tension. This movement, writhing and struggling inside that last skin, takes place inside a layer of gas. Imagine a man put into a transparent diver's suit, which is then blown up with air until the suit is six inches clear of his body all round, and the man is then told to get out of that suit by unzipping it down between the shoulderblades. Well this is the sort of thing endured by an insect about to hatch. Through that outer skin can be seen the struggling insect, thrashing and writhing inside. No wonder that the fish, at eyeball to eyeball range, sees not a sleek slim insect but a fuzzy mass of movement, sparkling with trapped gases.

Then the miracle happens. The moment the outer skin is exposed to air – usually on top of the thorax, where the wing cases are – it dries and splits, and the insect can draw itself out. It can then stand on the tension of the surface film, as the blood pumps up the veins in the wings which expand to their full size, and the insect is then capable of flight. From my own observations, the wings as soon as they are of full size also dry out, and the veins shrink again. I have seen the wings of midges come out of the shuck an orangey colour, only to fade rapidly to their natural grey with black or dark grey veining. While this is going on, the insect is standing on top of or very close to the skin it has just discarded, giving an impression of a jumbled mess of legs, tails, body and wings, all seen twice – duplicated by the skin it has just climbed from.

Is it any wonder, then, that fish *seem* to prefer a shaggy mess of hare's fur wrapped on a hook, to a neat, clean, sharp, beautifully tied nymph? I do not think so. So for my own fishing, I tend to choose shaggy nymphs for fishing near the surface, and sleeker, neater ones for deep fishing. It works for me, and I am happy in my mind that by doing so I am giving myself the best chance of deceiving a stupid ignorant trout, whose brain is pea-sized compared to mine. Then, every now and again something happens to tell me that we have not yet found the total answer, and the relative size of the human brain has little to do with my ability as a nymph fisherman!

Fishing a nymph can be done at almost any depth. If you cast to a rising fish with an imitation of a nymph on your leader, you may as well be fishing a wet fly, as the same methods will apply. If, however, as most nymph fishermen do, you are prospecting, searching for a feeding fish which you have not seen, a slightly different set of rules apply. The key to success is depth.

It is important to realise that nymphs are feeding insects. From the moment they hatch from the egg, they have to feed in order to grow, and different nymphs feed in different ways, and on different foods.

Some nymphs feed on the weeds and stems of underwater plants. Those plants, because of their need for light, will be found only in relatively shallow water, say a maximum depth of ten feet. Some nymphs feed on the bottom, grubbing around for tiny particles of vegetable or animal matter. This is possible in depths up to perhaps fifteen feet. These two broad classifications cover almost everything which we can class as a nymph except for the midges; they are totally different.

Midge eggs are laid, as a general rule, over deep water. When you see swallows taking flies near the surface, away out over the middle of the reservoir, it is almost certain that those flies will be midges. Not for them the lush shallows, they prefer the depths where the bottom is composed of soft ooze. The eggs sink to the bottom and hatch out into the larvae which we call, in their tiny form, jokers (get that on a hook, mate? You must be joking!), and in their slightly larger form, bloodworms. They are that colour for a reason. They have, unlike most insects, haemoglobin in the blood, and can survive in an environment of much less free oxygen than can other insects. So the midge larva is happiest when it is burrowed into the soft mud, in the darkness many feet below the surface. There it feeds by sifting through the mud exactly as earthworms do. Then comes the time for it to pupate, to turn into the equivalent of the butterfly's chrysalis. It builds itself a little foxhole in the mud and sits there with its breathing filaments sticking out, waving in any tiny current, until it is ready to hatch into the adult midge. Then it starts its long, perilous journey to the surface far above. It could be that it needs to cover as much as fifty feet of water, occupied by fish eager for a meal, and it is indeed fortunate that midges hatch in their millions, as many of them get eaten long before they reach the perils of the swallows, swifts, house martins and wagtails.

It is said by some that a midge pupa will ascend to the surface and return to the bottom several times before finally hatching, but I think this happens only rarely. Most of nature is deadly logical, and I prefer to believe that this journey to the surface is undertaken only once, although it might well take a long time, 24 hours perhaps. During the ascent, the pupae are sometimes writhing around and sometimes just drifting motionless in a curved attitude; and while a pupa is impossible to imitate while it is moving, the typical curved shape is easily conveyed by using special curved hooks on which to dress the imitation.

The nymph fisherman can, therefore, do much to increase his chances of success by being selective in where he fishes and what nymph he chooses from his flybox. If fish are seen rising over deep water, it is almost certain that they are feeding on midges at some stage of their development from pupa to adult. It would then be folly not to put a midge pupa imitation on the leader. I am not saying that only a midge pupa will work, but you are increasing your chances by offering the trout a food form similar to that on which they are feeding.

Over shallow water, say less than ten feet deep, the insects currently on the menu can be anything from the various sedges, upwinged flies, damselflies, shrimps or waterboatmen. You take your pick depending on the rise-form you see, the insects flying round, the empty shucks you see floating on the surface, or by sheer hunch when you peer hopelessly in your flybox for inspiration!

It is occasionally possible to be completely fooled by conditions. I recall one day on Grafham seeing fish feeding on the downwind shore. There was an occasional wink in the waves, and my detective work told me that the food form was most likely to be upwinged flies, as I had seen these under the leaves of bankside bushes. My pheasant tail nymph was completely ignored. Finally I got my nose down among the waves breaking on the shore and saw midge shucks. The pupae must have been coming up to the surface in deep water a few yards off shore, and were then carried by the strong surface current into the shallows before managing to hatch. I started to rise fish as soon as I put a midge pupa on my leader, in about four or five feet of water. Apart from occasions like this, the rule applies: over deep water, use a midge unless you are certain that the menu says something else.

That something else can be almost anything if the water is shallowish. Sometimes you can be fortunate and start the day with a lucky guess, and on other days you can change from pheasant tail nymph to sedge pupa to shrimps to waterboatmen, and all the way back again before you find the key. Spooning the first fish is absolutely vital: it is highly likely that you will find that you caught the fish by sheer accident, and that its stomach contains nothing at all like the fly which caught the fish! But examination of what that fish had been eating for the last hour gives you concrete information – you can go to your flybox with a particular pattern in mind, knowing that it will give you the best chance of further fish.

There is, of course, the school of thought which says that, having caught a fish, you must already be using the right fly, and that it is folly to change now. Perhaps so, but I know that I fish with more confidence when I have a fly on the end which is as close as I can get to what the stomach contents have told me is the favoured diet of the moment.

One day somebody will invent the 'chocolate biscuit fly'. Let me explain. If you were to examine the stomach contents of a gang of small boys immediately after a school lunch, you might well find that every one had been eating egg and chips. Offer the boys another plate of egg and chips, and they may well refuse it. But if you put a chocolate biscuit in front of them they would take it! In the absence of a 'chocolate biscuit fly', I prefer to think that the trout are like those small boys, but in the middle of their school lunches. They are half-way through a plate of egg and chips, and if offered another mouthful they will swallow it without thinking. I think this is a better analogy for spooning a trout. Find a trout before he is full, and he will take another mouthful of whatever it was he was tucking into before the mouthful on which he was caught, because his appetite was locked on to a food form which was plentiful around him.

The key to successful nymphing is, of course, not only the pattern you put on your leader. It must have more to do with 'how' you fish that pattern, and the first part of that 'how' must be *depth*. Nymphing trout seldom make journeys vertically in the water. They cruise at a chosen depth, and they glug down nymphs as they come across them. That depth will be determined by the insects, not by the fish who go where the food supply is most plentiful, or most freely available with minimum effort.

Let us now consider the various insects commonly imitated under our broad nymph classification, and how best to fish them.

MIDGES

I do not think there is any doubt that in the majority of our waters midges or midge pupae form the largest part of the diet of stillwater trout. Yet for generations of anglers, the midge was largely ignored. It could be that many midges – hatching out of deep water, out in the middle – are never even seen by the bank angler. By the time the empty shucks have drifted into the shore, many of these will also have been eaten by trout, and the rest which have formed a scum on the downwind shore which will just be regarded as scum, nothing more, and will be ignored by the unobservant. These rafts of scum will be composed of millions of empty shucks, yet where are the adult midges which hatched from them? Probably many feet up in the air over the middle of the reservoir, engaged in their mating swarms, being eaten by swallows which look like tiny specks in the sky, until darkness falls and the females descend to the water to lay their eggs and die.

I think it is thus true to say that the majority of midge hatches are never observed by human eyes. I have often sat in a boat on some of our larger reservoirs, and seen midge pupae coming to the surface to hatch. They hatch only when the sun is hidden behind a cloud. Once the sun comes out, the pupae seem to sink for a few inches, only to drift quickly up again to the surface when the sun dims again. Approach a stillwater at dawn, and you will frequently find rafts of empty shucks which were not there the previous evening, showing that lots of midges hatched during the night. In the pre-dawn dark, you can hear fish rising and they will still be at it when the light greys to almost full daylight. As soon as the sun rises, and the first rays of sunlight strike the surface of the water, all activity stops as if somebody threw a switch. The adult midges which hatched a few minutes ago in the pre-dawn glow are nowhere to be seen, and the fish are no longer rising. What has happened to all those countless thousands of pupae which failed to hatch before the sun came up? Have they begun their slow sink to the bottom to await the onset of darkness once again, when they can run the gauntlet and have another try?

Although the rise appears to have stopped, the fish will certainly not have stopped feeding. The growth rate of trout in some reservoirs indicates that trout must feed all the time, continually stuffing themselves with whatever food is available. And freely available to them, in the circumstances we have just described, are millions of midge pupae, slowly sinking again to the depths! These will be followed down by the trout, so while the 'rise' has stopped the fish are still feeding avidly beneath the surface, going deeper and deeper as the light strengthens. Get the message? In bright conditions fish a midge pupa deeper than you would in dull conditions. Up to as much as twenty, thirty or even forty feet deeper!

I think it is also a reasonable rule to accept that the deeper the water the midges hatch from, the larger they might be. I have seen trout caught while lead-lining near the bottom in forty feet of water which spewed out hundreds of black midge pupae. Huge ones, over an inch long! I have never seen an adult midge that size in my life. No wonder, if they hatched out in total darkness when I was tucked up in bed, mated at an altitude of 500 feet, and returned to lay eggs and die in total darkness on the following night. The swallows always seemed so busy up there high in the sky, and now I can deduce what they might be feeding on.

I have caught many, many trout which had been feeding on empty pupal shucks. Clearly seen in an autopsy, these must have some food value if eaten in sufficient quantity, and once the rise has finished at least the shucks make easy pickings. I cannot for the life of me think that it would be worth tying a fly pattern to imitate one, but I could be wrong, as the last wild brown trout I caught had perhaps 50 percent of its stomach contents in the form of these distinctive, almost transparent, empty bits of skin. The other 50 percent was made up of an assortment of waterboatmen, complete midge pupae, a beetle or two and a leech. Yet I caught it on a Pink Baby Doll! What that tells me I am damned if I know, but I do have the little niggle at the back of my mind that, one day, I should sit down and attempt to dress an imitation of an empty pupal shuck to fish on the surface after I have missed the bulk of a midge hatch.

The other peculiarity about midges is that they can be quite localised. You can catch a fish in one bay at Rutland on a black midge pupa (for instance), and when spooned, sure enough, it has been eating black midge pupae. Go half-a-mile along the shore to the next bay, and the black midge pupa no longer works. Change to a green or claret pupa, and you can start catching fish again. On spooning these you find that they have been feeding on a different colour of midge from their friends in the previous bay. Why? I have no idea. The bottom seems the same from what I can see; the depth seems the same; the weather conditions are the same. Yet fish in this bay are feeding on nothing but green midges. I could quite easily understand different colours of midge hatching at the same time in the same place, but how can they be so localised? Beats me, but it points to the need to be ready to change flies frequently, and not to become fixated with one pattern or colour.

Let us now, in the light of what we have discussed, think about ways to fish an artificial midge pupa, or a fly which could be taken by fish as a midge pupa, which is not at all the same thing! I shall return to this particular aspect in the chapter on artificial flies.

First and foremost, let us abandon the concept of fishing pupae in the surface film. This seems to work only in a midge hatch, when rising fish can be seen and is, for all intents and purposes, to be regarded as wet fly fishing with a midge pupa. Within a foot of the surface you are not nymphing, in the accepted sense.

Nymphing with a midge pupa should be done to imitate the pupa as it ascends to hatch, or descends after failing to hatch, and falls victim to the trout which is feeding at least a foot below the surface, down to as deep as we can fish with any reliability of indication of a take. It is my humble opinion that most midge pupae are tied too lightly - they should be weighted in some way. This is not to save time while they sink to fishing depth, but to make sure they get there at all.

If we assume that midge pupa imitations are normally dressed on hooks from size 16 (if you are finicky), to perhaps size 8 (if you think you are being bold), it can be said with some confidence that they will not sink very far in normal fishing. Even if you sit there like a heron for five minutes, with a floating line lying out immobile in front of you, the fly on the point of a 12 foot leader will still be perhaps as little as 4 feet or as much as 8 feet under the surface. If you are a typical reservoir angler with a compulsive left-hand draw, it may be as little as 2 feet unless the fly is weighted, as midge pupae seldom are.

A fly with some weight in it, even if this is only six turns of fine lead wire under the thorax, is capable however, of drawing a leader down until it hangs almost vertically in the water. Thus we have taken our midge pupa down to at least 10 feet, it could be 12 feet. We now have a method of fishing a fly down as far as the length of the leader. Lengthen the leader and we could go even further down. This cannot be done if the line is other than absolutely stationary, of course, but that can be arranged. Having let the fly sink steadily to the desired depth, a slow, very slow, draw with the left hand will cause the pupa to rise in the water as if it was on its way to hatch - exactly what the fish have been seeing for the past hour or so! Takes are signalled by the sudden stopping of the line, or an impression that the tip of the line is going down through a hole in the surface. The movement is sometimes tiny, but it is there.

Immediately this is seen, the tip of the rod should be raised. It helps to have fighter pilot's reactions, but whatever you do, strike if in any doubt. The worst that can happen is that you have to cast and start all over again. If you wonder if that tiny movement was a fish, it was, and you have missed it! A fish will spit out your fly like lightning, added to which it does take an appreciable time for the take to be signalled along the leader and to be detectable on the end of the floating fly line. For this reason, I always fish with as short a leader as I think I can get away with – if I guess that the fish are feeding 6 feet down, I will fish a 9 foot leader. To fish a 15 foot leader in these circumstances is to invite more missed takes, as the slack in the leader absorbs most of the indication of a take. Equally, it is important to 'de-kink' the leader before starting. The straighter the leader material the more reliable will bite indication be, so do not be afraid to pull your leader through a

This angler at Eyebrook is standing well back from the edge, and there were fish rising well within reach as a result. One pace further back would have been even better, and then his line would not be at risk of being caught on tree roots sticking out of the bank below his feet. A thinking angler.

folded part of a wader-top – if you are wearing one – to remove any suspicion of coils in the nylon.

Just as reliable an indication of a take comes when the fly *stops sinking*. There must be a reason, and that reason will be a fish. If you have degreased the leader, it should all sink at the same rate, and you will soon get used to the rate that the nylon seems to disappear under the surface. If it seems to stop sinking for an instant, strike like lightning.

When I use the word 'strike' I do not mean a great wrenching heave, as I have said before. I mean a swift but gentle lift of the rod tip. I try to hold my rod in a loose grip, in order to make sure that my strike is gentle enough. If you clench the fist tight as you strike, you will almost certainly put too much snatch into the process. Keep telling yourself that you have to move the average trout hook about a quarter-of-an-inch in order to stick it in over the barb, and that this does not need six feet of rod movement to achieve! Although it does if you have a couple of yards of slack line lying around somewhere, so all slack should be avoided.

How can it be arranged that the floating fly line stays absolutely immobile if there is a wind blowing! Simply fish with the wind at your back, so that the line is not affected by wind-drift. Avoid casting sideways to the wind, or the line will belly on the surface, the fly will not sink as fast or as far as it should, and the belly will be a source of slack line to reduce hooking ability.

It helps your visual indication of a take to ensure that the fly line is buoyant right to the tip. Some floaters are made deliberately with the last foot designed to sink, and these should be avoided. Well greased, most good fly lines will float right to the end, where the leader joins on. If yours does not, you can tie a little piece of wool onto the butt of the leader and treat it with dry fly oil. This is then a little float which, when it bobs under, should result in a fish for the pot! Other devices are successful, like little pieces of self-adhesive foam stuck onto the leader butt, little sections of brightly-coloured fly line threaded and Superglued onto the leader – there is no end to the ingenuity you can display in order to give yourself a better visual indication of a take.

Remember what I said earlier about fish seldom looking downwards, and start shallow and go deeper and deeper as you search for fish. Do not do this by adding a yard at a time to the tippet – you will end up with too many knots in the leader. Remove the tippet and replace it with one a yard longer each time. Then you still have only one knot to worry about. Cut up the discarded nylon by rolling it around your fingers and cutting it into two-inch lengths, or take it home and burn it, better still.

By standing with your back to the wind, or sitting in an anchored boat facing downwind, you can handle leaders of a much greater length than you can cope with if there is any cross-wind or upwind casting to do. Fishing a deep midge pupa therefore is the only time I ever fish with a leader longer than about twelve feet. The weighted fly also makes it easier to cast a reasonably straight line downwind – aim high in front and let the wind take it away. When the fly plonks into the water, start to concentrate like mad on that leader slowly creeping down through the surface. If in doubt, *strike.* Once you are certain that the leader is hanging down as vertically as it will do, start a very slow draw with the left hand, and again, if in doubt, *strike.*

SEDGE PUPAE

Sedges hatch from the egg and turn into a little caterpillar-like creature, with legs only at its front end. Almost as soon as these hatch from the egg, they build themselves a house, glueing bits of sand, rotting vegetation or pieces of reed stem in the form of a tube, using a form of saliva. As they grow, they get too big for their homes and either abandon them altogether and start again, or go through a constant series of extensions to the front porch. I am not aware of any species of sedge larva which is free-roaming without a protective case in stillwaters: there are some in streams and rivers, but as far as I am aware, all stillwater sedge flies have taught their grubs to build homes for themselves. After growing to full size, the grub pupates (the equivalent of the butterfly's chrysalis). It does this by sealing off the front door with a little silken mesh, and retiring for a period of somewhere between a couple of weeks and a couple of months. In that time the caterpillar-like creature turns into a folded-up version of the adult fly, with wings all ready in the wing cases, and long legs (particularly the rearmost pair which act as oars during the pupa's trip to the surface to hatch). When the pupa is fully grown, and triggered by some combination of time, temperature, atmospheric pressure or, more likely, light level, the case is left, and the pupa starts its perilous journey to the surface. How quickly it ascends I am not sure – it may go up like an express lift, or it may drift up slowly – but of one thing I am sure, when it gets to the surface it wastes no time. The skin splits as soon as it touches the air, the insect climbs out, spreads its new wings and is off across the surface like a flying boat, all in seconds, running and flying at the same time until it is airborne. I am told that there are species of sedge which crawl up a weed stem to hatch at leisure, but I have never seen this happen and even if it does, the fish do not get much opportunity to eat these, so I have ignored them in my fishing. It is the swimming ones which are fish food.

It seems a particular habit of sedges to hatch after lunchtime. Many of them, I am sure, hatch in total darkness, but I cannot ever remember seeing a sedge hatch in the morning. They are flies of late summer afternoons, evenings and those balmy nights when it does not seem to get dark until an hour after we promised our partners we would be home!

Mating takes place almost always in the evenings or at night, and the egg-laying females then fly back and forth over the water, dipping their rear ends into the water from time to time to wash off the eggs. Big trout feed avidly on egg-laying females if they stop for a second, and that heart-stopping wallop in the darkness signals a trout with a smile on his face and — at the same time — the end of life for a sedge fly.

So how should we fish a sedge? There have been imitations, from time to time, of the sedge larva - often called a caddis grub - made by dressing a long slim body on a hook, then coating it with glue and rolling it in sand or grit. I have never found this a worthwhile exercise as I lack the patience to twitch something like that slowly enough along the bottom. Some people do it, and are successful, and perhaps the easiest dressing is given later under the title Stick Fly. It is not one of my favourites, despite many of my autopsies having shown that trout have picked up many of these creatures by grubbing along the bottom. Fish can be caught on a Stick Fly pattern at almost any time of the year, but the success of the pattern is not limited to an impending sedge hatch. Fishing a Stick Fly successfully must be done on a weed-free bottom; acid Scottish lochs or Lake District lakes are a good example of this habitat. And I am not at all certain that fish caught on stick flies did think they were caddises in their cases!

I much prefer to fish a sedge pupa imitation. Limited, of course, to months when the real sedges can be expected to hatch, and also limited to after lunch! In the early days, Doctor Bell's Amber Nymph was perhaps the first deliberate pupal imitation, but we have advanced since then. My favourite, called the Shaggy Sedge, was invented by my son Gordon after we had studied some pupae, heads together over the kitchen sink as I gutted some trout after one particularly enjoyable evening on a small lake. I am not sure how much of the success of the fly can be attributed to the curved hook on which it is dressed, and how much to the deer-hair head or green fuzzy body, but it certainly is a great fish-catcher. Fished in the same basic way as I described under the heading for midges but a bit faster, the trout wallop it. The extra speed of sink and lift is, I think, quite critical, and I have never found it necessary to fish it any deeper than perhaps six feet. Many takes will come within three or four feet of the surface.

I am not sure why many successful sedge pupa patterns have green bodies, but they have. If a green one does not work, however, be prepared with some flies tied with a gingery-coloured body - amber if you like. These seem to be the two basic colours for success, but green is my favourite.

Once the sedge has hatched which, as I said, takes only seconds, the fly is off, scuttering along the surface in a frantic race for survival. Great success can be had by dragging an oiled Muddler Minnow or bushy sedge pattern along the surface. The wake caused by knots on the leader does not seem to matter. The fish chase and wallop the fly in a heart-stopping way if they are in the mood.

There is one great drawback to sedge hatches, so far as I am concerned. The best hatches, and the most exciting fishing, always take place long after I have told my wife that I will be home. I then have the choice of telling myself that she will not worry unduly if I am two hours late, knowing that she will be imagining me in a car crash, or being a dutiful husband, being home on time but with the thought gnawing at me that I am missing the most exciting fishing of the season. This is the only occasion I can think of when it might pay to be a bachelor!

OTHER NYMPHS

Under this heading I include the nymphs of upwinged flies like the lake and pond olives, anglers' curse, claret duns; the nymphs of damselflies, shrimps and beasties like waterboatmen.

Fishing these artificials is a matter of finding the correct depth, and then moving the artificial in the same way as the real insect moves. It is highly unusual to see a waterboatman move in three-foot pulls, for instance!

Most of the other nymphs are denizens of the weedbeds. Find a weedbed and you find nymphs, shrimps and waterboatmen. When they are feeding on these insects you will also find trout there. Weedbeds are not found in very deep water, so these nymphs are the ones most used by the bank angler.

When loch fishing in Scotland, one dodge to find the correct fishing depth is to stick an oar vertically down into the water. If you cannot touch bottom it is too deep. And over the generations, Scottish anglers have happily fished with the maximum amount of confidence in about six feet of water, knowing that this is where most of the trout food lives. In clear water, you should be able to see the bottom easily if it is only six feet deep: but if you can see the bottom, the fish can see you, so it pays to stay back from the edge a bit and not to wade unless you really have to.

Perhaps for best results when nymphing, you should try to find a gap between two weedbeds. Imagine a two-foot wide channel, in which fish swim, feeling rather as visitors to New York feel when they walk along Fifth Avenue with the skyscrapers towering on either side. Insects can be found crossing from one weedbed to another, and are frequently chomped by trout who have occupied that particular sentry beat. Every now and again, a trout will dive into the weed and grab some morsel which has caught its eye, and the other nymphs in the vicinity will scurry in panic, to be chopped in their turn when they find themselves in open water without cover.

Polarized glasses help greatly when looking for such feeding trout, enabling you to see the quick glint of the silver side of a rainbow or the gold side of a brown, as they turn and slash at an insect. Other good signs are a sudden little calm patch in the ripple over a weedbed, as water wells upwards from a sudden fishy movement or even, as I have sometimes seen, a great tail waving above the surface as a big trout gets its nose down into the top of a weedbed. These tailing trout can be a problem.

Some weeds grow to quite a height, and it is not uncommon to find the weeds exposed on the surface later in the season. Trout will feed around the edges of such weedbeds, providing the water is more than a couple of feet deep, but care should be taken to fish only the sides and the edge nearest you. If you are ever tempted to fish the far edge, your leader or line will lie over the top of the weeds and get hooked up on every backcast. If you do hook a fish it is likely to dive straight into the weeds, and then you are in trouble. So fish the sides and near edge only, unless you are in a boat and can drift over the weeds and hoe with a landing net!

There are some clues to look for when first approaching the waterside and seeing a nice-looking weedbed, but no trout visibly active. If the water is calm, it is sometimes possible to see tiny dimples on the surface, rather like little raindrops.

The bull elephant. He arrived and waded straight in with great strides until he had only three inches of freeboard left on his waders. Then, while the shockwaves of his progress were still advancing in front of him, he started to cast as far as he could. There had been fish feeding a foot under the surface to ascending olive nymphs just where he eventually stood to fish, but he caught nothing in the following hour. An unthinking angler.

These are often caused by waterboatmen doing a racing turn at the surface after replenishing their bubble of air. It is unusual to see this in areas where the waterboatmen have to travel more than perhaps three feet between air and home. This, of course, can be in ten feet of water if the weedbed is seven feet tall, so it pays to analyse just what that weedbed looks like underwater if you can.

Shrimps and damselfly nymphs, alder fly larvae and the nymphs of upwinged flies will be found in any depth up to perhaps ten feet. Shrimps and alder fly larvae do not require weedbeds, but are happy on a slime-covered bottom. It is best if the slime is green but I have seen them on brown slime. If the slime is dark grey, black or rotting and giving off gas in bubbles, I have not found many of these insects. It pays, therefore, to try and analyse the kind of bottom in front of you before starting to look in your flybox for a nymph imitation.

Having said all this, we hear frequently of anglers catching fish in completely open water, miles from any weedbed, with a small pheasant tail nymph. There cannot possibly have been real nymphs around in that situation, so these were simply cases of a fish coming across something which looked like food and having a go at it. Many nymph fishermen fish in just this way, hunting for fish which they might catch by accident. I would submit that anglers would catch more fish, and get more satisfaction from doing so, if they put some thought into just where to fish what nymph in the first place!

A floating line is almost essential. It is not necessary to use a sinker to fish a weighted nymph six feet down, and the technique I have already described should be used, with one major difference. Once the fly is at the depth you judge to be correct, do not move the fly in a long slow draw as you would with a midge or sedge pupa. Short starts and stops, little twitches or even a figure of eight retrieve will convey much more lifelike movement for the insect you are using: and lifelike movement will help to overcome any defect in your fly, if it moves like a shrimp, it might be taken as a shrimp, even though it doesn't look quite like a shrimp. Better if it does both, of course, but movement is one of the keys to success.

Imitations of waterboatmen (and the Chomper is an excellent one), can be taken on the drop, and this should be watched for. Concentration combined with quick reactions to any slight difference in the behaviour of the leader and line will put many fish in the bag, and the strike indicator mentioned earlier does help in detecting takes.

Tailing trout can be a problem. They are obviously engaged in eating something, and that something is only as far below the surface as the length of the fish. There cannot be much depth of water there, in fact the water is probably only a foot deep. Shallow water means an easily frightened fish, so approach only as near as you really have to, and stay low. Try to put a shrimp imitation or a small fancy fly like a Butcher, March Brown or Invicta, as close to the fish as you can, and do it like thistledown. Heavily leaded flies will tend to frighten tailing fish far more than a slimmer, lighter fly which makes no disturbance when it lands beside the fish. Let the fly sink until it is as deep as the trout's eyeballs, and draw away very slowly. Watch the tail, and if it suddenly seems more agitated draw more quickly. The acceleration of the draw is all that is needed to stick the hook in if the fish has taken the fly, and will not alarm it if it hasn't. Tailing fish are a great challenge, often found in the shallows at the head of a reservoir or loch, and seem always to be whoppers!

Please do not think nymph fishing is easy. It demands the most intense concentration on the end of the line, and it is a certain recipe for missing a fish if you spend your time watching other anglers, aeroplanes, or just daydreaming. You are not there for a rest, you are there to catch fish, so work at it. When you realise that, to catch a bag limit on most reservoirs you have to catch only one fish in each hour, it shouldn't be difficult, should it? I hope you can see my sardonic grin when I say that!

C·H·A·P·T·E·R

13

Lure Fishing

We are breeding a race of anglers in this country who have never fished with anything but a lure. Their flyboxes are crammed with gaudy nasties – in sizes ranging from huge to indecent – and to suggest that they might try a dry fly is to mark you down as a mad decrepit from a bygone age.

Please do not think that I dislike lure fishing. When it is the method which works best, and there are days like that, I love it. I love any method which catches fish. All I am saying is that there is more satisfaction to be had by using the *best* method for the conditions prevailing: and sometimes that will be a dry fly, sometimes a wet, sometimes a nymph and sometimes a lure: but not a lure *all* the time.

I do not think that lure fishing would ever have happened without the rainbow trout. It seems a particular trait of the rainbow that it will grab anything at all if it is brightly coloured enough. I have had rainbows slash at the tuft of red wool on the end of a leader while I have been giving casting demonstrations – and I never can resist striking! Brown trout will not take lures to nearly the same extent, unless they are recently stocked and starving (with two glaring exceptions, the great browns living deep down in some reservoirs will take only a lure, and wild brown trout will belt a Pink Baby Doll sometimes with a ferocity which always amazes me, but more of these later).

The trouble with lures is that they make good magazine copy. They are bright, big and exciting, and new ones are being invented every day. People write about them, and then have their photograph taken with a double bag limit of poor stock fish with tails which look as if the fish had leprosy. I am always sad for those who grin into a camera over the evidence of their mass murder of the innocents: did they kill them all just to prove what great anglers they were? Of course, we all like to have a bonanza day every now and again, and I have done it too – once. I now find myself looking for the fish which have had time to grow into pink-fleshed, tearing acrobats, and stay well away from where the stock fish were poured in yesterday; and that is, perhaps, how we develop as anglers with a sense of maturity in our fishing.

There are days when only a lure will work. Conditions in early spring may be so cold and dour that no insect hatches, the trout are frozen stiff and so are we, and the only chance of catching anything is to belt a lure out into the blue, let it sink and pull it back in the hope that some trout will try to see if it is edible, or chomp it for its cheek in being a trespasser on the trout's territory.

Equally the weather can change suddenly in mid-season, when a cold spell will switch off all insect activity for a while, and lower the metabolism of the fish, depressing their appetites. . .Lure time.

In late spring or early summer, the daphnia blooms into a population of countless billions, and the water turns a greenish colour. Trout swim along and sieve the soup of daphnia which contains a marvellous content of proteins and carotene. They put on lots of weight, turn as fat as butter and their flesh goes pinker. Lure time again, as we cannot imitate daphnia. A bloom of algae creates just the same effect. It matters not to the angler whether the cause of the coloured water is daphnia or algae, but different flies are called for in each bloom.

In September, trout are avid feeders, building their reserves of fat for the winter, developing eggs and milt, and require hormones and vitamins in big chunks. Minnows, sticklebacks and the fry of coarse fish provide such big chunks. Lure time again, but a slightly different lure, this time designed to look like a small fish.

Let us start with the early-season, frigidly cold day. We are well wrapped up, long-combs on, as we try to deduce where the trout may be. Remember the wind and water temperature, and go where the water will be warmest. Then think what colour of lure is likely to be the most successful – the odds are that it will be black! If black is the colour, it does not really matter which black lure you use. I have never been able to detect much difference in success rate between, for instance, a Black Chenille lure, an Undertaker, a Sweeney Todd, a Viva or any other lure which is predominantly black. Go well away from the lines of other anglers standing like herons in the water – up to the tops of their waders – they will have scared fish away from them. Remember that if the wind is colder than the water you fish with your back to it, and preferably into deep water. Put on a sinking line, and whether you choose a slowish sinker, a medium sinker or a fast sinker is up to you, but I would, as a first stab, opt for a medium sinker unless I knew it was very deep in front of me. The leader should not be too long, I prefer about nine feet, and the fly is tied on the end with a careful knot, no matter how cold your hands are! Belt the line out not, to start with, as far as you can, but only half as far as you can. As soon as the line lands on the water, start counting, and start by counting ten slowly. Then draw the fly in through the water. Repeat this in a fan shape in front of you, searching for a fish: then cast again in that fan shape, counting to

Two more thinking anglers. As soon as one of them caught a fish, they put their heads together over the stomach contents. The spoon was homemade and worked well. A little water in the flask top, and the contents were stirred to separate the hundreds of midge pupae: then why the blank blank did the fish take a pink lure? One of angling's imponderables. The fish did not get itself caught entirely by unlucky fluke, but fell to a thinking angler who had searched for the colour, the depth and the speed of retrieve which the fish wanted at that moment. Now rinse that cup well!

fifteen: then again, counting to twenty. If you hook the bottom or the fly comes back with weed on it, you have counted too far. Keep searching until you have found the *depth* at which the fish are taking a fly. Only after you have searched the short arc in front of you do you try to cast as far as you can, and perhaps count slightly higher as the water can be expected, on most occasions, to be deeper further out. After you have searched the far arc thoroughly, you have a choice: if you are on a bare shoreline, with no promontories or bays, you should move to another spot and search that. If you are in such a position, on the point of a promontory, as to think that a shoal of rainbows following a contour line underwater may be channelled to you in time, by all means stay where you are, casting until the shoal arrives. This can be a bit mindless as, after a while, you realise that there are no fish there at the moment but that they might just swim to you. Then again they might not and I get itchy feet after a short while. I find it pays to get your thinking cap on again and do some more detective work on a likely hot spot. Many people are too busy fishing to stop and think.

If you can find a current blown by the wind off a point, carrying a trace of coloured water with it, it pays to fish hard along the edge of the colour. Cast well beyond this edge, into clear water, allowing the fly to sink to the desired depth, and then expect takes as the fly approaches the wall of colour: it is almost as if fish think that they had better grab the fly before it disappears into the murk. And casting across the murk like this helps to conceal your presence. I have found that, in murky conditions, the darker the lure the better – bright colours do not seem to be as visible in cloudy water.

If your chosen fly does not work, be bold in your change of pattern. If a size 8 Undertaker does not work, it is no good putting on a size 10 Undertaker. Try a size 8 white lure, or a fluorescent pink one. Keep ringing the changes until you find the colour for the day, which does vary. If you have been catching fish on a black fly and then the takes stop, change to a different colour as the bad news travels fast underwater: 'Charlie and Joe both disappeared with a scream when they ate an orange thing – we had better not eat any orange things.' They may well be fooled when a white thing appears among them!

Early season fishing can, I find, be a bit of an ordeal. Standing there with the sleet turning the side of your face into raw meat is a stark contrast to the air of eager anticipation the night before, when you watched the weather forecast with the central heating going full chat. You were so eager to get fishing again, after a long winter, that conditions did not seem to matter, until you have been flogging away for four hours and start to wonder if you are not a bit insane to be there at all. Then you get a pluck from deep in that icy water, lift the rod, and a three-pound bar of silver comes up like a Polaris missile. The adrenalin starts to flow, and you immediately feel sorry for all those people sitting in their warm houses watching football on television! They could, like you, be out enjoying themselves, even if you are a bloody fool to be there.

Just occasionally – it seems like once in a hundred years– we have a mild winter followed by an early spring, and fishing seems good right from the first day. You will find one peculiarity. Fish after a mild winter are likely to be in poorer condition than they are after a hard winter. The answer, which took me years to work out, is that in hard weather, perhaps with a layer of ice on the water, the fish slow right down and lie dormant on the bottom for long periods of time. They do not need food, so they do not hunt actively for it, and thus use up less of their reserves of fat and body tissues. In a mild winter, the fish are active, looking for food which isn't there and swiftly use up their reserves. Simple, yet when first realised, it seems so illogical, but it isn't. And fishing is better after a mild winter because the fish are hungrier: They must replace those depleted reserves, which is why the fish you will catch on opening day after a mild winter are skinnier than they would have been after weeks of ice and snow. Recently stocked fish, unless they are bred in spring water at a constant temperature, will be smaller after a hard winter, as they will not have grown as fast in the hatchery. This gives rise to much complaining by anglers, many of whom are not accustomed to having to measure a fish to see if it is above the minimum size limit for the water: too many of today's anglers feel that all fish in a water on which they have paid to fish should, by right, be of killable size.

Later in the season, white lures may well work better than black ones, and flies like the Baby Doll, White Chenille, Missionary or Jack Frost, could well be the first choice. If you get a cold snap in May try a white lure. The same tactics as in early season will apply, but it may now pay – in warmer water – to fish a bit nearer the surface. Do not, whatever you do, let this last statement prevent you hunting by depth, you should still count down as this is a basic requirement of sunk lure fishing.

Orange flies can work well on bright days in early summer, and the Whisky Fly is deservedly popular. I have found that a Whisky Fly works best when retrieved fast, but again you should experiment to find the speed for the day, as well as the depth. In an algae bloom, when the water turns greenish, you should try a Whisky Fly first, and if it fails, try a Leprechaun. If the fish do not like orange then they might prefer lime green. One or other seems to be the colour to try in an algae bloom, or when daphnia are in their population peak. Orange is a colour which seems to trigger rainbows to attack. There seems no logical reason for it, but certainly in May and June it is a favourite lure colour.

On a windy day in summer, it can sometimes pay to put a buoyant lure on a floating line and try to skip the fly from wavetop to wavetop. Fish can sometimes be seen chasing the fly, and it takes a lot of self-control not to whip the fly out of the fish's mouth but to wait for the take, which can be a great jolt as the fish takes the fly and immediately turns away. It is a mistake to use fine nylon for this game. If there is a good wave the thickness will not put them off, and 8 lb breaking strain would be a minimum for me in a good rolling wave with a big Muddler on the end.

At any time in the year you can see trout slashing into the margins. A great commotion, and then everything dies down, soon to be followed by little dimpling rises. If you were watching that spot when everything started to happen, you may have seen little fish showering out of the water, and falling back like silver raindrops. The little fish can be of almost any size from pin-headed little roach fry to four-inch long minnows. What has happened is that a trout has decided it is time for solid protein in its diet, and spied a shoal of little fish. In the trout charges, slashing from side to side with that great shovel tail, stunning the little fish. They have, at the last moment, seen the predator coming, and tried to get out of the way by jumping clear of the water. Some of the little fish are stunned by the thrashing rush of the trout, and do one of two things: they either sink to the bottom, or they float to the top. Just occasionally, one will see a little fish quivering around in an aimless circle on the surface, but most of them lie inert. The trout cruises quietly back and picks up these stunned or dead little fish. And that trout can be surprisingly easy to catch if you follow one golden rule.

Standing well back, cast an imitation of a little fish to a point on the farthest edge of where the little fish showered up into the air. Use a floating imitation if the little fish are floating, or a sinking pattern if you cannot see any little fish on the surface; *then do not move it*. That's the key – total immobility. The minute you start to pull with the left hand, you have destroyed the impression which you were trying to create, that of a stunned small fish. Stunned small fish do not swim, however slowly, they just lie there.

I once stood on the boat dock at Grafham, and there were big trout slashing into shoals of minnows among the tethered boats. One of the bailiffs, a lovely man, was trying to help an angler catch one of these, casting for him and then handing the rod over ready for the confident slow rise to the floating fly. The angler just could not resist a slow draw with his left hand, and finally the bailiff slapped his hand away, and more or less ordered him not to hold the line until he saw a fish take. Then he caught one, and it went like a train.

Standing well back and watching, we had to grin at the language used by the bailiff.

'Don't pull the line, just let it sit there.'

'I said don't pull the line.'

'Dammit, get your hand off the bloody line.'

'Stop that damn pulling, will you,' and so on, in increasing frustration. . .

He knew the key, and the angler just could not stop pulling the line and moving the fly. So wait until either you see the fly taken from the surface, or until the leader starts to draw away before you move at all, then the movement is a strike. The water is usually quite shallow where shoals of small fish are slashed into, and a floating line with a leader of a maximum of nine feet will be found to be best.

In lure fishing from the bank there are, therefore, some broad guidelines:

1) Search for depth by counting each cast down.
2) Keep changing flies until you find the colour for the day.
3) Vary the speed of retrieve until you find the speed for that fly and that depth.
4) Fishing a stunned fry imitation, *do not move it*.
5) Remember that a shooting head can be cast much further than can a dressed

line, and will allow you to search many more square yards of water in that fan shaped arc in front of you.

6) Don't find yourself too busy fishing in a mindless fashion to think about what to try next.

7) If somebody near you catches a fish on a black lure, do not despair if you have not got one exactly the same. The key is in the colour, and far more important is to ask him how deep and how fast!

Finally, one tip. When you are stripping a lure in, keep your elbow straight. If you pull by bending your elbow, you will get 'tennis elbow'. Kept straight, it will not be painful by the evening and force you to take time off work the following day! What is more, you can pull further with a straight arm than you can with a bent elbow, and fish frequently prefer their lures to be moving in long pulls of a yard at least.

C·H·A·P·T·E·R

14

Boat Fishing

So far we have considered only the bank angler. Far more anglers would choose to fish from a boat if only boats were not so expensive to hire; but the hire costs are dictated, not only by the high cost of boats when bought, but by the high cost of repairs after anglers have maltreated them! Not just by running them aground at high speed, but by wearing studded boots, chewing away at gunwales with big C-clamps and dropping anchors on the floorboards: losing oars and rowlocks, smashing propellors and shearpins in shallow water, not tying the boat up securely at the end of the day: you name it, and it happens regularly. The cost of maintaining a fleet of boats on the larger stillwaters in Britain is astronomical, and has to be shared out among those who hire them, good and bad alike.

If you can afford to hire a boat for a day, it will give you several advantages over the bank angler. Not only can you carry more tackle, and bigger flyboxes, you can reach fish which are impossible from the bank. You can move more quickly from place to place – even a rowing boat is quicker than a man trudging along the bank – and it opens up more methods of fishing. All these factors combined should put more fish in the bag at the end of the day, but how often do they?

Stand at any boat pier on a large stillwater, and watch anglers arriving for a day's fishing. You will see them screech to a halt in the car park, rush around to the boot of the car and start unloading hundredweights of gear. Anchors, drogues, sacks of chain, leeboards if they are allowed, long planks and swivel seats, all in addition to perhaps three rods each, flyboxes made out of suitcases, and a tackle box which would buckle the knees of a Mount Everest Sherpa.

After buying their tickets and loading the boat, one will look at his pal and say, 'Where do you reckon we try first?'

After scanning the blue horizon for a moment, his friend will answer 'How about the trolling area off the valve tower?'

And off they go, at peak revs on the motor, blissfully happy that they have the spray on their faces again after a long week's work. Once the flurry of their departure dies down, the trout start to rise again beside the boat pier! Something wrong somewhere, isn't there?

I do not think I have ever seen, even once, boat anglers pull up in the carpark, get out a pair of binoculars and start to do a visual reconnaissance. Yet I would submit that this is just what they should do. If you hire a boat, you have an even larger financial investment in the success of the day. Why should you do *less* homework than you would as a bank angler? The answer is that you should do even more, if you are to get proper value for money from that boat hire.

Much of the key to successful boat fishing lies in what used to be called watermanship; nowadays called boat handling, much of which is common sense. It will pay you to start by considering this aspect alone. The purpose of this

All set for a day on Rutland Water. You can see the eagerness in their step. This was their second journey to the boat, the first time they were laden down with anchors, drogues, chains and boards to sit on. But do they really need five rods for two of them? All made up, ready to have an anchor dropped on one of those black sticks, each of which cost a hundred pounds? And would a telescopic landing net not take up much less room in the boat? Think about it.

chapter is to help you to get a better return for almost a day's pay, and a sore bottom!

Firstly, let us say quite clearly, that you cannot expect the boats on any reservoir to be fully equipped to give you the very best chance of coping with all conditions, with a maximum chance of catching fish. There are things which you must provide for yourself.

The standard boat anchor seems to be about twenty feet of rope, with an old paint tin filled with cement tied on the end. This is done because it is the cheapest way of replacing all those anchors with which the fleet started out when new! In anything better than a gentle breeze, or in water deeper than ten feet, this is not enough. You should have your own anchor.

Find a pal who has access to welding equipment, and have an anchor made. Start with a length of mild steel rod, about three feet long, and form a two-inch diameter ring on one end. Bend the other end into a hook shape. Then take two more lengths, about two feet long, and form them into hooks too. Weld the shanks of the hooks together, just like a treble hook. You now have an anchor which will hold almost any boat even in a good wind. If you err at all on the measurements, then make it bigger for, within reason, the bigger the better.

Next, beg, borrow or liberate a length of chain. Good solid chain with welded links, each link a minimum of 1½ inches long. Try to get thirty feet. When you stagger away carrying it, you will realise that it weighs about half a ton, but you will come to bless it. The chain does two things. It slows the boat down on a drift when used on its own, and it will hold the anchor down so that it grips the bottom better.

A length of rope is next. I prefer polypropylene rope, as it floats and is less likely to end up around the propeller, but nylon will do if you are careful. Fifty yards is not too much. Not the thin stuff sold by an ironmonger to replace a clothes' line, but good solid rope which would tow a car. The fatter it is the easier it is to grip with wet cold hands in a bucking boat. You cannot heave hard on thin rope, but it should be thin enough to go through the links of your chain.

A drogue is regarded by many people as an essential. If you use the chain in the cunning fashion I shall describe, you will not need a drogue. If you do decide you need a drogue, get one made of rot-proof material, as it is nearly always put away wet. Get a nice big one, at least four or five feet square, and with a hole in the middle. I have seen drogues with an adjustable hole, and most of these were falling to bits, so avoid them. It is essential that the four rigging lines, attached one to each corner, should meet in a good swivel - some conditions of wave and wind can cause the drogue to go round in whirligig fashion, and the swivel is needed to prevent the whole drogue screwing itself into a ball behind the boat.

As a little insurance, the next thing you need is one of those plastic buckets with a tight-fitting lid and a wire handle in which some brands of emulsion paint are sold. If you visit the town dump, or have a word with a friendly decorator, you should be able to get this for nothing. (I have refrained from suggesting that you save one of these when next you decorate the house, as anglers' houses tend not to be decorated very often!) Lying in the boat, this bucket will seem a bit of a nuisance sometimes, but it will be very valuable in an emergency. It can be used to throw at somebody in the water, and will keep a man well afloat for hours, unless he gets so cold that he lets go! Tied hurriedly to the end of your anchor rope before you abandon it and flee, it will mark where your precious anchor, chain and rope are, and there is a chance that they can be recovered when the wind goes down. Do keep the lid on the bucket at all times, it's too late to fiddle a lid on when a friend has gone over the side and the boat is drifting away from him at a rate of knots.

These, then, are the essentials for good boatmanship. Now let us consider your own comfort.

Begin with something to sit on, to pad your bottom. An old cushion, well wrapped in a dustbin liner and sealed with freezer tape has served me well for years. If you are very rich you can buy a special boat cushion. I have seen it suggested that a boat seat can also double as a lifebuoy, and should be buoyant. I do not agree. I tie my cushion to the seat so that it cannot shift around as I shuffle on it, and it could not be detached quickly enough. Better to use the plastic bucket I mentioned above. Each corner of my cushion has some thinnish nylon string attached, so that I can lash it firmly to the thwart. (OK, landlubber, the plank you sit on!) I always lash it with the knots behind me, so that the knots and loose ends of the string cannot catch on stripped-in line when I am fishing.

Many people advocate owning a long plank – at least a foot longer than the width of the boat. They sit up on this plank, which is balanced across the gunwales, thus gaining perhaps six inches of height. I have never felt secure on one of these, and would never use one. Equally, some folk carry a specially converted typist's swivel seat, clamping it to the thwart of the boat and sitting up on it like a newly crowned king. Again, I have never used one since I found myself swinging to and fro in a good lop, feeling most insecure. I prefer my bottom firmly sat on the original boat thwart, but padded with my cushion. Then with my feet spread well apart I can move with the boat and concentrate on my fishing. That is what I am there for.

Some people advise making a huge rudder, or lee board, and attaching it to the boat with large C-clamps. They do this so that they can drift at an angle to the wind. I have never found the need for one of these devices, as an oar wedged out at an angle can achieve similar results, but without all the damage I have seen caused by C-clamps – splintered gunwales and cracked fibreglass. And I personally agree, wholeheartedly, with those boat-owners who ban such things to avoid their boats being chewed along the sides and stern. Outboard motors can also eat away at the woodwork, though there is usually a special reinforcement put there for that very purpose. Even so it pays to check the motor clamps before starting the motor – every time you start the motor!

On Rutland, and some other places, the rudder or tiller can be wedged with a block of foam rubber. This does no harm, and achieves almost as good an effect as a special rudder or lee-board.

All this kit is, of course, in addition to the normal fishing tackle, and the sheer weight and bulk of it all explains why boat anglers often take half-an-hour to load the boat before setting off. The boat allows one to take more tackle too, and this is often done, with rods sprouting all over the place.

I do believe most firmly that if I do take an extra rod into the boat with me, it should not be made up, but should be still in its solid plastic tube. Then I can drop an anchor or an oar on it and not cry my eyes out for the rest of the day. All kit should be stowed carefully, and in such a way that a slop of water over the side will not land in an open flybox, on a camera or my sandwiches! Life in a boat can be soggy enough without extra water where it can be avoided. Make sure that the rope for the anchor can pay out cleanly, by coiling it properly in the first place. It is too late when you see your flybox or thermos flask flipped over the side by a rope paying out fast in a good wind. The butt end of the anchor rope should be well tied to the ring in the bows before you set off, and the chain shackled to the anchor. All ready, in fact, for anchoring quickly if you have to. Again, it is too late when the motor dies and you are being pounded against a lee shore with rocks coming through the bottom of the boat. Unfortunately, it is too common to see people all eager to set off from the mooring who neglect this aspect of boatmanship: off they go with noses up into the slipstream, the engine roaring at full chat, and then they do not fish properly on the first drift as they are too busy getting the boat organised. Far better to do it all first, and fish the first drift diligently.

Equally, I think it is prudent to get dressed before even setting off. Too often I have seen people overbalancing backwards as they try to put on their waterproof overtrousers while the boat is leaping over the waves on the way to the first fishing spot. Not only is it dangerous, but they probably get wet right at the beginning of the day. Putting your waterproofs on then is too late, and a chill follows in a couple of hours.

The secret is proper organisation of the boat and its contents right at the start, before you ever leave the moorings. Your detective work will have told you what method you are likely to use, and therefore what line the rod should be threaded up with. The leader is attached and a guess made of the fly to start with and all tackled up, the kit is stowed where it will be behind me when I am sitting fishing.

I then run through a quick mental kit-check leading to, 'My God, I have forgotten my grub – it's still in the boot of the car!'

This mental check can avoid a ruined day. An old friend of mine once went to Loch Leven for the day, a distance of perhaps a hundred miles from his home. He and his fishing buddy were promised a special lunch for such a grand day, and a parcel wrapped in aluminium foil was tenderly placed in the lunch basket by his wife. The fishing was good, and it was well into the afternoon before the stomachs rumbled enough to demand lunch. Thinking of the roast duck which his wife had told him about, the foil parcel was tenderly unwrapped by the angler, to disclose a large ginger cake! Even when washed down with copious amounts of highland whisky, that cake had to be forced down by the third slice. . .and now my old friend stands over his wife and checks the lunchbasket with a beady eye! If he is looking forward to roast duck, he is going to get roast duck, and he leaves nothing to chance. His wife grits her teeth and then smiles understandingly when she sees him unpack everything, examine it and wrap it all up again!

Why is all my kit behind me when I am fishing? Because I swear have seen the buckles on a fishing bag actually reach out to tangle with a fly line dumped at my feet. I have seen the line go around the end of one of the slats of floorboarding on four retrieves out of five. I have seen the drips off my right index finger, as I retrieved line in long pulls, go off at 45° just so that they could land in my open flybox. In short, in a boat, if it can go wrong, it will. If two things can go wrong at once to cause a real mess, sooner or later they will. Things which go wrong in boats can, at one end of the scale, cause lost fishing time: at the other end of the scale, they can kill you.

There is one golden rule which I see being broken every day on every stillwater. People stand up in boats. They stand up to fish; they stand up to net fish; they stand up to change places in the boat. I cannot stress enough how stupidly dangerous this is. To see a boat drifting with the wind down one of the arms of Rutland Reservoir, with two men standing up, facing downwind and casting in turn, fills me and anybody who knows the slightest thing about seamanship with horror at the risk they are taking. One lurch, and they have overbalanced and gone over the side, perhaps even banging their head on the side of the boat as they go, perhaps by trying to avoid breaking a favourite or very expensive rod. By the time they hit the water they are unconscious, and they never surface, or they surface perhaps twelve hours later, with their faces the colour of putty, all ready for the mortuary slab.

Even in a boat moored at the dock, get in and sit down. Then stay sitting down until you get out of the boat. If you want to change places with your fishing companion, reel in, hook the fly onto the rod, wind all slack line in, lay the rods down tucked well along the sides and, when you are both ready, move one at a time, staying low and holding on as you do so.

Please believe me when I say that accidents do not happen only in a good wave which rocks the boat. Your companion can suddenly try to cast a little further to reach a fish he has seen, and this is enough to make you lose your balance for a second. Even in flat calm, *do not stand up in boats, ever.*

When you are sitting down in a boat, fish will often rise right beside you: when you are standing up, you have to cast at least twenty-five yards to reach unfrightened fish. So, not only will you live longer, you will catch more fish close to the boat, and will end up much less tired from over-long casting.

One other little word of advice from an old hand – and forgive me if I preach,

The most dangerous practice of all. Standing up in boats can kill you. Even in a gentle breeze, it only needs a slightly more powerful cast by your companion to make you lose your balance, and over you go. These anglers were having to cast a long way to reach fish which had not seen them: if they had been sitting down, the fish would have been rising under their rod tips.

but if half-way through a drift you think to yourself that a change of fly would be a good idea, do it right then. Do not fish the drift out first. Not only might you forget, but you have wasted fishing time with a better choice of fly. Sitting in a boat drifting gently with the breeze can be a soporific pastime, and you will find yourself too busy fishing to think. If you do think of something which might improve your chances of a fish, do it straight away. Even something as apparently complicated as changing lines - do it. If you feel conditions are too cramped to thread the rod, take the rod apart, thread the butt section and then the tip section,

This is the safe way to fish, sitting down. Except that the stern man should have been casting over his left shoulder. Perhaps that is why his companion ducked every time that great heaving cast was made!

then join the rod together again; all while sitting firmly on your bottom! Then check the line is not twisted around the rod at the ferrule or spigot.

What should you do in a boat, which you do not do on the bank? It is, of course, easy to regard a boat as a mobile casting platform, taking you to a chosen spot where you drop the anchor and fish just as you would from the shore. Let us consider this for a moment.

Suppose we see a patch of rising fish. The patch is stationary and we think it would be a good idea to have a go at those fish. Do not motor up to them at full speed, cut the motor, chuck the anchor out with a splash, then pray the anchor rope is all run out before you are on top of them. This is exactly what a surprising number of people do. Make a wide circle at a slow speed – until you are a hundred yards upwind of those fish – then cut the motor, and start to drift silently down to them. Fifty yards to go, slip the anchor silently over the side, making sure that the links of the chain do not rattle on the gunwale. Feed the chain out hand-over-hand until the rope is reached, then let the rope run quietly over the gunwale. When you are within casting distance of the nearest fish, stop the rope paying out and tie it to one of the thwarts near the bows. Make sure that the boat is at a slight angle to the wind, or it will yaw from side to side. Once the boat settles and you and your companion agree that the position is right, quietly pick up your rods and start fishing. Nothing to it, and the fish can be within ten yards even on a calm day with no wave to hide you. Having done what you can to make a silent approach, keep silent. Do not shuffle your feet, particularly if you have studs on your boots (you shouldn't have studs in a boat in the first place!) If you change your fly, do not drop your scissors or fly box on the floor.

I once had a most frustrating day in a boat with an otherwise charming companion who, every time he changed his fly, chucked his big wooden flybox at least a foot, to land with a crash which must have echoed yards underwater. He could not cast far enough to reach unfrightened fish, and I could only just do it, so I caught a few fish and he didn't catch any. By lunchtime my patience was wearing thin and I asked him, quite politely, if he would please put his flybox

Safety in boats

It is essential that the flies never come back over the boat. In this drawing, the stern man must be capable of casting over his left *shoulder. The bow man should roll cast into the area to his right where a backcast could be blown by the wind into the sternman's neck! Note that there is no overlap area, this saves argument even between friends. The only time one man will cast into the other's area is when he is invited to do so because the owner is changing flies, or is otherwise unable to cover a fish which has risen.*

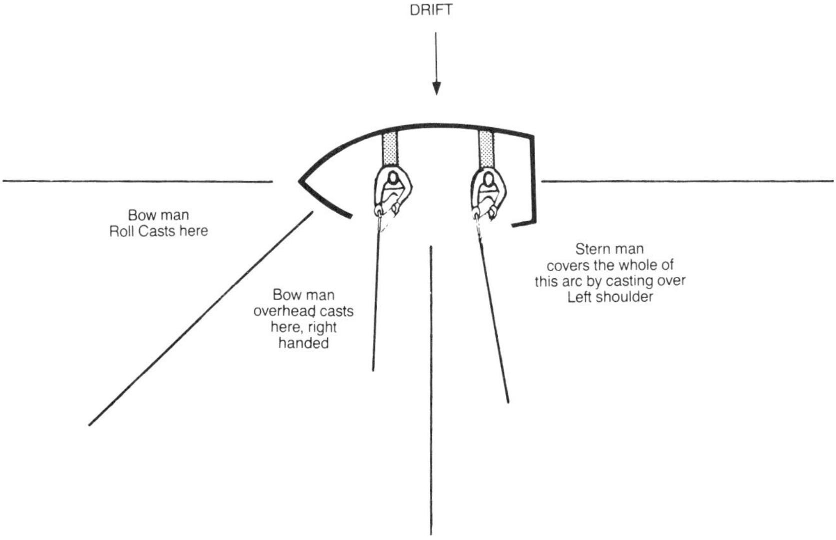

In a good wind, this is the safest way to fish. Not only is there least wind-resistance with the bows being upwind, and thus least chance of the anchor dragging, but both men can cast right-handed with safety. There is no overlap area, and neither man poaches in the other's arc unless he is asked to do so.

This arrangements can also be used when drifting with a towed chain or drogue, and each man can cast sideways and have his flies come around in the curve which is so often attractive to fish.

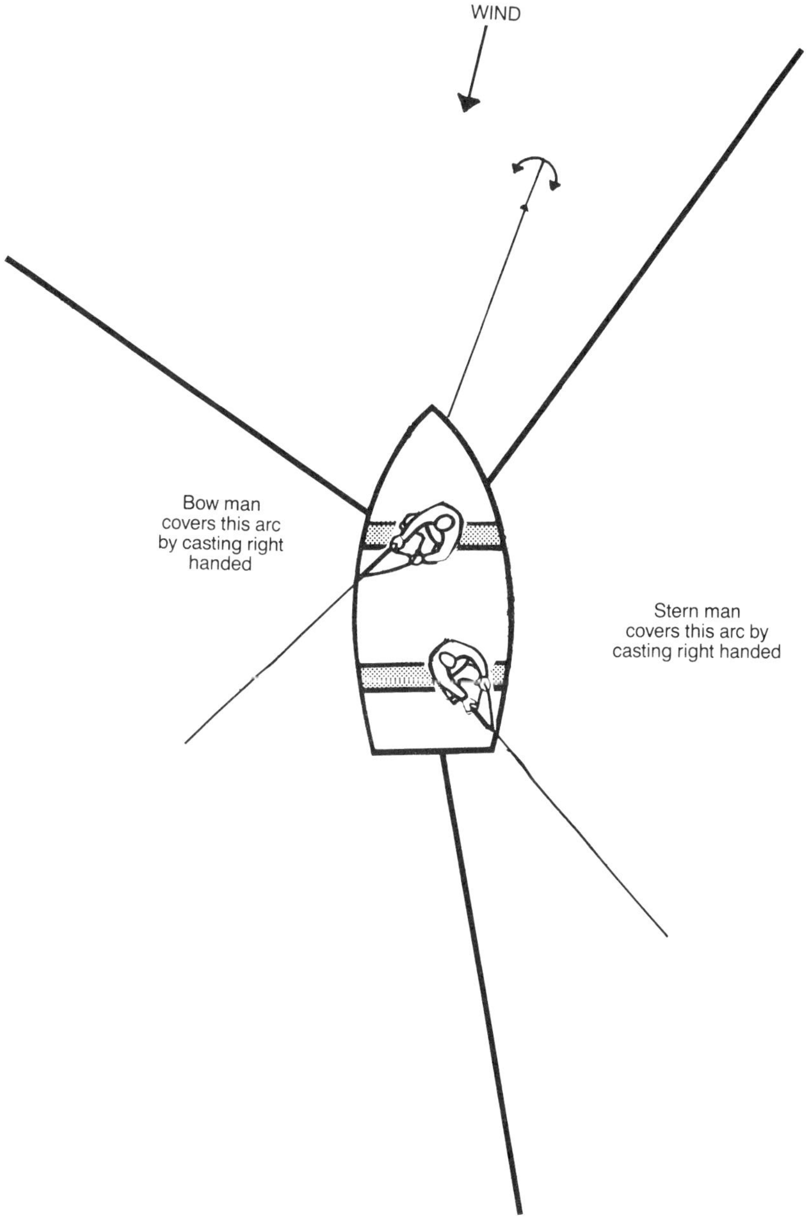

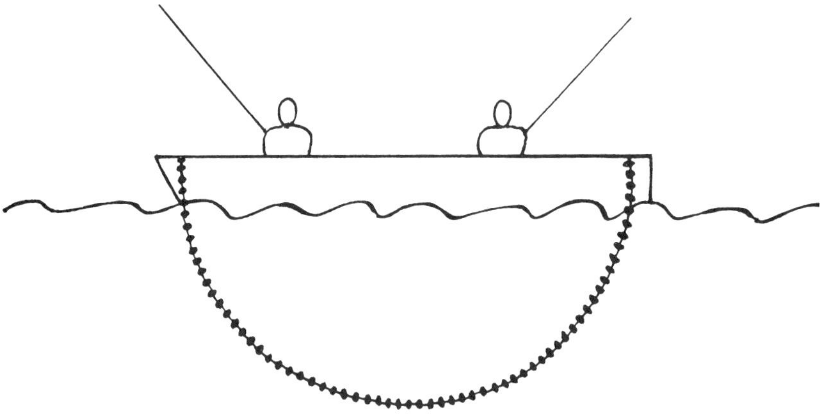

Loop of chain acting as drogue — deep water.
(Stern man casting over right shoulder
— Bow man casting over left shoulder

Loops of chain acting as drogue — shallow water.

Instead of dragging a length of chain by one end along the bottom, the chain can be used as a drogue. The more chain in the water the greater the braking effect, but it is vital that it should not be allowed to foul the bottom. In shallow water therefore it is much safer to tie the chain in loops, using quick slip-knots.

In an emergency, the motor can be started and the boat driven, if the chain is in multiple loops. It is a highly dangerous practise to use the motor with the chain hanging in a large single loop - if the chain fouls on an underwater obstruction the boat will tip over or lurch severely enough to throw the anglers out.

down quietly. He was most offended and told me that I was being too fussy. However, he obliged, and in the afternoon we caught fish steadily, all within ten yards of the boat. About a year later we had another day together, and all his movements in the boat were of exaggerated silence! And we caught fish again.

From an anchored boat it is possible to fish a dry fly, a wet fly or a team of wet flies, a nymph or a lure. Having said that, there is a great temptation to stay in one spot too long. It has taken a bit of effort to get there and the easiest thing to do is to just stay there, in circumstances which would cause the bank angler to move. By all means cover a patch of rising fish thoroughly, but if you catch them all (!) or they stop rising, then move. The rule that you will catch most if you show your fly to most fish applies just as much to boat fishing as it does to the man on the bank.

A very slow drift is often the way to achieve this, and here the chain comes into its own. It is possible, of course, to drop the anchor and keep a foot on the rope. Lift the foot to let a yard of rope pay out, then press your foot on the rope again. This works in gentle breezes but is hard work in a gale. Lowering the chain until some of it drags on the bottom is a handy dodge. Increase the length of chain on the bottom until the boat is moving at the speed you want, then tie it off. If the water shallows you will slow down, as more of the chain lies on the bottom: if the depth increases you will speed up. I confess that this is my favourite method of boat control, and I use the anchor less and less as the years go by. It must be there at all times for emergencies, of course, but the chain is nice and simple to control. Just adjust the length over the side to have almost absolute control over the speed of the boat. Come to think of it, I haven't used the drogue at all for the last couple of seasons.

The chain can be used as a drogue, after a fashion. If the chain is tethered to the boat at bow and stern and allowed to hang in a loop underwater, it exerts great drag, and will slow the boat considerably, providing the wind is not too strong. In a really good wind, where the drogue alone is not enough, the chain loop can be used in addition. Care should be taken over a rocky bottom, that the chain does not snag solidly underwater. It is a basic suggestion that when the chain loop method is in use, the chain should not touch bottom at all. It seldom snags on the bottom when being pulled straight, but I have found the occasional heart-stopping moment when it is dragging broadside. Not, luckily, heartstopping because of the danger, but at the thought of being jammed immoveably on the bottom and having to abandon all that money!

One more word about safety. When you are sitting down, the flies come lower in the backcast and forward cast, sometimes dangerously so. The golden rule that the *flies never come over the boat* must apply. The man at the right-hand end of the boat must lean his rod to the right so that the flies come back to the right. The man at the left-hand end of the boat must either be a left-hander, or must take his rod hand to his left ear so that the flies go to the left; never over the boat, ever. I have seen a Highland ghillie go through some exaggerated gestures of putting on a pair of safety spectacles and pull his hood up after he had been hooked in the hat twice, and he did not think it was funny. When the flies then stuck in his hood, he suggested that he might go ashore so that he could collect his motorbike crash helmet, as flies would bounce off this! Eventually the anglers swopped ends of the boat, so that the better angler became the left-hand man, and then he cast over his left shoulder. The ghillie visibly brightened up at the removal of the threat to his health, and was able to concentrate on controlling the boat for best fish-catching.

Firstly let us consider using the boat as a mobile casting platform. We use it to get to our chosen spot, then we anchor and fish in the method we choose. There is almost no difference between boat and bank when fishing a dry fly, a nymph or a team of (or single) wet flies. If you are a successful angler with any of these methods, you can get into a boat and be just as successful. With lure fishing, there is one basic difference, and that is the consideration of depth.

In water any deeper than perhaps 20 feet, when using a sinking line, it must be realised that the effect of that line sinking under the rod tip is the same as if you were bank fishing off a cliff. No sooner do you cast and the line starts to sink, than the fly starts to drag towards you while the belly forms under the rod tip. By the time the line has settled on the bottom in 20 feet of water, the fly is at least seven yards nearer you than it was when it hit the water. So you must be prepared to cast as far as you can when deep lure fishing from a boat. If you are fishing your fly at a depth of only a few feet then it makes no difference, behave as you would on the bank.

The same rule applies if you are fishing a nymph very deep on a floating line as, by the time the leader has all sunk, the fly will be almost vertically under the tip of the floating line, and your distance will have shortened by the length of the leader.

In boat fishing you can expect to see a fish rise anywhere. If it is in range, remember the trick of pointing the rod in the direction you want the fly to go, and then do a straight backwards and forwards cast. Changing direction is thus made easy, and it is important to get that fly there quickly, before the fish moves on.

With wet flies I am constantly amazed at how fast the flies can be moving and still be grabbed by fish. Frequently, when you decide it is time to cast again and have started the backwards movement of the rod, there will be a great thump and a fish is on. This decided me to experiment in pulling a team of standard wet flies very fast through the water as soon as they landed, and it worked! Fish can sometimes be seen chasing the flies, a huge set of jaws pointing at you with a bow wave on either side. The great temptation is to slow down the retrieve to allow the fish to catch up – don't. Just occasionally a sudden stop altogether will make the fish grab the fly it was chasing, but just slowing down seems to make the fish sheer away without taking the fly at all. Better to speed it all up even faster, to encourage the fish to chase harder. Fish seem, then, to lose some of their caution. The very worst thing to do is to strike when you see those jaws facing you, you will pull the fly right out of its mouth. If you see a fish chasing the fly, keep everything going at the same speed to be safe. The fish found it attractive enough to chase, so why alter anything at all? It takes willpower not to change something, I can tell you.

Drift fishing can be an art in itself. Not the fishing part but the boat-handling part, and it can make the difference between success and failure. Drift too fast and you cover too few fish, drift too slowly and you waste time. It is almost impossible, in this country, to drift too slowly unless it is one of those rare, flat-calm days. The main problem is how to slow the drift down to a speed effective for fishing.

The fastest drift will be with the boat broadside to the wind, with the biggest sail area. Stand up, and the sail area is increased, the boat goes faster and you risk falling in, so stay sitting down. . .

The second to slowest drift is with the bows leading, and the drogue or chain attached at the stern. This exposes the flat stern, the outboard motor and the occupants to the wind. There is a danger that the flat stern will cause waves to break with a great slop against the flat transom, and you will get much wetter as a result.

The slowest drift is with the bows into the wind, and the drogue or chain tethered in the bows. This gives the most streamlined aspect to the wind. You stay the driest of all, and this is the position I favour most. If you look at the diagram you will see how both anglers can cast right-handed and still be safe. They cover arcs on either side of the boat effectively, and this is an excellent way of surface fishing. It can also be used for fishing deeper, as I will explain.

Imagine casting a sinking shooting head out as far to the side as is safe, bearing in mind the wind speed on the back of your neck. Let the line sink, and when it appears that all the line is behind the boat, start a retrieve. What you have achieved is an undragged sink of the line for as long as possible, far longer than if you had to start pulling in to avoid the boat running over the line, as it would if you had cast straight ahead of the boat. You can expect the majority of takes to occur as the fly whips around the corner at the start of the retrieve. This is a simplified version of the mumbo-jumbo nowadays referred to as the Northampton Style, as if it was invented there. I was using this technique with a schoolfriend back in 1947, but the line we used was a braided hemp line intended for handlining mackerel, and we were after the big brown trout we were convinced lived deep in Scottish lochs! We didn't catch many, as we were using standard wet flies and three-yard casts. An example, perhaps, of getting something right, but not enough to make the experiment a success.

One word of caution. If you let the line sink like this, and only retrieve when the line appears to be coming from behind the boat, you could be said to be trolling, and in some places trolling is banned. So be careful about the rules. This method can also be used for wet flies, as it is an easy way to give the retrieve the curved path which fish seem to find attractive.

To achieve either a much deeper sink or else to retrieve only when the boat has drifted further away and there is thus less risk of showing flies only to frightened fish, you can pay out loose line as soon as you have cast out. Then when everything tightens up, you have put more line between you and the flies. A useful dodge this, as with a fastish drift it is sometimes just not possible to sink the flies deeply enough before the line tightens up and the flies lift on the pull of the boat.

Trolling is simply towing the flies behind the boat. That is a very simple statement of what can, with a little thought, be a most effective way of fishing from a boat. Start, for instance, by casting out at right-angles to the line of drift. Pay line out so the flies are sinking while the boat moves away. Once you reckon you have enough line out, clamp your finger over the line and just sit there. The flies will move at the speed of the boat, once the curve has straightened out behind. Up to a point the kind of sinking line you have on will determine the depth of a troll. The amount of line out will also determine the depth once again up to a point.

If you suddenly decide you want to fish deeper, strip line off the reel and dump it over the side. The line then sinks until everything tightens up again. It is important that you do not just sit there for hour after hour towing a fly behind in the hope that something will grab it. If you are not getting, say, one take every half-an-hour, you are doing something wrong, so keep experimenting with depth, colour of fly and speed, until you hit the effective combination for that day. You can troll by drifting, or by rowing, and I have seen people motoring a troll. While you should abide strictly by the rules, I have never found an outboard which would not oil its plugs when being used at a tickover for long periods, and I do not use the motor to troll. On the one occasion when I did, we needed the engine quickly to get us off a lee shore, and when the throttle was opened suddenly, the motor died on us. There followed some frantic unshipping of oars and hard rowing, before we got out of trouble we should have avoided in the first place!

It makes sense to use all the fishing time at your disposal and, when rowing back into the wind to start another drift, it pays to take it in turns to row and to fish, casting across the wind and letting the fly or flies swing round. Apart from a refuelling of coffee or a sandwich, I cannot just sit there letting my companion row us back to the top of the next drift. I have to fish while he works away at the oars: next time back, it will be my turn to slave for him!

This is an alternative method of using both rods to troll with, while going back to start another drift. Perhaps, if you are good friends, it pays to use both rods in a simple towing action. Do make sure that the reels are hooked over a seat to avoid the rod leaping out of the stern if a fish bangs the fly. I have seen this happen once, and you might as well burn pound notes! The drill is that both lines are fishing out of the back of the boat. When a fish attaches itself to one of the rods, and usually no striking is needed, the oarsman ships the oars, grabs the unlucky rod and winds the tackle in as fast as he can to avoid tangling with the fish being played, then gets the net ready. The non-rowing man has nothing to do except to play the fish. It sounds easy, but it does require teamwork. Sod's Law says that fish will only be hooked at a spot where the boat will run aground if rowing is stopped for more than a second or two, and if this happens it is probably a sign that your drift was perhaps too far from shore. It may be a day for fishing where the waves are breaking on a downwind shore, or where the insects are being churned up by the undertow. And that might just be a day when you should have been bank-fishing in the first place and saved the cost of the boat!

One last method of boat fishing, which I should like to mention, is used to great effect in Ireland for brown trout, and in Scotland for seatrout and occasional salmon. I refer to dapping. There is no reason why this should not be effective in reservoirs for rainbows and browns. The aim is to allow a fly to dibble on the surface of the water, held away from the boat by the wind. It is not as easy as it seems, but the essentials can be grasped in ten minutes of practice.

To start with, a long rod helps. Scottish dapping rods are normally seventeen or eighteen feet long. If you have a fifteen foot salmon fly rod, or a fourteen foot match rod, you can use this reasonably well for dapping. Then you need at least 25 metres of nylon attached to the end of your fly line on the reel. The idea is that you should have only monofil running up through the rings of the rod, so that when you lift the rod to a near-vertical position, you do not have heavy fly line sliding down through the rings to the butt; and when you are playing a fish, it is a bad idea to have knots clunking their way up through the rings, when line has to be yielded as a fish runs. Then you need a few feet of special floss, which has to be knotted every foot or so, or go to a sewing shop and get a few yards of ¼ in. wide ribbon, the sort which is threaded through the decorative edges of baby clothes, so that you can tell if it is a boy or a girl. Get the boy's one, pale blue. If the wind is strong, you will need perhaps four feet of ribbon: if the breeze is gentle, then ten feet would make a useful starting point. Then, last of all, add a leader of 6 lb nylon to the end of the ribbon. The leader should be only three feet long. On the end of this short leader attach a bushy fly of some kind. Proper dapping flies are really bushy, perhaps as many as ten hackles wound on a lightweight hook, but then why a seatrout takes them is anybody's guess. For rainbows and browns, a daddy-longlegs tied with two hackles and well oiled will do just as well.

Drift the boat broadside on the wind, sit well balanced with your feet wedged, lift the rod and let the fly sail out in front of you. Then lower the tip of the rod until the fly is just skipping on the surface. As the boat rolls, you will find yourself gently rocking in time with the swell , lifting and lowering the rod so that the fly sits still on the surface, or skips only a couple of inches off the water each time. It is reminiscent of a stabilised gun turret on a tank moving over rough ground.

Takes can be a determined wallop accompanied by a great wrench. These are by far the best, as you do nothing except play the fish. Unfortunately they are also the rarest form of rise. Far more common is to see a great head come slowly out of the water, rising vertically with an open mouth. The mouth slowly closes and the head sinks slowly out of sight. Most people strike long before the mouth is shut.

The rule for striking while dapping is not to! It will require a certain amount of self-control, but you should do nothing except feel for the fish long after the fly has gone. Allow time for the fish to turn his body length, so that it points downwards, then when you do tighten vertically upwards you should, I repeat, you should, pull the hook into the scissors and hook the fish well.

You will often get a fish slashing at the fly and missing. By not striking you will give the fish the chance to turn around, and take quietly the drowned fly. This seems a common habit, particularly at daddy-longlegs time.

While all my own dapping has been done with the artificial fly, it is possible to dap with real flies, lightly hooked on a fine-wire hook. In Ireland they use mayflies sometimes – two or three on a hook – or a single grasshopper. I visualise great amounts of time spent catching daddy-longlegs in sufficient quantity for a decent fishing spell (even during bob-a-job week, when small boys can do the work) so I prefer to stick to an artificial fly. Well oiled and cunningly dapped, this works well enough for me. My artificial daddies are dressed either with the legs spread out for dapping or dry fly fishing, or with the legs all trailing backwards for wet fly fishing.

For most of the season boat fishing allows you to do one thing which is impossible from the bank, to fish for the bigger trout which are reputed to live deep in some of the larger reservoirs. Certainly at Rutland the big brown trout seem to spend most of their time deeper than ten feet below the surface. Many are, of course, caught by bank anglers when they come inshore to feed, but this tends to be a lucky accident. If you have your heart set on catching a big brown, you have to go boating to do it.

Having got into the boat, remember the depth at which you want to fish. Search for depth and concentrate on this aspect. Start with a slow sinker and after trolling with that for a while, go to a faster sinking line, and then eventually to a lead-core line. But get that fly down deep. What fly? There is an old saying that the bigger the fish the bigger the bait, and this applies to the sort of specimen hunting you are now engaged in. Brown trout of over five pounds do not get fat by eating tiny scraps of food: well they can, but it takes longer. They prefer their food in big chunks, like the fry of coarse fish, big minnows and other juicy mouthfuls. So your fly should be huge, perhaps a couple of longshank 8s in tandem with a big marabou wing and a muddler head; and the favourite colour is white, perhaps with a touch of silver glinting in it; or jet black, which seems to work better sometimes, in really deep water; or a brightly coloured fly; perhaps with some fluorescent material in the dressing, for when the sun goes down a bit, and it gets dark in the deeps while it is still quite light on the surface. (Something to do with the angle of the sun causing reflection of the light from the surface, instead of light going down through the surface as it would if the angle was steeper.)

Some of the big brown trout caught at Rutland have been caught on a huge fly, trolled very deep, perhaps as much as forty feet. And when they have been banged on the head, they have spewed out thousands of big black midge pupae, so presumably they could also have been caught on a big black midge pupa, if it had been possible to fish one of those reliably at a depth of forty feet! This is food for thought, and the man who perfects nymphing at that depth will become famous. (I do not mean just towing a big nymph on a lead-core shooting head, which is not nymphing as I mean it.) Those midge pupae have been up to an inch long. Such a midge not often seen by the angler, as midges spend their adult lives high in the air, and return to the middle of the reservoir at dusk and in darkness to lay their eggs. Ask a modern jet pilot what size of flies his plane smacks at 500 feet, and he will tell you that they are big ones. Not the usual ¼ in. midge which hatches in the day time and is seen around the margins, but midges of over ½ in. and up to 1 in.

long. It is a good job that they don't bite, or they would be a bigger problem than clegs and horseflies!

So the key to big fish for most of the year (and at least part of most days) is depth. If you can get down to them you can catch them, and so the specimen hunter uses lines which sink fast, and searches the deeps.

However, for part of the year at least – usually the latter half of the season – even the biggest fish come within the range of a boat angler who is fishing quite shallow, or of the bank angler. It pays, therefore, to treat every fish as a potential whopper until you are sure of its size. Which brings us to the subject of striking.

Too many people strike with a huge heave of the rod, accompanied by a sharp pull with the left hand. They do this because they have to heave so much slack line before they can stick the hook in. Look at any trout-sized hook. From the point to the bend is a maximum of a quarter of an inch, often less. That, in theory is the distance you have to drive the hook in order to get a firm hookhold! So why wrench the rod tip back by eight feet? The key is always to fish without slack line between the rod tip and the fly. Then a movement of the rod tip is translated into a movement at the hook. It is all very well for people to talk about lines stretching, but they don't stretch that much, not even the monofil behind a shooting head. Fish following a fly take it and turn away, the line keeps going one way and the fish the other. The fish should hook himself. All you do with that great heave is to snap off. It is my belief that there is no such thing as a 'smash take'. If the tackle is balanced (using the rule of numbers), fish should not break you when you strike reasonably.

Equally, you see anglers playing fish by holding the rod back over their shoulders, and hand-lining in with clenched fists and white knuckles. This is called, in the more flamboyant fishing magazines, 'horsing fish in'. Don't do it, you are not fishing for horses. Play fish from a boat just as carefully as you would from the bank, with the rod tip at no time bent at more than a right angle to the butt. Get the net well sunk and, when the fish is ready, draw the fish gently over the net and lift the net smartly. It is courtesy for the boat's other partner to get his line and flies out of the water as soon as a fish is hooked, and this avoids tangles. These tangles result in playing a fish on two rods, and with no hands spare for the net, which is exciting but not good fishing technique!

To summarise boat fishing:

1) Stow your kit where it will be out of the way and dry, and cannot reach out for loose fly line.
2) Check before you set off from the boat dock, that you are properly dressed and that you have got everything.
3) Think where you are going, before you motor off at high speed.
4) Approach fish gently, by drifting down on them not by motoring up to them.
5) Beware the down wind shore – if you are caught there in a blow and the motor packs up you will have to pull your hearts out at the oars to get out of trouble.

6) Have the anchor ready for instant deployment in case you lose an oar, or one of you goes over the side. Make sure the butt end of the anchor rope is securely fastened to the boat before you set off.

7) Make sure you have the empty emulsion paint bucket handy, with lid well on.

8) Above all, *never stand up in a boat.*

9) If the wind and wave suddenly get up, and you decide that discretion is the better part of valour, do not leave the decision until it is too late. By the time the bows are thrashing up and down, with breakers sloshing aboard, you run a grave risk of killing yourself just heaving the anchor in, particularly if Sid's Law has operated, and the anchor is stuck fast on the bottom. I know of two anglers who were lucky to escape with their lives when fishing the Tweed. The anchor stuck in a fast current. One man could not pull it up alone, so his companion went into the bows to help. The combined weight, plus the downward pull on the bows, dipped the bows under, the boat filled with water like lightning and before they knew where they were, they were swimming for their lives. In a good blow, this can happen just as easily on a stillwater as on a river, so if you have decided to run for shelter, tie the plastic bucket to the end of the anchor rope and go back for it later in calmer conditions.

And all that without even mentioning the fishing part of it at all! That's the easy bit. Enjoy yourself, and think depth before you worry too much about fly pattern. How's that? Too easy? Perhaps. But fishing from a boat is meant to make it easier for you to catch fish than it is on the bank – that's one of the reasons you are willing to pay more to do it, isn't it?

C·H·A·P·T·E·R

15

Fly Patterns

I could fill a book by doing a bit of research into the many thousands of fly patterns which have been invented since the early days of Chew and Blagdon, but that is not my intention. All I am going to do is to suggest a few fly patterns, which are favourites in my own flybox, and when to use them. Easy to say. . .but what you are going to get in the next few pages has taken me nearly fifty years to learn!

One thing I have learned, and sometimes the hard way, is that there are too many fly patterns around today, and the beginner becomes thoroughly bewildered by them all. Contrast today's flyboxes the size of suitcases – and I saw one Rutland angler with three of them in his boat – with what happened to me when I was a boy.

I was taught to trout fish with a fly by a lovely man who used to wade up the middle of the stream in a pair of old army boots. He carried all his fly tying kit in an old Elastoplast tin in his jacket pocket. He cut his rod on the first day of each season from a hazel clump, and he plaited his line from horsehair. His favourite saying to me was, 'Any fly will do as long as it has a badger hackle, and you match the body colour to the fly on the water. . .If in doubt, use a Grey Duster.'

He caught his trout by stealth and fieldcraft, and he used the fish to feed his family. He was a working man with a heart of gold, who took a small boy, aged then about thirteen, under his wing and, with endless patience taught me how to catch those wild trout, to the point that my bag went from a frequent blank to perhaps twenty trout in a day. Rationing was severe in 1944, and the protein was appreciated. If we caught twenty trout each one weekend, we could to it again the following weekend. There was no shortage of trout in those pre-DDT, pre-anti-blood sports, pre-farm sprays and fertiliser days. There was, of course, also very little fishing pressure. If we met one other angler a day on four miles of stream, we wondered who he was and where he came from!

Changed days if you look at a typical stillwater on opening day and see the crowded car parks and watch the anglers standing like herons ten yards apart along miles of bank! However, those flies which fooled little wild trout will fool stupid fish-farm rainbows which have been brought up to think that every man on the bank is a friend who is going to throw food at their heads.

Many of the flies lauded in the fishing magazines are transitory. They are here today and gone tomorrow, and many of them have been thought of before and are re-inventions around an idea which was forgotten years ago. Having said that, there is far more human brainpower being devoted to fishing nowadays than ever before. All over this country, twenty-four hours a day, there are men driving trains and lorries, working at machines, staring at dials, or working in offices, and every one of them is thinking about one of three things, money, women or fishing. And more and more of them are thinking about fishing! Yet despite all this human intelligence being devoted to fishing, the trout seem just as difficult to catch. Perhaps because most of us are on the wrong track.

If you spoon a fish you have just caught, it is highly unlikely that you will find only one food-form in its stomach. A typical autopsy would reveal perhaps fifty midge pupae, two snails, half-a-dozen nymphs, and one minnow or stickleback. All that shows us is we just caught that fish on a sedge pupa by sheer fluke. Because the fish didn't see a sedge pupa, it saw food. Period. So why all the agonising over the exact fly pattern?

Would it not be better if all that human brainpower was devoted to our ability to present a fly so that the fish thought 'food' more often, instead of following it for a while wondering, 'What the hell is that multicoloured thing – is it edible? Should I have a nibble to see if it is? Now I come to think of it, a similar one ten yards along the bank stung me when I took a nibble at it, so I won't bother!'

Is it all that wrong to allow trout the power of such reasoning? I do not think so. All wild animals go through life on the edge of terror: any inkling of danger and their adrenalin starts to flow and they get ready to flee.

The art of fly presentation is to avoid that flow of adrenalin, keeping the fish in a happy carefree feeding mood. So that, whatever fly you put in front of it, the trout will think food and grab it with confidence. This is the real challenge of fly fishing, and regrettably I do not think it is achieved by the majority of stillwater anglers in this country. They would catch far more fish if they did concentrate on presentation, whatever fly they had on the end.

Having said that, I must admit that there are days when no fly seems to work, and at the end of the day you meet a man who has caught a bagful on some fly you have never heard of: but was it the fly alone? Might he not have discovered some slight variation in depth which you missed? Might he not have found a shoal of fish which passed you by? Might he not have been fishing in the one spot where fish were feeding? Yes he might, but sometimes it is just that the fish were locked on to one food form, and you did not imitate it well enough for the fish you showed your fly to. This happens on very few days a year, is maddening when it does, but you should approach any angler seen catching fish, and ask him what fly he is using. Don't disturb his fishing and if there isn't a competition on at the time, he might just give you the right answer! Some folk think it is funny to deliberately mislead such enquirers, and a Church Pheasant Tail Nymph with fluorescent red thorax is referred to as a kind of nymph, when it is tied on a size 8 longshank and stripped in yard-long pulls. So watch *how* he is fishing, at the same time as you ask about the fly.

It is a rare angler indeed who would tell you, 'A red Church Pheasant Tail, size 8, four feet down, in foot-long pulls with five seconds between each pull'! The average reservoir angler hasn't the faintest idea how deep his flies are. It pays to ask him what line he is using, and count how long he lets it sink, and that might give you a better clue to the depth. If he tells you he is using a Super Aquasink, and you have only got an ordinary medium-to-fast sinker, then allow more time for your flies to get down to the depth at which he is catching fish.

While the study of insects is an absorbing hobby, I do not think it pays to become too immersed in the subject. If you learn the major groups of insects of the waterside, in English, that is good enough. Do not be put off if you meet some idiot who talks in Latin, he is just trying to impress you. Don't whatever you do, feel inferior to the man who refers to a hatch of *Caenis macrura*, when all you have seen are angler's curse shedding their skins on your fishing jacket that summer evening: you are both talking about the same insect, and if you are catching fish on a little Hare's Ear nymph, and he doesn't catch anything on his immaculate size 24s then great, you are a better angler than he is, and he is a nut.

A study of the groups of insects will show you that there are several which deserve your attention, and if you look at the pictures in this book you will grasp the essentials quite easily. I have tried to match up the real thing with an imitation which works well for me most of the time (there is no pattern on earth which will do a perfect job *all* the time). And I have found over the last few years that the majority of anglers, certainly in their first few years of experience, need to be told; 'If I see an insect which looks like this, then I should try an artificial which looks like that.' So the pictures are designed to help in just this way.

For those of you who tie flies, there is then a series of recipes for the patterns, and suggestions on how best to fish with them. Even if you do not tie your own flies, it will pay you not to skip reading the recipes. They will give you an insight into the makeup of the flies in your box. (If you are not learning how to tie your own flies, you should be, as no facet of fishing will help you more than this.)

Let us discuss the major families of insects, not in any particular order.

MIDGES

Without any doubt stillwater trout eat more midges than any other insect. This is because there are more of them, not because they like them more. Every little bit of static water has its midge population, from the little wiggling things found in an abandoned tin on the town dump, to the smoke cloud stationary over the south arm of Rutland, made up of millions of midges in their mating dance.

I have already gone through the midge's life cycle, from egg to bloodworm, to pupa, to adult midge. It remains only to say that it is the pupa which is *the* important trout food. I have not had much success with imitations of the adult, fished as dry flies, but have had great success fishing them as wet flies in a good wave.

Midges can vary in colour, and if in doubt go for black. In high summer there are ginger ones, olive ones, grey ones, brown ones and multicoloured ones. In all sizes too, but the bigger it is, the more likely it is to be black or dark grey. Just to confuse you further, a pupa is not necessarily the same colour as the adult which gets out of it. A black midge can hatch out of a grey pupal shuck, which can look almost silvery just before hatching, so try to see the colour of the pupa if you intend to fish a pupa, or the adult if you intend to fish an imitation of the adult.

The best way I have found to catch a midge flying past your head, is not to try to grab it or even to catch it in your hat - wet your hand and swipe, the fly will stick to your wet palm and will not be damaged too much.

When dressing a midge pupa, I have found it better to aim at a slim body and a plump thorax, and to tie it on a curved hook (Yorkshire Sedge Hooks are specifically designed to give this curved-body effect, and I use them for all my midge, sedge and shrimp patterns). The following pattern is typical, and can be varied by colour to match any midge pupa on your water.

MIDGE PUPA

Dressing

Hook Yorkshire Sedge Hook, any size from 8 to 16.
Thread whatever colour you want the pupa to be.
Body fine underlay of tying thread, overwound with clear High Power Gum.
Thorax any fur to match the thread colour.
Breathers small tuft of Yorkshire Dollybody or any white fine fibres, figure-of-eighted apart.

Small wing buds can be added for extra realism, and these can be conveniently made from small slips from the leading edge of a big stiff feather, like a primary feather from a goose quill. Called goose biots, they should always be a chestnut colour to imitate the colour of the wing buds with the blood in the veins of the wings which are packed inside them. Tie them in, pointing down and back, one at each side, protruding from the rear of the thorax, and then trim them to shape.

The thorax can have a few turns of lead or copper wire wound first under the fur, for a faster sink rate. Fish the fly *very slowly*, as real midge pupae cannot swim. They just float gently to the surface.

As a general purpose midge pupa, you cannot do better than a Cove Pheasant Tail Nymph, dressed with a body of pheasant tail fibres with a copper wire rib, and a thorax of rabbit fur left with shaggy ends to represent legs. A wingcase of the body material waste ends is often used but is incorrect – midges do not have wingcases on top of the thorax. See note on pages 171–2.

ADULT MIDGE

Bob Carnhill has made some beauties during his work on midges. The following pattern follows Bob's ideas closely, and he is to be congratulated on his work.

Dressing

Hook Yorkshire Sedge Hook, any size from 8 to 16.
Thread whatever colour you want the midge to be.
Body fine dubbing of fur, or a winding of feather fibre ribbed with the waste end of the tying thread.
Wings two blue dun cock hackle points, tied in to lay flat along the body, but splayed in a Vee.
Thorax bulky fur dubbing, of the same colour as the body.
Hackle only a few turns of cock hackle, usually of a colour to match the body and thorax. The hackle can be bearded in, instead of being wound.

I suggest that you fish the adult midge as an imitation of the drowned adult, just under the surface. This is most effective in a good wave which has tumbled the fly under the water when it was trying to hatch, or in a flat calm when the surface was too oily for the insect to struggle through. Fish either *very slowly*, as drowned flies do not swim, they are dead!

If you are caught out in a midge hatch without a pupa or adult imitation, all is not lost. Try a Mallard and Claret, a Partridge and Orange, or a Black Pensioner. Fish them as wet flies, and also very slowly. If the midges are grey or olive, a Grey Duster will also work. These are the traditional flies which have worked for generations of anglers before we even thought of imitations on a more realistic scale which, in any case, only happened within the last twenty years!

SHRIMPS

These are a standby food of trout around weedbeds in calcium-rich water. They can also be found in acid waters, but there they will not be nearly as common. Much argument over the years has been devoted to the correct colour to tie shrimp imitations, and many people stick to olive tones. I have spooned fish and found shrimps which were orangey-pink in colour and was quite prepared to believe that they had been bleached this colour by the trout's gastric juices, until I found some orangey-pink shrimps in a bunch of weed which came up on an anchor! Following the dictum which says that trout will eat what they can see, I am a great believer in making my fly just a bit different or a bit bigger than the naturals around in such quantity, so I now use only one shrimp pattern, and it is a orangey pink colour. It works well for me providing it is fished slowly, in little twitches of the rod tip.

ORANGEY PINK SHRIMP

Dressing

Hook Yorkshire Sedge Hook, size from 8 to 16 (but 12 is my standard size).
Body a mixture of seal's fur orange, pink and white, perhaps with a touch of olive if you are fussy. (I use Yorkshire Bug Fur, shrimp pink).
Overbody a thin strip of polythene brought over the top and tied in at the head.
Rib fine gold wire, over both body and overbody, to give a segmented effect. Pick out the fur underneath, to shaggy it as legs, and varnish over the overbody to strengthen it.

The hook can be weighted with fine copper or lead wire before tying the fly. Shrimps swim sometimes on their sides, sometimes upright and sometimes upside down, so it matters not in the least which way up your imitation goes in the water. If the fish think it is moving like a shrimp moves, they will have it.

If you are stuck for a shrimp imitation, put on an Invicta or March Brown wet fly and fish in the same short twitches.

GOLDHEAD

Dressing

Hook any roundbend hook larger than a 12. Smaller hooks will not allow the gold bead to be threaded around the bend and along to the eye, where the bead is secured by turns of thread fore and aft, and if desired, a touch of Superglue as well.
Body dubbed with hare's fur. Gold wire rib optional. Tail of guard hairs or partridge hackle fibres also optional.

I am not sure who invented the Goldhead, but it was originally intended as a sedge pupa imitation for the fast rivers in Austria such as the Traun. Like some other specialist patterns it has been found to catch fish in circumstances far removed from its original surroundings. Whether fish in our stillwaters think a goldhead is a sedge pupa, a shrimp, an alder fly larva, a damsel fly nymph or whatever, they seem to look at it and think *food*, and that is all that matters. Goldheads seem to fish best in bright weather.

Some fly tying materials suppliers sell gold beads made of gilded plastic, but I have not found these satisfactory as the gold colour comes off after a couple of fish. Much better to use metal beads – the ones I favour are made of solid brass, and make the fly fish in a sink and draw fashion.

WATERBOATMEN

There are two basic sizes of these fellows, big ones ½-an-inch long which can give you quite a bite and tiny ones about a ¼-of-an-inch long which are far more common. They both are air-breathing creatures, and have to come up to the surface every now and again to replenish the bubble of air they carry. They can also fly, as they are actually submersible beetles, and the apparently hard shellback is a pair of wingcases. They are quite strong swimmers, moving in little jerks of one inch at a time. The big ones move in two-inch jerks. Usually straight upwards towards the surface or straight downwards towards the bottom, so the imitations should be fished the same way.

No better imitation has yet been invented than Richard Walker's Chomper, a great pattern, and very simple to tie, although there have been many variations.

CHOMPER

Dressing

Hook standard wet fly hook size 12 (for the whoppers, a size 8).
Underbody any white wool or chenille, to give a plump sausage shape.
Wingcases brown raffia or brown feather fibre drawn over the back.

Legs are not necessary, but little paddles of peacock herl or feather fibre can be added but make no difference to the fish. Sometimes a little glint of silver tinsel near the rear of the body does but again this is optional. Weighting of the fly with fine wire can be done if you want to fish it sink and draw.

If you are a real devotee of sinking lines, you can carve a little body out of buoyant foam, slit it and glue it to the shank and put the wingcases over. This should then be fished on a sinking line and a short leader, and it should swim back over the weedbeds, or a couple of feet off the bottom. This style of fishing is now commonly referred to as Booby fishing, as a common buoyant fly with large polystyrene beads attached at the head is called a Booby. Fishing in this way you have to rely on touch for detecting takes, and as I prefer to watch the end of a floater, my Chompers are weighted, rather than buoyant.

A Black and Peacock Spider will work sometimes when fish are feeding on waterboatmen, but whether the fish think it is a waterboatman or a beetle cannot be ascertained. It's food, and that is good enough.

UPWINGED FLIES

As far as I am concerned, there are only three of these that I ever bother with, mayflies, olives and anglers' curse. I know there are lots of others but I have tried to be strong-willed and ignore all suggestions about claret duns, sepia duns and all the other upwinged flies there are around, and I have stuck to these three to keep things simple for myself.

MAYFLY

Whether your stillwater has a hatch of mayflies or not, and most of our stillwaters have not, you can catch fish on a mayfly nymph. Again, Richard Walker's pattern can't really be beaten and is grabbed with gay abandon by fish which cannot ever have seen a mayfly, or a mayfly nymph, in their lives.

MAYFLY NYMPH

Dressing

Hook Yorkshire Stronghold size 8, or longshank 8.
Thread brown.
Tails three or four strands of cock pheasant centre tail, tied short.
Body and thorax lemon yellow Fuzzy-Wuzzy or angora wool, wound or dubbed.
Wingcases and legs cock pheasant centre tail fibres.

The body can be weighted with copper wire, and the waste end of the wire can be used to rib the body. It seems important that there are a couple of touching turns of wire or thread near the rear of the body to convey the effect of the second and fourth segments being darker in the real nymph.

This nymph is seldom seen by the trout unless it is migrating to a new home or coming up to hatch, but the artificial is eaten cheerfully if it is just being fished sink and draw, or in short pulls. Again, I think it is taken because it looks edible, which is the secret of all good general-purpose patterns.

MAYFLY DUN & SPINNER

Again there are many patterns for this fly, from the simple spider patterns to monstrosities with great fan wings. I have never been able to fish a fan winged pattern without it propellering in the air and turning the leader into a nightmare of twisted nylon, so I avoid them like the plague. The most successful pattern I have found, both on stillwaters where there is a mayfly hatch and on rivers, is a Light Pensioner. I shall give the dressing later, under Olives. A good Mayfly pattern is as follows:

Dressing

Hook longshank lightweight hook, size 8
Thread black.
Tails a bunch of guard hairs from a chocolate or black labrador.
Body very thin Ethafoam, cut into a strip and wound.
Rib thick black sewing thread, or rod-binding thread.

Hackles three hackles, one olive, one badger and one hot orange, all wound together on the same spot to give a really bushy effect. Then the hackles below the hook are cut off so that the fly lands upright every time, and the thick hackles do not act as hook-guard.

For a spinner pattern specifically, omit the orange and olive hackles, use black only and figure of eight into a bunch either side, after winding.

OLIVES

There are several olives which hatch regularly from our stillwaters. They all look like little yachts as they sit there drying their wings, and the trout cannot tell the difference between any of them! Neither can I without using a magnifying glass, so I have standardised on just a couple of patterns when olives are around.

OLIVE NYMPH (Frank Sawyer's Pheasant Tail)

Dressing

Hook wet fly size 14
Thread fine copper wire, no thread at all.
Body & wingcase cock pheasant centre tail fibres.

This nymph will catch fish at any time of the year, and at almost any depth. Frank Sawyer invented the 'induced take' which involves allowing the fly to sink, then drawing it upwards in front of the fish, who find this almost irresistible. It will, of course, catch fish when it is just twitched along in very short dashes. Almost as if it fled for two inches, then stopped and peered around to see if it was still alive, before making another two-inch rush!

It is possible to experiment with the nymphs of the lake olive and the pond olive, many of which seem to have little blobs on the ends of the tails. Try using tippets as tails, preferably those of the Amherst pheasant, dyed olive. If you are prepared to go to this length, you can dress a very effective olive nymph imitation using any greenish fur in various shades of olive, with any dark feather fibre as a wingcase over. Just occasionally the fish take a liking to bright green numphs, and you could have a few of these in your box as despair flies. A Hare's Ear nymph will work too when olives are around.

OLIVE DUNS (Light Pensioner)

For the adult of the olives, you can do no better than a Light Pensioner. It works for me at all times of the year, any time of day, in any water, with great reliability. Although invented as a dry fly, do not neglect its ability to catch fish when sunk. Cast into rise rings and drawn slowly away, fish grab it even more reliably than they do if it is sitting perched up on the surface. Do not worry if the olives on the water are small – the Light Pensioner will catch fish even when dressed in my suggested size.

Dressing

Hook dry fly hook size 12.
Thread olive.
Tails a few strands of Greenwell hackle feather.
Body hare's fur, with a fine gold wire rib.
Wing a tuft of white mink-tail hair, but any white hair will do if it is fine enough, and not brittle.
Hackle Greenwell cock, parachuted around the base of the wing.

It is vital for the durability of this fly that the hackle stem be laid up beside the wing before the rest of the hackle is wound around. Tie in the hackle tip behind the head in the usual dry fly way. Then bring the stem down to the same point and tie that in too. Varnish the whip finish only underneath the body. Using this method, every turn of hackle is locked in position at the base of the wing and cannot migrate up the wing as is common on wrongly-tied parachute flies.

If you are stuck for a fly during an olive hatch, there are other choices of fly among the old favourites – Greenwell's Glory, Pheasant Tail, Blue Dun, Grey Duster and many others, but I have had such success with the Light Pensioner that I seldom use any of the others nowadays.

ANGLER'S CURSE

The tiny white fly which sheds its last skin on your fishing jacket on summer evenings. Once seen it is unmistakable. Called *Caenis* by the knowledgeable, this little fly is the cause of more swearing on summer evenings than any other. The duns hatch in the evening, about the same time as the sun goes down. They moult the last skin, and fly their mating dance for much of the night, mating just before dawn, laying their eggs and dying on the surface. Actually it is only the females which die on the surface, but males and females look alike anyway.

In the evenings, when there is a curse hatch on, the fish are seldom taking the adult flies. They are feeding on the hatching nymphs, and the anglers who are doing the swearing are trying to catch fish on imitations of the hatched dun. It seldom works. The way to catch these fish is to use a little Hare's Ear Nymph, and to land it a foot ahead of a fish which is cruising along sipping the nymphs in the film. It can be fascinating fishing, and the Hare's Ear is the only fly which has worked with any reliability for me.

HARE'S EAR NYMPH

Dressing

Hook standard wet fly or dry fly hook, size 14 or 16.

Body & thorax the fur from between a hare's ears, or on the forehead, or the finer hair behind the ears. The body should be dressed fıom pale-coloured hair, and the thorax from darker-coloured hair. A fine gold wire rib can be put on the body if desired, but is not essential.

You will find anglers around you are trying flies tied on size 20 hooks or smaller because they have read magazine articles extolling the virtues of exact imitation for the Anglers' Curse; but they will not catch nearly as many as you will be able to with good observation, accurate casting into the path of a fish and the good old Hare's Ear Nymph on a size 14 or 16.

Many nymphs in the act of hatching have one detail in common. As the fly climbs out of its nymphal shuck, the shuck has an orangey tinge. Within seconds, that colour fades to the watery grey colour we associate with the empty skin.

A most useful variation of the Hare's Ear Nymph is the addition of an orange tail, made of either golden pheasant tippets, or some orange fibre from a dyed cock's hackle or squirrel tail. Nymphs with this orange tail, although designed to be fished right in the surface film, seem to be just as effective when fished deep! And the addition of a tippet tail has, for me, just about doubled the catch-rate on this fly. I call this fly the Orange Ear, and it is steadily taking over the Hare's Ear Nymph section of my flybox.

At dawn, when the spinners are dying on the surface, the fish will again become preoccupied. Sip, sip, sip, one every foot they go, and you can go mad trying to catch them. Try the nymph as a first choice, of course, and if that doesn't work you have to go to a Grey Duster. Do not oil it but fish it flush in the film, and try to put it down a foot in front of your target fish.[3]

GREY DUSTER

Dressing

Hook dry fly hook size 14 or 16.
Thread olive.
Tail a few strands from the large end of a badger cock's hackle.
Body hare or rabbit fur, with a fine gold wire rib optional.
Hackle badger cock, wound sparsely.

Yes, I do know that the proper Grey Duster does not have a tail, but mine have, as the fly will not sit correctly level if it hasn't.

DADDY-LONGLEGS (Crane Fly)

In some years there are millions of these flies around, and in others there is a scarcity of them. On a day of high wind in the summer, they are likely to be blown onto the water, and you will see them being taken with a slosh: they are a good mouthful, and the trout don't want to miss the opportunity. Often not eaten on the first slosh but just smashed into the water, to be picked up at leisure five seconds later.

I have only one basic Daddy pattern, but I tie it two ways for my own flybox. For use as a dry fly or dapping fly, the legs are spread out around the clock, two backwards, two straight out at right angles and two pointing forwards either side of the eye. For use as a wet fly in a good wave, the legs are all tied in trailing backwards. Apart from that both versions are exactly the same.

Dressing

Hooks longshank lightweight hook (mayfly style) size 8.
Thread olive.
Body a bunch of deerhair lashed along a needle, whipped crisscross, and varnished. When dry, slide off the needle and tie onto hook as a detached body.
Wings two cock hackle points, the best colour being pale blue dun. Black will do.
Legs six fibres from a cock pheasant centre tail, with two knots tied in each fibre. Use a small crochet hook for this eyeball-straining job.
Hackle gingery to light red game cock hackle, wound bushy.

This is one of the few dry flies which can be fished with movement, providing the leader is sunk so as not to leave a wake from the knots in it. Only the fly should leave a wake. I tend to use the wake effect as a desperation-method, if leaving the fly sitting still proves not to work.

SEDGES

The sedge in its various forms provides exciting fishing any time from the end of May in the south of Britain or the end of June in the north. Very early in the season, anglers who drag Stick Flies along the bottom can kid themselves that they are fishing a sedge larva (caddis) imitation, but I am not sure that the fish the anglers catch thought they were eating a sedge larva, most likely it just looked like a creepy-crawly kind of food. My reason for saying this is that, of the hundreds of anglers I have watched fishing a Stick Fly along the bottom, not one has ever moved his imitation at the speed of an inch a minute! Real sedge larvae have to haul a huge house around with them, and they look tired after three inches of struggle, never mind the standard figure of eight retrieve of four inches every two seconds!

However, if you do want to kid yourself that you are imitating a sedge larva, and fish a Stick Fly as slowly as you can, you will catch fish.

STICK FLY

Dressing

Hook longshank lure hook size 8, or Yorkshire Stronghold size 8.
Thread olive.

Body hare's fur, dubbed in a long thin body. Two turns of yellow or green fluorescent floss at the head of the body, just behind the hackle.
Hackle a small black cock's hackle, one turn only.

When the larva has finished pupating, the pupa is ready to hatch, and is food for the trout as it rises to the surface. You now have a choice of several patterns depending on size and colour, from small grey silverhorns to the whopping-big large red sedge. You can take your choice from among the following:

SMALL SEDGE PUPA

Dressing

Hook Yorkshire Sedge Hook, size 12.
Thread to match the body colour.
Body any fine fur, in colours of grey, fawn, green or dark olive.
Antennae two strands from a bronze mallard feather, tied sloping back, and long.
Thorax any fine fur, in a colour slightly darker than that chosen for the body. Tease the thorax fur out below to imitate legs.
Wing buds can be added if desired, using goose biots in a chestnut or grey colour.

Fished sink and draw, the fly can be weighted if you want to. This pattern is a standby on summer evenings, when fish can be seen rising with a bit of a slosh.

SHAGGY SEDGE

Dressing

Hook Yorkshire Sedge Hook size 8.
Thread olive.
Body olive-dyed ostrich herl, ribbed in an open spiral with a thin strip of polythene so that the fuzziness is still left intermittently.
Antennae two strands of bronze mallard feather, tied sloping back, and long.
Thorax a loosely spun deer hair head, in muddler fashion, but barbered carelessly to look shaggy. Leave some strands pointing downwards to represent legs.

If you weight the fly to make it sink quickly, do so under the rear of the hook, not where you are going to spin the deerhair. Deerhair should be spun on a bare hook or it will not spin properly.

SHREDGE

Dressing

A slight modification of Tony Knight's pattern:

Hook Yorkshire Sedge Hook size 10.
Thread olive.

Body dubbed seal's fur or substitute, in a light cinnamon colour (tobacco). Aim for a thicker front end, or a fat carrot shape.
Wings any pale grey feather, laid well back. Best of all to tie one wing in at a time, on the sides, not on top.
Hackle bearded, a pale ginger colour, known nowadays as Carnill Ginger. Hen hackle is best, but cock will do.

The fly can be weighted, and fishes best in the summer months, and after midday. It is not known whether the fish think it is a sedge pupa, or a shrimp or just food. I have had most success fishing this pattern very slowly, in a sink and draw, and shrimps do not usually swim this way!

If you are stuck without proper patterns for the sedge pupa, do not despair, one of the following will probably work if moved in the correct way: Wickham's Fancy, March Brown, Invicta or a large Hare's Ear Nymph.

So much for the patterns of the sedge pupa, but now we come to perhaps the most exciting and the most frustrating fishing – that of a dry sedge. Usually in the late afternoon or evening and continuing until total darkness, the sedges all have one thing in common, they hatch fast and get out of there as if Old Nick himself was chasing them. If you see what looks like a moth scuttling along the surface, half running and half flying, it is a sedge. They can range in size from little tiny ones to things about two inches long, and *really successful* dry sedge patterns have, in my opinion, still to be invented. It might, of course, be the way we present the patterns we already have, and not the flies themselves which are wrong. It is most difficult to draw a dry sedge pattern along the surface without leaving wake from the fly line, the leader or the knots in the leader and unless there is a good wave these seem to put the fish off totally. So I always degrease the leader well, have a minimum of knots in it and, when I cast out, I allow time for the leader to sink a bit before starting the draw. Even so I have seen fish sheer away from my imitation which, a few seconds before had slashed a real sedge as if it was to be their last meal on earth. There is something wrong and I cannot fathom out what it is, but one day I shall find the key, and will be able to approach dry sedges with the same total confidence with which I view a hatch of olives or mayflies. Don't get me wrong, I do not fail to catch fish in a sedge hatch, but I just do not catch as many as I think I should!

One of the problems of fishing a sedge hatch is that it often takes place at last light, when you cannot see a dry fly very well. We have a customer, a Roman Catholic priest who is a dedicated angler, and he and I were discussing this lack of visibility. I advised him to go to the eastern shore, and kneel down, so that he was looking at the reflection of the last of the light in the evening sky, and would see his fly silhouetted. He grinned hugely, and told me that if he knelt down facing west, he would be struck from above by a giant fist! Having said that, it is still my advice that you face west and kneel down to get the last of the light!

A useful sedge pattern is as follows:

DRY SEDGE

Dressing

Hook dry fly lightweight hook, any size from 14 to 8.
Thread olive.
Body dubbed hare's fur, a gold wire rib is optional.
Wing one small feather from the top leading edge of a hen pheasant's wing, tied on to lay flat over the body, and to be longer than the body.
Antennae the two stems of the hackles, tied in to protrude forward, before winding the hackle.
Hackle two cock hackles with half the stems stripped to act as antennae, wound bushy, in front of the wing roots.

John Goddard's Deer Hair Sedge is also an excellent pattern, but if you are stuck, a dry March Brown, a Soldier Palmer or a dry Wickhams Fancy, will all catch fish. I have caught fish in a sedge hatch with a Daddy-Longlegs after I cut the long legs off – the result was just a bushy brown thing. Some people swear by a Muddler Minnow dragged across the surface or just under, and Goldheads are becoming popular as a sunken imitation of a sedge pupa.

DAMSEL FLIES

We have all seen those lovely electric blue flies with the long bodies hawking over the water on summer days, and have also perhaps seen trout coming up like rockets to try to catch them. It has been my experience that only the little, over-enthusiastic fish will do this. When they grow up they realise the futility of trying to catch damsels in mid-air. Better to wait near a weedbed for a mating pair to land on a reed and for the male, the blue one, to shove the female, the khaki one, below the surface to lay her eggs, Then they can be chomped quietly and at leisure, as they are too busy to notice the danger of those great jaws coming up from below.

I have spent many hours at the fly-tying bench, trying to make the perfect copy of an adult male damsel; and have used up lots of materials doing so, with a singular lack of success. Sure, I caught fish on most of them, but only poor ignorant stock rainbows. Cunning brown trout, or rainbows which had been caught and put back a few times, tended to ignore my best efforts. It was only when I looked at the male damselfly in the proper way that I got the key. They are electric blue on the top and sides, but underneath they are a chalky pale blue, almost a duck-egg blue! And if I had looked at the damned fly from the trout's point of view to start with I would have saved myself hours of work at the vice.

One of the reasonable patterns for an adult damselfly proved to be simply a bunch of pale blue bucktail hair lashed to a hook, with a blue dun hackle wound bushily in front. I caught a few browns on this, but it is still not what I would call a successful pattern. I have, over the years, more or less decided that when the damsels are on the go, I am better sticking to the nymph to catch fish.

There are lots of patterns for the Damsel Nymph, but one which is as good as any is:

Dressing

Hook Stronghold size 8, or a longshank 8.
Thread olive.
Tail three olive cock hackle points, tied to splay out, each one vertical.
Body olive seal's fur, tied slim, with a gold wire rib optional.
Thorax olive or claret seal's fur, or Yorkshire Flybody Fur.
Wingcases any brownish feather fibre brought over the top of the thorax.
Hackle bearded, and splayed out to the sides, olive cock hackle fibres.

This is one nymph to which I do not usually add weight, as the real insects tend to swim around just under the surface at the times when the fish are locked on to them. There is considerable variation in the natural colours of the damsel nymph, and it will be found that they can adopt the particular green of the weed they are living in. Exact colour is not, therefore, all that important.

If you are stuck for a damsel imitation, try a stick fly or any large green nymph you have in your box. I would urge you not to bother trying some of the fancy, time consuming dressings which endeavour to give a wiggling movement. I went through a period when I was cutting hooks to bits to add separate bodies, but all they achieved was a lot of extra profit for the hookmakers! If you do want a wiggle, take a small Waggy Lure and colour it green with a spirit-ink felt pen, it will work much better than all those jointed things.

SNAILS

There is a time of year when, for some reason known only to themselves, the snails will float in the film and be blown by the wind. Quietly rising trout head-and-tailing in the ripple with no flies apparently responsible, should cause you to bend down and search at water level for snails drifting just under the film. You really have to look hard to see them as there may not be all that many, but the trout see them alright and enjoy eating them.

There are many patterns for the snail – seemingly invented by people with lots of time on their hands – involving wound bootlaces, cut foam, Superglue and all the rest, but a Black and Peacock Spider tied as a wet fly, oiled to float in the film, will work every bit as well. It must not move, but just drift quietly in the film at the same speed as the naturals, having been put down in front of a trout on his patrol beat if possible.

BLACK AND PEACOCK SPIDER

Dressing

Hook standard wet fly hook size 10 to 14.

Thread black.
Body tie in three or four strands of peacock herl (I use herl which has been dyed black), twist it into a rope and wind the rope. This gives a bulky body which is still light in weight. Do not bother with an underbody of floss, this weighs too much.
Hackle black cock or hen, shortish for the size of fly, and sparse.

You now have a fly which can be used as a wet or as a dry fly. Leaded patterns should have a different colour of head so that you can tell which is which before you take one out of the box.

HAWTHORN FLY

There is a period in Britain of about a fortnight in late May or early June when the hawthorn bushes are in blossom and this can provide some exciting fishing if a good breeze is blowing. The hawthorn flies are blown onto the water, and trout love them.

A very similar fly hatches out of the heathery slopes around many Scottish and Welsh reservoirs and lochs. It is of the same *Bibio* family but, unlike the hawthorn fly which is all black, the heather fly has red stocking tops. I developed a pattern to do for both, and it has proved most successful, always providing it is fished properly.

These two flies have some things in common, they are poor fliers, they have long back legs which trail down in flight, and when they land on the water they *do not float on top of the water.* They plonk in the water and sink into the film, lying flush in the surface, usually struggling feebly. This is the key to successful presentation of an imitation of a hawthorn fly or a heather fly. Take a black dry fly, oil it, and then cast it gently so that it sits perked up on its hackles and the trout do not want to know. Take a black dry fly, do not oil it, and cast it so that it sits *in* the film and you can have a ball.

My pattern for both of these naturals is as follows:

Dressing

Hook Yorkshire Sedge Hook size 10.
Body black seal's fur, dubbed thinly for nearly all the body. At the head end, wind one turn of fluorescent magenta floss right behind the hackle.
Hackle sparse winding of black cock's hackle.
Head more black seal's fur, dubbed in a little ball behind the eye.

I did go through a stage when I tied a pair of long legs in, trailing backwards, but I have found that these are not necessary. If you want extra fiddle at the vice, and perhaps more aesthetic pleasure from your fly tying, you can add legs made of cock pheasant centre tail, dyed black, or strands of deer hair, dyed black.

If you are stuck for a pattern to use in a fall of hawthorn flies, try a Black Pensioner, any black spider or even a Black and Peacock Spider, they will all work, provided that they are *in the film*, not sitting up on it.

DAPHNIA

On most evenings I walk my labradors around the lake. I confess that I do not do this only for their good but also for mine, as I learn something on most evenings. My wife, looking out of the bedroom window to see where on earth I have got to, is often treated to the sight of my bottom sticking in the air, as I kneel, nose at water level, shining a torch into the water or horizontally across the surface. Beside me – with expressions of utter boredom on their faces – sit the labradors, but then they do not appreciate the details of insect life I am studying by torchlight!

One of the most fascinating subjects for me is the behaviour of the daphnia. Smaller than pinheads, they look like little drifting specks in the water, but shine a torch into the water and they are attracted by the light, moving steadily into the beam as it shines down through the water. Move the torch away, and then back again, and the daphnia will be seen as a solid column of tiny specks where the torch beam had been. I have often pondered the problem of imitating this soup of protein, much loved by trout who swim through the water filtering the daphnia out, and growing fat and pink-fleshed in the process.

The short answer is that daphnia are impossible to imitate on a hook, but you do not have to. Fish a lure in one of two colours and you will catch trout which are feeding on daphnia, every time. The two colours are lime green and orange, and the patterns I favour are as follows:

LEPRECHAUN

Dressing

Hook Stronghold size 8, or a longshank 8.
Tail fibres of fluorescent lime cock hackle.
Body fluorescent lime chenille, with a silver wire rib.
Hackle bearded fluorescent lime green cock hackle.
Wing pair of fluorescent lime green cock hackles back to back. Peter Wood's original dressing used four hackles, but I find two will do. If you are careful, the fly can be dressed using black thread. Squirrel tail, bleached and dyed fluorescent lime green, can be used for wing and hackle, and makes a more durable fly.

WHISKY FLY

Dressing

Hook Stronghold size 8, or longshank 8.
Thread orange.
Body flat gold tinsel.
Hackle hot orange, or fluorescent orange cock hackle fibres, bearded.
Wing hot orange or fluorescent orange dyed, bleached squirrel tail hair, or cock hackles. This is a simplification of Albert Whillock's pattern.

Fishing for daphnia-feeding trout requires that you find the correct depth, and strip the lure quite fast. Bear in mind that these tiny creatures, although they can swim, cannot progress against a surface current of any kind found on most stillwaters in anything stronger than a gentle breeze. They will, therefore be found in greatest density (thicker soup) on the downwind side of the lake.

LURES

Talk of daphnia, and the lures required to catch fish, leads us on to the lures which find regular places in my flybox. I have already said that the basic colours for lures are black, white and orange, but it is not quite as simple as that. I have already listed the green lure, the Leprechaun, and the orange one, the Whisky Fly, and here are the others.

BLACK LURES

For the simplest black lure of all, take a longshanked hook and lash all black materials on it. It does not really matter whether you use wool, seal's fur, chenille or floss on the body as long as it is black. Any fibre will do for the wing and hackle, from marabou to cock hackles, to hair of any kind. Just so long as the whole fly is big and black. You can put a silver or gold rib on the body if you like, and you can incorporate some of the new flashy materials into the dressing if you wish. If black is the colour of the day, you will catch fish on it. You can add a touch of colour, and put a tail of fluorescent lime wool on, and it will be a Viva (or nearly a Viva). You can tie a black Baby Doll, add a silver rib on the body and you will end up with an Undertaker. There is nothing to choose between all of these as far as the fish are concerned; and moved at the correct speed they will all catch trout as well as each other. My own little variation is to dress a black lure with the fluorescent at the head of the hook instead of at the tail so that, in theory, the trout would get themselves hooked better, and not nip at the tail and miss the point of the hook. (I have never really believed that it is possible for a trout to nip at the tail of a fly and miss the point of the hook a quarter of an inch away, if a trout wants something to eat, his mouth opens wide as he sucks it in, and I feel that 'tail-nipping' is caused far more by blunt hooks than by anything else!) Here are two that I like:

BOWLER HAT

Dressing

Hook Stronghold 8, or longshank 8.
Thread black thick thread, or buttonhole thread.
Body made of the tying thread with a few turns of fluorescent lime floss or chenille under the wing roots.
Hackle some strands of black squirrel tail hair, bearded in.

Wing black squirrel hair, tied no longer than the bend of the hook.

I invented this fly in 1975, and was racking my brains for a name when I spied my bowler hat at the back of the wardrobe. Black with a sheen of green mould around the brim, the name seemed appropriate! Since then the fly has caught lots of fish, but it is just another black lure among many.

ABBOT

Dressing

Hook Stronghold size 8, or longshank 8. Will also work smaller, down to 12.
Thread black.
Body black thread.
Wing black squirrel tail hair, dressed no longer than the bend of the hook.
Head Muddler-style, of white deer hair, clipped into a ball shape.

Invented by Mr Abbott of Feltham, Middlesex, this is a highly successful lure for those days when all-black seems not to work as well as it should.

Other black lures which are excellent are Richard Walker's Sweeny Todd, and the Ace of Spades by David Collyer.

WHITE LURES

Starting with one as simple as a Baby Doll in its original form, there are dozens of these. Again you can tie whatever you like with various materials, so long as they are white. As a thought-starter, I have found that when a white Baby Doll gets grubby, it loses much of its fish-appeal and should be changed for a new, clean one. I then soak the dirty ones in biological detergent and when rinsed and dried they are as good as new. I am sure that it is renewal of the white fluorescent dye which makes all the difference, and most modern washing-machine detergent has white fluorescent dye in it. If your shirt glows purple under ultra-violet in a night club, the detergent used for your shirt has this dye, and you can happily pinch some to soak your Baby Dolls in!

Bodies can be of chenille, wool, floss, ostrich herl or even of marabou wound or dubbed. Ribbing can be added to strengthen the body material. Wings can be of hair, feather fibre, marabou, hackles or anything else. White lures can also have a touch of colour in them, added to the tail, hackle or body, and orange or yellow are favourites. I have no favourite white lure, but tend to use one with a white marabou wing, chenille body and no hackle or tail.

COLOURED LURES

Many years ago (I think it was in 1975!), I was shown some fluorescent pink material which had been bought from a market stall at Doncaster market. I looked at it and screwed up my eyes, it was truly a hideous shocking pink, in the form of a fine floss. At the time I was working on making Baby Dolls smoother than is possible with the normal baby wool, and this floss intrigued me. I tied a Baby Doll with the pink material, really only to see how smooth a fly it would make, and having tied one and been delighted with its sleek appearance, I tucked it into my flybox without much thought. A little later there occurred one of those maddening days when the fish are totally uncooperative, I just could not catch anything, and nobody else could either. In sheer desperation I tied on the Pink Baby Doll, and the fish loved it. I saw fish come at it over ten yards in the clear water, with an attitude of total aggression. Bash and another fish was hooked. I then tried it on wild brown trout and, against all the rules, they loved it too. Since then I have caught fish on a Pink Baby Doll with unfailing regularity, rainbows, brookies, seatrout, even grayling. While part of its success must be the simple fact that the fish can see it so clearly, and many of the fish caught on it have been fry feeding in some form (sticklebacks to sandeels), I cannot for the life of me deduce why such a colour – one of my friends calls it 'heaving pink' – should be so attractive to fish. But it works, and I am delighted that it does. The material is now sold as Yorkshire Dollybody and is available in white and a range of colours.

PINK BABY DOLL

Dressing

Hook Stronghold 8, or longshank 8.
Thread black.
Body, back & tail fluorescent pink Yorkshire Dollybody.
Head black, tied small.

PINK DOG NOBBLER

There has been much controversy over Dog Nobblers. Copied from American flies with lead heads, designed for fishing through holes in the ice by jigging up and down, they were popularised in the UK by Trevor Housby. He wrote the first article extolling their virtues and giving them the name then trade-marked by Sid Knight, who tried to prevent anybody referring to the fly by this name unless he had tied it. Magazines who are guided by their legal departments tend, therefore, to refer to these flies as 'Leadheads', but as I have called these flies 'Dog Nobblers' ever since that first magazine article by Trevor Housby, I shall continue to do so.

The original way of weighting a Dog Nobbler was to superglue a split shot just behind the eye of a long-shank hook. It did not need many low backcasts before the split shot disappeared, and there must be flyboxes all over the country containing Dog Nobblers which lack the essential lead head and are waiting to be worked on with another BB shot and Superglue. Some years ago, a Lancashire angler, Colin Wilson, developed a method of adding a weighted ball to a hook in such a way that it never fell off. It forms an integral part of the hook, and using these hooks has transformed my tying of Dog Nobblers from a fiddly chore into the same pleasure I get from 'normal' fly tying. The hooks are nowadays called 'Tinhead' or 'Steelhead' hooks, and are wholesaled to the trade by Bob Church.

Dog Nobblers come in all shapes and sizes, and are given all sorts of crazy names by the press, but my favourite is a Dog Nobbler tied in the normal way, with a tail of marabou, a chenille body, a palmered body hackle and a tinsel rib. All except for the palmered hackle should be a bright, fluorescent pink. I tend to think that the palmered hackle looks better in black, but I have not the slightest shred of evidence for this statement. In the early days I used to go to considerable trouble to paint the heads pink and dot a black eye on; I no longer bother. I find the fly just as effective if the tin head is left bare and shiny, a silvery colour.

On one day I shall long remember, I was one of a party of friends fishing Farmire, and it was one of those days when one is reaching for a 'despair fly' after a couple of hours. We were chatting to each other on adjoining casting platforms, and I announced that I was going to change my fly again. 'OK, you dry-fly purist, what are you going to try next?' Bending over my flybox, I announced that I was going to try a pink dry fly, and that silenced them for a minute or two while they racked their memory banks for a pink dry fly. When I finally cast out my pink Dog Nobbler, I cast as gently as I could, and it did land like thistledown, and floated, buyoed up by the great bunch of marabou. The ribaldry which greeted this 'dead flamingo' was suddenly silenced as a great pair of jaws engulfed the fly and I found myself playing a seven-pound rainbow which won the bottle of scotch for the largest fish of the day. 'Of course it was a damn dry fly – it was floating, wasn't it?'

Just in case a beginner, reading this, does not quite understand, I hasten to add that a Dog Nobbler is intended to sink, is fished in pulls, long or short depending upon what the fish want at the time, and can be fished on a floating line or a sinking line. Obviously it can be fished much deeper on a sinker, but when fished on a floater, the fly drops when stationary, and rises when pulled, and this rising and falling action is sometimes what drives the fish to attack.

While pink is nowadays my favourite colour for a Dog Nobbler, I confess that I am never without a couple each of black, white and orange, which I can try in the rare event that a pink does not work. Within the last five years, I have had one day's fishing when the fish wanted only black, and two days when they wanted only white.

YORKSHIRE FLASHER

Dressing

Hook Stronghold Lure Hook, size 8.
Thread copper wire
Wing and Hackle Lureflash Mosaic, or any dark multicoloured fine tinsel.

This is an 'in case' fly – not one of my favourites, but I have caught enough fish on it to include it here. The body is made of touching turns of copper wire, and the wing is tied in also with the wire. The waste ends are then brought down and bound in pointing down and back to form the hackle. The fly takes about thirty seconds to tie, and is best fished deep and fast in bright weather. This fly is the result of a conversation with John Harris in the early 1980s, and I have caught browns, rainbows, grayling (by accident while trout fishing) and one seatrout on it.

FALKLANDS FLASHER

Dressing

Hook Tinhead hook, size 8, or a longshank hook size 8 with a BB shot attached behind the eye.
Thread white or grey.
Wing and Hackle Lureflash Multicolour Silver Pearl.

At times this is the most exciting 'despair fly' I have ever used. I saw my first pattern of this when I was sent a sample by its inventor, who was at the time working on the new airfield on the Falklands in 1983. I do wish I could remember his name, as he was a dedicated angler and fly dresser who was having a ball on the seatrout of the Falklands rivers. The original fly was not weighted. It takes at least thirty seconds to tie. Put a Tinhead hook in the vice, start the thread just behind the metal blob, tie in a bunch of twelve to fifteen strands of the Lureflash or Flashabou material with half-a-dozen quick pinch-and-loops, draw the waste ends down and back and lash them down with a further twenty turns of thread, then whip finish and add a dab of varnish to the whipping.

I knew, from correspondence with the originator, that it would catch seatrout, but I confess that I was amazed when I first tried it on a stillwater, as it was chased by brown trout, grayling and rainbows. Of the fish which chase it right to the bank, maybe one in four will actually take it, and on some days the faster it is pulled the more likely it is to be grabbed by a fish.

Traditional anglers, of course, look at it and see that as it is made entirely of man-made materials with not a trace of feathers or fur, it cannot be a fly, and should not be fished on 'fly-only' waters! I prefer not to become involved in this argument, but still have a few Falklands Flashers in my box for those days when 'traditional' flies will not work.

My last experience of this fly was very recently when I was invited to fish the Davidson River, in the Blue Mountains of North Carolina. My host, two of his friends and I fished hard for three hours in this small tumbling crystal-clear river, with not a fish between us. We had lunch beside a large pool, where fish could be seen rising occasionally to flies too small to see. My companions were all using their traditional flies for these conditions, size 20 or 22 would you believe, when I was struck with a wicked thought – what would happen if I put a Falklands Flasher through that pool? I quietly removed my fine tippet and tied on a Flasher. At the first cast, a large fish chased the fly to the edge and then turned away. Second cast there was a thump and I was playing a fish. After that I removed the fly and gave it as a souvenir to my American host. It just did not seem right to be using a fly like that on prime catch-and-release fly water. (Later in the day I found that I could catch fish regularly on a Light Pensioner, and thus proved to my own satisfaction that British patterns fool US trout as well as UK ones.)

I do not think that there can be any doubt that trout think that a Falklands Flasher is a small fish, but this thought triggers another in my mind. Why should they want to chase and catch a small fish which is swimming as fast as I can strip line? All the established gospel states that trout are attracted to wounded and sickly fish, so why should they chase and grab a Flasher if it is sprinted through the water, and ignore it if it is fluttered slowly? Beats me, but questions like this, cropping up in my mind, will keep me sane in a ten-person queue at the supermarket checkout.

When to use the Yorkshire Flasher and when to use the Falklands Flasher? There is no simple answer, except to say that I do not use added weight (apart from the copper wire) on a Yorkshire Flasher, so when I want a surface glittery lure I tend to reach for that fly. When I want to fish deep I tend to reach for the Falklands Flasher with its metal head. Salmon anglers have exactly the same decision to make when deciding upon a silver or copper lure for spinning, and we find the answer most often by pure hunch, being unable to rationalise our decision if we were asked to.

If I was to summarise the Falklands Flasher in one sentence: the fly to put on when you might otherwise be lying down on the bank for a sleep, and I guarantee it will keep you wide awake.

FANCY FLIES

All I am going to do here is to list the flies I normally carry against a rainy day when the flies I have already listed will not work as well as they might, and my catch rate is getting depressing. Some of them will be recognised as traditional flies without which no self-respecting angler would dream of going fly fishing, but they form a basis for a serious attempt to cover the requirements of the average stillwater angler, while omitting all the nasties which work once or twice and then fade from view.

Coachman
Peter Ross
Butcher
March Brown
Zulu
Blue Zulu
Soldier Palmer
Invicta
Black Pennell
Lead-headed lures, in various colours
Mallard & Claret
Cinnamon & Gold
Greenwells Glory
J. P. Special
Black Spider *or* Williams Favourite (a black spider with a silver rib)
Partridge & Orange
Church Pheasant Tail Nymph, with both red and lime thoraces.
Muddler Minnows, in various colours

Nor is a range of sizes required. I carry only one size of each of these flies, and have never found a situation where another size of one of them would have made any difference to the size of the bag.

You might call me an old square because I do not list any of the magic new lures invented by anglers in the last ten years. Frankly I have covered them all when I describe, for example, a 'white lure'. If it is a white lure with a touch of colour here and there it is still only a white lure, and it does not matter what the other colours are. You can invent your own quite easily, and there is no need to cry if you happen to hear that an Appetiser is catching fish, and you haven't got one. Match the general white colour and you will catch fish if you get depth and speed correct for the day.

Fly tying materials are in just as bewildering an array as fly patterns, and here you should experiment a bit. There is a trend developing for the addition of flash in lures, and it does work. But do not believe that the patterns written about in magazines are the only ones which will work. Get yourself some of the new materials and tie some flies, letting your imagination run riot while you sit at the vice. Not only will you find this an absorbing part of fishing, but you might discover some basic truth about angling which has been hidden to us: then, and only then, should you rush into print and let the world have the benefit of your new-found knowledge.

The worst thing you can do as a thinking angler is to believe every article you read, dive to the vice and tie some of the new, new, magic fly, and pin your hopes on them the next time you go fishing, to the detriment of your planning and thinking beforehand. You then run the risk that you will be too busy fishing to think!

'It must be right, I saw it in the paper,' is a belief which is the enemy of the enquiring mind, and this applies just as much to angling as it does to current affairs. . .

Note:

Suspender buzzers are a modern development of the midge pupa pattern, and are not difficult to tie. You need some small polystyrene balls, and a pair of ladies' nylon stockings. How you get the stockings is up to you, but the polystyrene balls can be found in packaging, some makes of padded envelopes, or can be bought as fly tying material.

Cut a one-inch square of nylon stocking, put a polystyrene ball in the centre of it and lift the corners up so as to wrap the ball in the mesh, keeping a tight grip until the parcel can be offered to the shank of the hook and firmly lashed on with several pinch-and-loops. Then the thread is taken along the shank of the hook, tying down the waste ends of nylon stocking. Trim off any excess, then work back up the body tying a normal midge pupa as you go. You end up with a midge pupa with a round float on top or just in front of the thorax, which fishes in the surface film just like a real hatching midge.

A useful addition to any midge pupa pattern is a shaggy dubbing of seal's fur or similar in the thorax area to represent legs. Two colours for this dubbing seem best – claret or ginger, and these can be added to any colour of pupa.

C·H·A·P·T·E·R

16

Knots

The two-turn thumb knot: *used for forming the loop at the butt-end of the leader. Two turns must be used. If only one turn is taken, the loop will sit at an angle. With two turns the loop lies more-or-less straight. Cut the waste end quite short even though it does lie pointing straight down the leader and does not snag on weeds.*

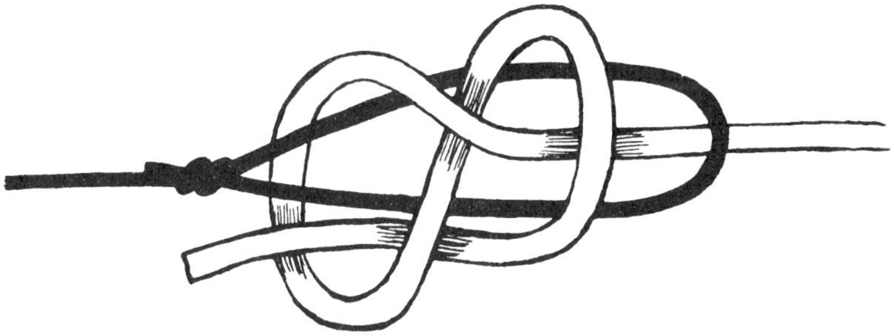

The figure of eight knot: *used for attaching the fly line to the loop on the end of the leader. It has the advantage that the waste end of the fly line lies pointing down the leader, and does not stick out at an angle to catch on weeds. Tied carefully, with a short waste end, it can still be unpicked when changing leaders. Unpicking the knot prevents the fly line's fine point being eroded away.*

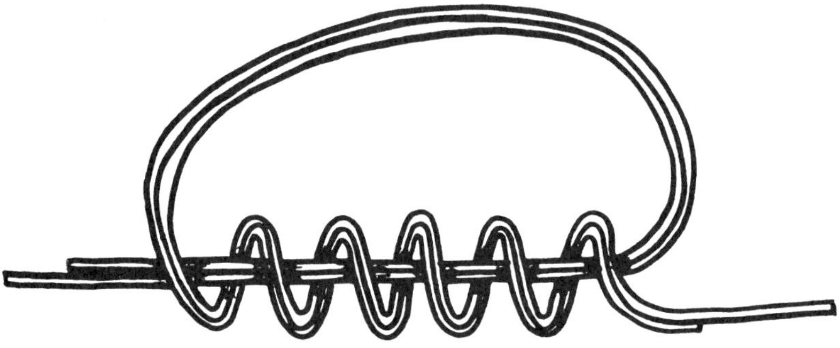

The five-turn water knot: *used for joining lengths of nylon, or for adding a tippet to the point of a tapered leader. Can be used to join lengths of different thickness. The waste ends lie snug along the standing ends, and do not catch in weed if they are cut short. Not to be used for forming droppers – for this purpose a grinner knot is best.*

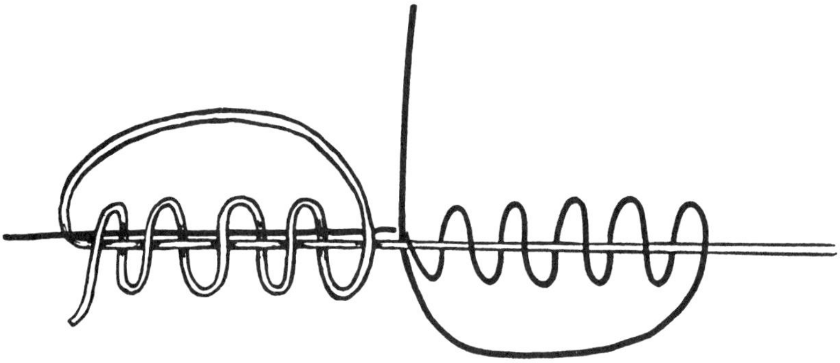

The grinner/half-blood knot: *in this illustration, the big butt leader comes from the left, and is shown in black. The dropper fly goes onto this waste end. The tippet goes off to the right, and the waste end of the grinner knot is cut off short. When tying this knot, it helps to hold the dropper end as the whole knot is snugged up, to prevent the dropper length being too short when the knot is finished.*

The tucked half-blood knot: *used for attaching the fly to the leader. The finer the nylon, the more turns should be made – up to six turns when very fine nylon is being used. Do not forget the final tuck, the waste end can be cut as short as you like. Avoid leaving a long end on the nylon, as this can act as a hook-guard, and bounce the fly out of the jaws of the fish before the point of the hook digs in.*

C·H·A·P·T·E·R

17

In Conclusion

Having gone through what I have written, I am reminded of the elderly man who called at our showroom a while ago. He looked depressed, and said that it was his 80th birthday. We all congratulated him and then he was asked if he had any ambitions left unfulfilled.

'Yes,' he said, 'When I die, I would like to be born again, knowing what I know now – then by the time I am 80 again, I might be a good angler!'

We all roared with laughter, and so did he, but there is so much truth in his wish. I too, believe, that one lifetime is not long enough to learn it all.

What I have set out in this book is as much as I have learned and been able to remember. If I have not remembered something, I did not learn it well enough! And the symptom of this is the sudden memory, while going home in the car after a poor day, of something else you could have tried and didn't think of at the time. We all do it.

The thinking and preplanning which should go into a fishing day will help to organise your mind, so that the things you remember afterwards become fewer: you will have tried more things while you were there. Almost inevitably, your catch rate will go up, and you will have fewer blank days.

It is usually true that 10 percent of the anglers catch 90 percent of the fish. It might be 20 percent catching 90 percent, but the principle is there. What we must do to become better anglers is to determine that we will become one of the 10 or 20 percent. Not one of the very great majority who go fishing time after time with only a few fish to show for their efforts, who often do not bother to fill in a catch return because it would show a blank anyway. I also know anglers who fill a fictitious catch return after a blank day, showing that they caught a limit, in the hope that this will increase the stocking density to make future fishing easier. Both of these tricks, no return at all or a falsely high one, are forms of self-delusion, and the perpetrators are themselves the losers in the long run, usually by an increase in the cost of their fishing!

In most fishing, there is a circle of events which must link up correctly to yield success. It goes roughly like this: place, time, pattern, colour, depth and speed, if all correct equal fish in the bag. Break the chain with one item wrong, and there are no fish in the bag: and only your own powers of deduction, experiment and perseverance will tell you what you got wrong. In reverse order then, you should stick at it, not go to sleep on the bank and wait for conditions to improve; you should keep varying your methods, and not just stand there flogging away in the hope that a stupid fish will tie itself on the end; and you should think. Keep thinking about what you are doing, and why. Above all you must not allow yourself to become so soporifically grooved into your habits that you are too busy fishing to *think*.

Talk to other anglers whenever you can. Pick their brains unashamedly. It does not have to be somebody famous because he writes articles or books on fishing, any thinking angler will do, which could even be a small boy on his first outing, who is perhaps even more likely to notice something about the surroundings, the weather or the insects which you have missed.

There is so much scope for further experiment. Our specimen-hunting coarse fishing friends are often far more dedicated than fly fishermen. They consider one aspect which the fly fisherman totally ignores, let me explain.

How often have you been fooled by a plastic apple? It looked like an apple and it was in a fruit bowl, where you expected it to be. So you picked it up. You just did what a recently stocked fish does, usually only once, you made a mistake. If the weight had not given it away you might have taken a bite at it, and if your mind was on other things you may even have done this. If you did, you were fooled as even the most cunning trout is occasionally.

The taste buds of a fish are on the outside of the mouth, so a trout has only to bump against something to detect if it is food or not. In some cases it only has to come close to it in order to detect smell or taste. (Two inches behind a lure being pulled through the water?) So a trout following a fly may well not only be looking at it, but smelling it. . .what do your flies smell of?

It could be mothballs from your fly tying kit, tobacco from your hands or salami sausage if you have just had lunch! But what do real flies, shrimps or minnows smell of? The dodge of dipping flies into Oxo or Bovril might just be a good idea, except that we do not know what they *should* smell of! If you picked up an apple and it smelled of salami, you might just hesitate before biting into it. But I do think that there is a future for experimentation into smells to be added to flies.

I am not talking about the smell to be added to an imitation of a trout pellet to be used on recently stocked fish, that is definitely Bovril!

The standard of casting around our reservoirs and stillwaters is very low. The average American angler thinks nothing of signing on for a weekend fishing school before actually going fishing. There he or she is taught to cast with reasonable proficiency, lectured about insects, taught how to tie knots and is thus set off with a good grounding in the essentials. Compare that with the procedure of the average British stillwater angler. He has a friend who fishes and who offers to take him. He watches his friend for a while, borrows a rod, reel and line, and puts on the fly which his friend recommends. Then he proceeds to thrash the water into foam, trying harder and harder to get the fly out there. He hasn't the foggiest idea of the theory of casting or any knowledge of fly life, and if he catches something on his first outing it is a miracle. He starts to read a fishing magazine or two, and is bamboozled by the photographs of grinning faces poised over double bag limits of stock fish. He starts to think that he should be able to catch as many fish as that and, if he cannot, then the stocking policy is wrong where he has been fishing. He tries other waters, in increasing desperation, and then one of two things happens – he gives up, thinking it is all a big con trick, or he develops a small measure of luck and efficiency over the next few seasons and becomes an angler. He is most likely to turn into one of the anglers who form the 80 or 90 percent who catch very little.

I do hope that what I have written will help in some small measure to shorten the odds a little. Having said that, I have been guilty of laying down some rules to follow and I must now say this. All the rules formulated by the mortal mind of man will apply to trout, only when the trout want them to. But the mortal mind of man needs guidance sometimes, and the rules should be followed until they are proved not to work that day, then we try something else!

Anglers are a happy breed. They are invariably honest, friendly, helpful and sincere in their desire to see other anglers enjoying themselves. I have often been on the receiving end of that help in years past, and have seen men give up hours of precious fishing time in order to help a beginner or a small boy. Fishing seems to breed an inner contentment which carries over into the next few working days. Equally, fishing can cause an inner restlessness in the few days before the next fishing trip, and Friday afternoons can be an ordeal of impatience!

While fishing is really about *enjoying* yourself, much of the enjoyment comes from a sense of achievement, which is absent if you catch nothing at all. It is all very well to return home blank and say that you have had a marvellous day, it would have been even more marvellous if you had caught something. So the learning process must never stop. The more you remember of what you have learned, the better angler you will be on the next outing. Keep a diary and write down everything you can remember about the day before it fades from your memory. What you did right; what you did wrong; what flies other people caught fish on, and how they fished them. Next year, you can look back at that accumulated knowledge when you are doing your homework for the forthcoming day, and avoid making the same mistakes as you made at this time last year. Better by far than a new fishing rod is a casting lesson. If you cannot afford a casting lesson, start a fishing diary in an old exercise book: best of all have the lesson *and* start a diary, then you are really on the way to becoming one of the top 10 or 20 percent.

Don't think that the experts never make mistakes, they just never write about them. But we all hear the experts swearing from time to time too! We all make mistakes and we will continue to do so as long as we pursue trout.

I was once giving a small boy a casting lesson on our lake. He mastered the basics very quickly, and was putting out a delightful line. It became time to try to catch a fish so that he could learn what to do with the fly once he had put it out there, and how to strike and play and kill a trout. Everything went well, the fly landed like thistledown near a rising fish, the fish took it, was hooked and went off like a train. The lad was so excited that he clamped his hand over the line and hung on grimly. There was the inevitable 'ping' and as everything went slack, a voice from the other side of the lake said, 'OK you've taught him how to fish, now teach him how to swear!'

And that put it all into perspective not only for me but for the lad as well. He turned to me, all four feet nothing of eight years old, and said 'I know how to do that – I have heard me Dad doing it.' Bless him, he will one day be a great angler.

I wish you tight lines, screaming reels and happy fishing.

Appendix A

Essential flies, as suggested by a selection of 22 stillwater anglers. This list is the total of 350 years of experience of fishing stillwaters in Yorkshire and elsewhere. What flies would you find most useful? Only if there was general agreement was a fly included, so each fly in this list was looked upon as essential by all 22 anglers.

April
Muddler Minnow
Baby Doll (bright day)
Any Black Lure (dull day)
Midge Pupa
Mallard & Claret
Mayfly Nymph (Richard Walker's)
Pheasant Tail Nymph (lure size)

May
As for April, plus:
Whisky Fly (bright day)
Shrimp (in alkaline water)
Black & Peacock Spider
Butcher
Peter Ross

June
As for April and May, plus:
Damsel Fly Nymph
Invicta
Daddy Longlegs

July
As for June, plus:
Dry Sedge imitation
Sedge Pupa in varying sizes

August
Black & Peacock Spider
Midge Pupae in various colours
Sedge Pupae, ditto
Mallard & Claret
Butcher or Peter Ross
Black Pennell
Daddy Longlegs

September
Baby Doll or Polystickle
Muddler Minnow
Whisky Fly
Any black lure
Peter Ross or Butcher

Yet we see men at the waterside with flyboxes the size of suitcases! I am not, of course, suggesting that these are all the flies you will need, but 22 good anglers agreed that these were the essentials. Plus a suitcase of 'despair flies'!

Appendix B

If you are a dedicated fly tier, you may come across books written about the turn of the century, where the hook size recommended for a pattern does not look right to you. There may be a reason.

A man called Hall invented the up-eyed hook, and he became so wrapped up in hook sizes, that he suggested a new scale of sizes. This 'New Scale' was taken up by the chalkstream dry fly purist and by almost nobody else; but as the chalkstream caused most of the angling literature for the next few decades, you come across the New Scale of sizes from time to time.

The Redditch scale has survived the test of time, and anglers still work to it, although there are confusing variations with some hook ranges.

Hooks in uneven numbered sizes are no longer made, but it pays to remember that they did once exist and have a bearing on sizing today, particularly when describing hooks not of standard lengths. Therefore a hook described as Size 8 2X long, is a size 8, but with a shank length normally used for a size 6. The gape will be a size 8, but the shank is 2 numbers longer, and one of those numbers will be the uneven number which is not made any more!

Redditch scale (Sometimes referred to as the 'Old Scale')	*New Scale (by Hall)*	*Straight shank length not including the eye. Even sizes only*	
		In.	**mm.**
5/0	19	1½	38
4/0	18	1⅜	34
3/0	17	1¼	30
2/0	16	1⅛	28
1/0	15	1"	23
1	14	⅞	22
2	13	¾	20
3	12		
4	11	19/32	15
5	10		
6	9	17/32	13
7	8		
8	7	15/32	11
9	6		
10	5	11/32	9
11	4		
12	3	5/16	8
13	2		
14	1	9/32	7
15	0		
16	00	7/32	5.5
17	000		
18	0000	5/32	4

If you see the Redditch scale published elsewhere, the measurement will include the bend. Measure an insect and the body length equals the shank length of the hook you choose – one size smaller if you think the eye of the hook represents the head of the insect!

If you have ever thought that the knot in the nylon at the eye of the fly might be seen by trout as part of the insect, it might pay you to reduce the hook size still further! If you use a tucked half-blood knot, the knot will be about 1 mm long. Might this not be an argument for the use of a Turle knot around the head of the fly, so that no apparent length is added to the insect?

Appendix C

Many people find nylon sizes confusing. Some folk talk about the number of Xs, some folk talk about the diameter in inches or millimetres, and yet others talk about the pounds breaking strain or kilogrammes breaking strain.

This table will help you to translate from one to the other. Please bear in mind that the rule of numbers I gave in the book applies only to the pounds of breaking strain – surely the only important information needed by the reservoir and stillwater angler.

When next you buy some of your favourite brand of nylon, I would urge you to find a micrometer and measure the diameter. Then compare it with this table, and see if you are being conned by buying, say, 8 lb nylon labelled as 6 lb nylon – no wonder you think it is nice and strong. It will, of course be thicker than you need, and in some circumstances you will get fewer rises than you would otherwise!

This table of thicknesses refers to the nylon chemistry current in 1985/86.

Test breaking strain (after soaking for one hour)	*Dia. mm*	*Dia. in.*	*X scale*
2½ lb (1.1 Kg)	0.14 mm	0.005 in.	6X
4 lb (1.8 Kg)	0.18 mm	0.007 in.	4X
5 lb (2.3 Kg)	0.20 mm	0.008 in.	3X
6 lb (2.7 Kg)	0.22 mm	0.009 in.	2X
8 lb (3.6 Kg)	0.26 mm	0.010 in.	1X
10 lb (4.5 Kg)	0.28 mm	0.012 in.	Half-drawn
15 lb (6.8 Kg)	0.35 mm	0.014 in.	Quarter-drawn
22 lb (9.9 Kg)	0.45 mm	0.018 in.	Heavy salmon

To give you an idea of how chemistry has come to the aid of the angler. . .in 1931, the year I was born, 2X silkworm gut had a diameter of 9 thousandths of an inch, and a stated breaking strain of 2½ lb! And that for high-quality gut, the cheaper stuff broke even more easily. No wonder the emphasis in those days was for small flies, soft rods and delicate striking. The fish were, of course, wild brown trout of usually less than half-a-pound, but it made the landing of a fish of over a pound a notable achievement.

Appendix D

The AFTM scale is a cause of much confusion among anglers. If you bear in mind that the original scale was designed around grains avoirdupois and the table below shows these grains converted into ounces or grams, it will become clearer. Any rifleman or ammunition homeloader understands grains avoirdupois – there are 7,000 to a pound – and they should not be confused with grains apothecary's, as there are 7,700 to a pound of these! So the homeloader, who goes to his local chemist's shop to weigh his powder, ends up with a ten percent underload.

AFTM Number	*Weight in grains of the first 30 ft, excl. the level tip* Nominal	Range	*Weight in grams of first 30 ft, excl. level tip* Nominal	*Weight in ounces of first 30 ft, excl. level tip* Nominal
3	100	94 to 106	6.48	0.228
4	120	114 to 126	7.78	0.274
5	140	134 to 146	9.07	0.32
6	160	152 to 168	10.42	0.366
7	185	177 to 193	11.99	0.422
8	210	202 to 218	13.61	0.48
9	240	230 to 250	15.55	0.55
10	280	270 to 290	18.14	0.64
11	330	318 to 342	21.38	0.75
12	380	368 to 392	24.62	0.86

The first thing to realise, when studying this table, is the effect of putting more line outside the tip of the rod. Assume your rod is rated AFTM 7. If you aerialise ten yards of line you have 11.99 grams of line outside the rod tip: if you now aerialise another 4 yards, you now have 11.99 divided by 10, multiplied by 14 equals 16.79 grams of line outside the rod tip, equivalent to more than ten yards of AFTM 9 line! Actually the increase in weight is greater than this if you are using a double-taper line, as part of the first ten yards is the tapered bit.

The other message brought out by the table is that a ten yard head of No 9 line weighs just a fraction over half-an-ounce, so why all the acrobatic contortions to throw it a few yards?

Index

Numbers in **bold** refer to pages of the colour section